WHEN YOU'RE FALLING, DIVE

WHEN YOU'RE FALLING, DIVE

MARK MATOUSEK

Using Your Pain to Transform Your Life

HAY HOUSE

Australia • Canada • Hong Kong • India
South Africa • United Kingdom • United States

Published and distributed in the United States of America by:
Bloomsbury USA, 175 Fifth Avenue, New York, NY 10010, USA.

First published and distributed in the United Kingdom by:
Hay House UK Ltd, 292B Kensal Rd, London W10 5BE. Tel.: (44) 20 8962 1230; Fax: (44) 20
8962 1239. www.hayhouse.co.uk

Published and distributed in Australia by:
Hay House Australia Ltd, 18/36 Ralph St, Alexandria NSW 2015. Tel.: (61) 2 9669 4299; Fax:
(61) 2 9669 4144. www.hayhouse.com.au

Published and distributed in the Republic of South Africa by:
Hay House SA (Pty), Ltd, PO Box 990, Witkoppen 2068. Tel./Fax: (27) 11 467 8904. www.
hayhouse.co.za

Published and distributed in India by:
Hay House Publishers India, Muskaan Complex, Plot No.3, B-2, Vasant Kunj, New Delhi – 110
070. Tel.: (91) 11 4176 1620; Fax: (91) 11 4176 1630. www.hayhouse.co.in

Sections of this book have appeared in the *New Yorker, O: The Oprah Magazine, AARP
Magazine,* the *Utne Reader,* and *Common Boundary Magazine*

"The Layers," copyright © 1978 by Stanley Kunitz, from *The Collected Poems by
Stanley Kunitz.* Used by permission of W.W. Norton & Company, Inc.

"Love after Love," from *Collected Poems 1948-1984* by Derek Walcott, Copyright ©
1986 by Derek Walcott. Reprinted by permission of Farrar, Straus and Giroux, LLC.

"I was lost," from *False Prophet* by Stan Rice. Copyright © 2005 by Stan Rice.
Reprinted by permission of Alfred A. Knopf, Inc.

A catalogue record for this book is available from the British Library.

ISBN 978-1-84850-492-9

Printed and bound in Great Britain by CPI Group (UK) Ltd, Croydon, CR0 4YY

For
Marcia Horowitz (1948–1978)
and Marco Naguib

CONTENTS

Utram bibis? Aquam an undam?
Which are you drinking? The water or the wave?

—John Fowles, *The Magus*

INTRODUCTION

One afternoon when I was twenty, my eldest sister, Marcia, appeared at my front door, needing to ask an important question.

"What is it?" I asked, shocked by her appearance. In spite of the unseasonable L.A. heat, Marcia was wrapped in a bulky Mexican sweater tightly belted at the waist (just like a crazy person, I thought), her dark hair unkempt, eyes bloodshot: a dramatic decline from the attractive thirty-year-old banker she had been only months before. I sat Marcia down at my kitchen table, poured her a cup of tea, found a comb in my back pocket to run it through her messy hair, as she had once fussed over me as a boy. She had been my surrogate mother—ours wasn't really up to the job—reading me Aesop's fables before bedtime, packing lunches, explaining riddles (birds, bees, our disappeared father), comforting when my feelings were hurt. Now it was my turn to comfort Marcia. Her spirits had sunk so quickly that winter. I kissed my sister's cheek and asked her to please tell me what was the matter. Marcia seemed unable to speak, simply shook her head and drifted away to that no-man's-land where none of us had been able to reach her.

Marcia had been viciously betrayed by her husband, filed for divorce, had a nervous breakdown. She was hospitalized, then released prematurely when her insurance company refused to pay more. Now she found herself alone, unmoored, and terrified in a world that had always distressed her. The mensch in a family of hooligans, Marcia was the gentle, obedient daughter who did as she was told without question and cared for others more than herself. Newspaper tragedies sent her to bed. She wept for people she didn't know. I never once witnessed her being cruel.

My sister appeared to be sinking fast, unable to locate solid ground. I begged her again to talk to me. At last, Marcia looked into my eyes and spoke. "How do you do it?" she asked.

"Do what, honey?" I was confused.

"How do you live?"

The question froze in the air between us. In every life there are red-flag moments that seem to flash out, magnified, against the soft focus of everyday contentment, warning us to pay attention—that something essential is happening. I snapped to attention when Marcia said this yet had no earthly idea what to tell her. I was a wobbly piece of work myself at that age; the bravado my sister seemed to admire was largely a mask for bitter self-doubt. Having grown up as the only son in a fatherless, four-kid, welfare home, I believed that denial and monolithic ambition were the only tools at my disposal for surmounting such disadvantaged beginnings. Pessimism seemed to be evil juju that winners must avoid at all costs. Failure wasn't even an option, of course. Yet here was my beloved, defeated sister posing a heartbreaking question I hadn't yet dared to ask of myself.

I told Marcia that she had to keep fighting. No matter what.

"I can't," she said.

"You have no choice . . ."

Marcia opened her mouth to answer—then stopped. The kitchen fell silent; she slumped in her chair; that was the end of the conversation. I tried to distract her by rubbing her shoulders. She drifted away again. When she stood up to leave, I felt guilty relief as I followed her out to her beat-up Buick, parked hastily at the curb. Marcia fumbled in her purse for the car key, then sat there without moving, hands clutching the wheel. I asked Marcia if she was okay to drive. She stared at me without answering.

I leaned down to kiss her good-bye. "You'll be fine," I promised.

Marcia touched the side of my face. She attempted a smile, which wasn't much but gave me a bit of hope. Then she started the engine, waved good-bye, and disappeared slowly down the street.

"How do you live?" Marcia had asked. This question would haunt me in years to come—following some great loss or disappointment, some piece of unexpected bad luck—when I was exposed enough to wonder. How does a person survive his own life, the ceaseless surprises, uncertainties, struggles, reroutings in strange, inconvenient directions? What force is it, exactly, that flips a falling man back on his feet, reconstitutes him after disaster, helps him prevail in the face of challenges far beyond his previous limits? What mysterious strength is it that enables us to outsmart "the terrorists within" (as one psychologist described them to me), those destructive maniacs under the skin—cynicism, despair, resignation, terror—that threaten to stop us in our tracks? Finally, how is it possible not merely to survive our greatest obstacles but to prevail in circumstances that threaten to stop us?

This quandary intensified substantially for me when mortality paid an unwelcome visit. One afternoon in 1984, lying on a Jamaica beach with my best college buddy, John, I found a purple lesion on the ball of his foot that had not been there the day before. Lives, like buildings, have foundation walls; remove these crucial supports and the whole thing comes crashing down around your ears. In the instant that I saw John's lesion, in the seconds it took me to realize what it probably meant for both of us—though our friendship had been platonic—life as I'd known it cracked down the middle from chimney to basement; the house I'd lived in, the self I'd believed in, the future I thought was waiting for me, was suddenly condemned.

John was dead within three months. For the next ten years, I lived in a state of near-constant anxiety, waiting for my own demise, scared each morning when I looked in the mirror of what forbidding signs I would find there. Mostly, I couldn't breathe. In her famous essay on affliction, Simone Weil likened this acute state of dread to that of a condemned man forced to stare for hours at the guillotine that is going to cut off his head. You shake, you wait, you do your best not to pee in your pants while people are watching.

But no one can stay panicked forever. You're forced to find a way through your terror before any viable answers appear, while the floor is dropping beneath you. It's a sloppy, lurching, imperfect business; though not quite yourself, post-catastrophe, neither are you yet equipped to cope with the fallout from such seismic changes. You haven't grown those muscles yet or begun to reimagine your story. You're more like the common American lobster, *Homarus americanus*, which dives for a few days each year to the ocean floor to slough off its old shell and wait for a new one, a naked, pink-skinned glob of flesh trying not to get smashed too hard before its second skin grows back.

In my case this retreat took the form of spiritual seeking.

When John died, I was working as an editor at *Interview* magazine under the pop artist Andy Warhol. I'd chased the publishing carrot from L.A. to New York, worked my way slavishly up the masthead, yet found that in my frenzy to succeed, I'd ignored any sort of inner life. Now the prospect of leaving this world with so little clue as to who I was, what (if anything) this life meant, whether I believed in God, the soul, or self-transcendence, felt like adding insult to injury—like a sleepwalker stumbling off a cliff. I quit my job, left New York, and shifted gears from limousine chasing to authenticity (whatever *that* was) and confronting a problem I'd long avoided: Why, in spite of my worldly good luck, did I feel so secretly heartsick and vacant, so like an impostor, long before my diagnosis? Why was I so rarely truly happy? This question was an urgent one whether I was dying or not. I became a compulsive, nomadic seeker, living hand to mouth for most of ten years, trawling for wisdom from spiritual teachers around the world (wherever plastic was accepted), gulping it down in desperation.

These years were traumatic yet eye-opening. I kept a saying in my wallet—"In a world of fugitives, the man who goes in the opposite direction will always be said to be running away"—that seemed to let me off the hook. I needed to find out for myself if anything existed of a man beyond this booby-trapped bag of bones. As a skeptical agnostic, I dove warily into the question of whether anything *meta*physical truly existed, or if human beings really were just blips on the screen of a heartless creation, dying animals like a billion others born to eat and fuck and die, as I had been raised to believe. This philosophical question had struck me for the first time at age seven, when I lifted the lid off a garbage can and found my first dead thing, a blue jay's corpse swaddled in plastic and newsprint. I stood there a long time, staring down at the cat-chewed body, wondering whether the bird had been this pile of bloody feathers or the thing that had escaped? Which, more pertinently now, was I?

The primary insight that arose from those years had nothing at all to do with religion. In fact, the single most transformative idea to emerge from all that reading, meditation, and ashram-shlepping was simply this: that terror can be a door to enlightenment. While traditional cultures have long understood the empowering aspects of fear and wounding, the double-edged force of passage rites to galvanize and deepen the spirit, we are too often shielded from this secret knowledge. Our prevailing contemporary view of pain and loss as handicaps to be avoided at any cost is not only wrongheaded but deeply ass-backward, in fact. Terror is fuel; wounding is power. Darkness carries the seeds of redemption. Authentic strength isn't found in our armor but at the very pit of the wounds each of us manages to survive. As one widow put it to me, "Strength doesn't mean being able to stand up to anything, but being able to crawl on your belly a long, long time *before* you can stand up again." Transformation is in our wiring. Looking backward is a Humpty Dumpty waste of time. "You're gonna come out gold on the other side," one heroic man says in this book, "or you're not gonna come out at all."

This is not Pollyanna speaking. Science is finally catching up to what sages have been saying forever. Thanks to recent breakthroughs in fMRI technology, neurologists are now able—for the first time in history—to observe the human brain in the act of feeling. This has revealed a phenomenon known as neuroplasticity, which in turn has revolutionized how we think about personal change. Once believed to be lumps of gray matter cogitating between our ears, our brains turn out to be more like interlooping

Wi-Fi octopuses with invisible tentacles slithering in many directions at every moment, constantly picking up messages we're not aware of and prompting reactions—including illness—in ways never before understood. Contrary to the old wives' tale that humans are born with a fixed number of brain cells that only diminish over time, our bodies produce one hundred thousand new brain cells every day, in fact, until we die. Our brains are highly mutable, reinventing themselves on a regular basis, which is why *not* putting pain to its natural use—as grist for the evolution mill—is such an extraordinary waste of suffering. While hardship can certainly render us bitter, selfish, defensive, and miserable, it can also be used quite differently: as the artery of interconnection, a bridge to other people in pain, as blood in the muscle that propels us. Crisis takes us to the brink of our limits and forces us to keep moving forward. When people in extremis call it a blessing, this is the paradox they are describing. It's why men sometimes blossom in wartime and women are often changed by childbirth—they come alive as never before on that knife blade of danger and pain. There's vitality in facing life's extremes, including that of your own extinction. Crises pushes you to travel wide, fast, and deep, expands the heart and calls forth reserves of courage you didn't know you had, like adrenaline in the muscles of a mother saving her only child. Only you are the child, and it's your life—the life of your own soul—that you are saving.

This paradox is hard to swallow. When I used to tell friends, half jokingly, that HIV had actually saved my life, they rarely understood what I meant. I wasn't promoting an awful virus or claiming I was glad to have it. I wasn't pretending to be overjoyed by the prospect of an early departure. I was simply confessing an odd bit of truth that I wouldn't have believed myself had my own life not improved so dramatically. Without the threat of mortal loss, I would never have had the conviction—the fuel—to become the person I wanted to be or to find my way through terrible dread to something stronger than my fear.

On April Fool's Day, 1996, my roller coaster took another twist with the news from my doctor that treatments for the virus had finally appeared. Paul Bellman, who looks like Vincent van Gogh if the painter had gone to a Brooklyn yeshiva—ginger-headed, intense, and bearded—told me that although there were no long-term guarantees, it was now highly possible that I (and many thousands like me) might look forward to a ripe old age after all. I was, in other words, no longer dying, at least not yet and not from this illness.

I stumbled out of Bellman's office feeling like the man who fell to earth—reeling, confused, a little dizzy before the unmitigated expanse. A majority of survivors, regardless of their particular storm, recall this resurrection moment in eerily similar, jumbled-up ways, of being yanked back to earth once they thought they were leaving. There's numbness, thrill, and disbelief, joy intermingled with bittersweet panic. Aristotle was right when he compared good luck to the moment on the battlefield when the arrow hits the guy next to you. It's an abstract, outer-space, torn-in-half feeling, partly shattering, partly sublime. *Awe* is the only word that fits.

A gift returned is doubly precious, charged with the mandate not to be wasted. I was determined not to lose track of what I'd learned in the mortal zone, or forget the miraculousness of things in the blur of everyday life. For me, this became a new reason for living, to prove myself "worthy of my sufferings," as novelist Fyo dor Dostoevsky described his own resurrection moment. Arrested at age twenty-eight for revolutionary activities against Tsar Nikolai I, the impoverished epileptic author spent eight months in solitary confinement before his death sentence was announced. Marched into Saint Petersburg's Semenovsky Square on the teeth-rattling morning of December 22, 1849, along with twenty-three other condemned men, Dostoevsky stood in line for thirty minutes while awaiting his turn to climb the scaffold. "They snapped swords over our heads and made us put on the white shirts worn by people condemned to death," he later wrote to his brother. "Thereupon we were bound in threes to stakes, to suffer [our deaths]."

At the very last moment, the writer was informed that his sentence had been commuted; in fact, the whole thing had been a scare tactic. Suddenly, Dostoevsky was a free man. A fellow inmate went mad after this incident, but Dostoevsky's own madness took a different form: to survive brightened, revivified, by his personal brush with death. Obsessed with the image of one man executed, the other reprieved, the novelist made a lifelong commitment not to waste his gift, to conduct his life in terms of "what the condemned know," to become a survivor artist. "When I turn back to look at the past, I think how much time has been wasted," he confessed in that same letter. "Life is a gift . . . each minute could be an eternity of bliss. My old head has been cut from my shoulders . . . but my heart is left me. And the same flesh and blood which likewise can love and suffer and desire and remember. *On voit le soleil!*"

As I retraced my own footsteps in order to understand this turnaround, Marcia's question came back to haunt me. How does a person live full out in a world where uncertainty's king? How do we survive our own days once a fall has already happened? How is it possible to live with "what the condemned know" before we are confronted by crisis, through the course of everyday affairs, in order to live in this illuminated state? Finally, how can we keep our hearts "open in hell," as the Dalai Lama describes the existence of suffering, in the midst of trouble, when we need compassion most?

Survival, I came to understand, has less to do with cheating death than with living as brilliantly as possible. (How many oxygenated people do you know who do not appear to be fully alive?) There are new ways of seeing—of being—in a world turned upside down. There's an art to turning poison into a boon. Even during the worst of times, as I plummeted into some squall of fear, it never failed that some involuntary, irrational wave would sweep me up sooner or later as if out of nowhere. Other times there was satisfaction in the battle itself, a tenacious hunger to stay alive, when I was glad to simply be here, to fight—to *participate*—even when the going was tough.

Every situation has the potential for this greening, this *viriditas*, this bringing of beauty, insight, or healing from the manure of suffering. We're reconstituted after being crushed, fleshed out again after being stripped, by the mysterious, profligate, glowing, extravagant force that courses through and electrifies the phenomenal world. Though we're immersed in this power at every moment, survivors realize how profoundly quality of life is determined by how skillfully (and quickly) we harness ourselves to that evergreen force at the heart of things. Just as we recognize beauty when we see it, we respond to those who have tapped into this secret. They seem larger and more alive somehow, as if working from a more vivified palette. It's no accident that such impassioned, inventive people have frequently endured greater-than-usual doses of pain. Where adversity crosses paths with aliveness, there is the potential for art, as well as for artful living. Although we may not all be masters, we can learn from such enlightened souls and witness their greening survivor's genius for self-renewal.

When the hundred-year-old poet Stanley Kunitz tells me, for example, "Reinvention is my philosophy," how different is that from painter Auguste Renoir assuring students, "Pain passes, but the beauty remains"? When Dr. Rachel Remen, a physician who's lived with a painful physical condition for fifty years, promises that "optimism is not required for healing," how liberating is that for those who've scrambled to keep their own smiley-face masks in place when what they needed to do was scream? Seeking out masters of this art, following their various footsteps through their particular labyrinths, I saw there might be a way to compose a chorus—the aboriginals call it a song line—to serve as a map for people crossing their own wilderness, a voice map to this dark geography. "In a dark time, the eye begins to see," poet Theodore Roethke reminded us. With our illusions of safety exploded, outside the bounds of "normal" life (*way* out on King Lear's stormy heath), new abilities do indeed dawn in a person; values, intuitions, skills, perspectives that might seem unnatural—even perverse—to those who've led more sheltered lives.

But what do people like me have to teach? Something about the limitations of rational thought; our supreme powers of adaptation; the short shelf life of shock; the fraternity of the *anawim* (people who have experienced great loss); the enlargement of self through tragedy; the absence of guilt; the paradoxical thrill of endangerment; the actual flimsiness of the narratives each of us composes for his life, believing the dots to be connected (when, in fact, they're just dots); the paltriness of survival without spirit; the role of verve and imagination—what the French call *je m'en foutisme*, the brave art of not giving a damn once your back is already against the wall and you choose to move forward anyway.

Awe is so much vaster than pleasure. It is boundless, transcending clichéd ideas about good and evil, pleasure and pain, success and failure, redemption and loss. The line blurs between good and bad luck; bipolar Fortune spins her mad wheel, reverses, slows down a moment, then speeds up again in her maddening round. Survival requires a dose of madness—what cynics call "hoping against hope"—just like art does; you conjure your future from white space, locate the hidden person, yourself, against this unfamiliar background, peering through grief and loss at something greater. "Survivors are more urgently rooted in life than most of us," observed one Holocaust expert. "Their will to survive is one with the thrust of life itself, as stubborn as the upsurge of spring. A strange exultation fills [their] soul, a sense of being equal to the worst."

I knew this strange exultation myself, of being destroyed yet beyond destruction. Mystical as this may sound, even the hardest-headed atheists I spoke with would echo some version of this same awareness, a retrieved sense of sacredness, even transcendence, flooding the vacuum of survival where common protections had been stripped away. Terror does have its purposes. "If I cut you," Rachel Remen reminded me, "your entire healing system"—physical, emotional, spiritual—"will be mobilized instantly and become more alive in you, more activated than before." For this reason, survivors may be our greatest teachers in an increasingly terrorized world.

After the wounding by Al Qaeda, Americans watched our country morph overnight from a dozing, not overly conscious giant into a great hydra-headed survivor caught up in the fight of its life. Foreseeing the dangers of power and comfort, Thomas Jefferson had favored revolution every ten years to snap people to attention. Americans were now being called upon to ask themselves the sorts of questions survivors wrestle with every day—to think *heroically*, although they might not want to be heroes. This heroism has less to do with John Wayne, the default machismo of a people weaned on pioneer individualism, than with throwing off our bonds of fear, deepening through our so-called weaknesses, surrendering to "the thing with feathers" that lifts us beyond who we thought we were (and what we are capable of) and rouses us from our perpetual stupor.

We spend so much of our lives in a waking trance of retrospection, regret, distraction, idling, and disembodiment through a range of addictions that when the bottom does fall out, life assumes a sudden, counterintuitive richness, clarity where there was haze. We're starched into the present tense, where we stop and gaze around with wonder at existence on a mysterious planet. Epiphanies happen where life and death meet. The very walls we construct to protect our lives hide the full glory of those lives from us. It's strange but true that we live immured by our own best intentions, and that the human mind is so constructed—and our powers of denial so baroque—that nothing short of catastrophe has the power to snap us out of our trance. Marcel Proust described this anomaly best, as usual. "I think that life would suddenly seem wonderful to us," wrote the hypersensitive Frenchman,

> if we were threatened to die, as you say. Just think of how many projects, travels, love affairs, studies, it—our life—hides from us, made invisible by our laziness, which, certain of a future, delays them incessantly.

But let all this threaten to become impossible forever, how beautiful it would become again! Ah! if only the cataclysm doesn't happen this time, we won't miss visiting the new galleries of the Louvre, throwing ourselves at the feet of Miss X, making a trip to India.

The cataclysm doesn't happen, we don't do any of it, because we find ourselves back in the heart of normal life, where negligence deadens desire. And yet we shouldn't have needed the cataclysm to love life today. It would have been enough to think that we are humans, and that death may come this evening.

Confronting our own impermanence is the skeleton key to a secret life. After surviving his own vision quest, before reentering civilian life, Carlos Castaneda was advised by his Yaqui teacher Don Juan to keep death on his shoulder. Mortality becomes a muse—the notion that fear disappears is absurd. But how is it possible to stand up to the terrorists within? How do we live once the ground starts shaking? That is what Marcia wanted to know.

Today I would tell her that there is an art. There are song lines, principles, signposts, tricks, shortcuts, ways of making it better. Plato described such lifesaving wisdom as *techne tou biou*— meaning "the craft of life"—which is why, in the spirit of arts-and-crafts wisdom, this book is divided into a sequence of lessons that can be read either in order or hopscotch style, depending on the reader's taste. Since a story is worth a thousand rules, I've opted for parables, poetry, true-life tales, and autobiography to illustrate this *techne tou biou*. These concise chapters are meant to be seen as pieces in a larger mosaic, movable parts, independent lessons in the nonlinear art of self-realization.

As the world becomes more dangerous our need for such lessons only grows more urgent. There are great survivor artists among us whose lives stand as proof of this transformative power. As the reader will discover in the following pages, their strength is a precious, renewable resource available to anyone willing to learn.

MAGICAL THINKING

The impossible happens to everyone—when we're least expecting it. One minute, you're still the person you know; the next, you've been changed by some freak happenstance you never believed could happen to you.

You've become a post-catastrophe person. The mask of safety is torn away. There's nowhere to run and hiding is fiction. You search your own reflection for comfort, and the mirror whispers, *Adapt or die*. Feeling your way along in the dark, you dream your new life into existence, grow these strange new appendages slowly, see the world and your own being through unblinkered eyes.

Picture a husband and wife, both writers, sipping cocktails at the end of a long workday, a week after Christmas in New York City. For forty-two years this has been their routine, living and working cheek by jowl—editors, best friends, collaborators. On this particular evening, with snow attacking the windowpanes, John is reading by the fire while Joan, all ninety-five pounds of her, tosses a salad in the kitchen. Both of them are exhausted. Their only daughter, Quintana, is in a nearby hospital, suffering from septic shock following an infection gone wrong. After dinner, Joan and John go back to the hospital. Now it's time to eat and relax.

Joan carries the salad into the living room. John closes his book and waits to be served. Joan is a woman who thrives on routine, as order is an antidote to dread. Mundane details form the daily grid behind which, if she is careful, Joan believes she can barricade her family and herself from the chaos she has glimpsed since girlhood, lurking under the surface of things. The daughter of pioneers (her great-great-great-grandmother brought a cornbread recipe and a potato masher across the plains from Arkansas to the Sierras), Joan was raised to be strong, and has always been stronger than she looks, but suffered nevertheless from a kind of hypersensitive dread, the intuition of hidden yet imminent danger. Joan negotiates this unease through writing, throttles her fears in tight, gimlet-eyed prose, and maintains her cool front in a frightening world. "We tell ourselves stories in order to live," she wrote a long time ago, and now, lighting the candles for dinner, Joan may be thinking (for the thousandth time) of this man she has known for all these years, her husband, and how he actually understands her, allows for her insecurities, loves her anyway.

John looks up from the table and catches his wife watching him. Joan hands him a second drink. Beginning to eat, John lifts his fork, slumps to the side, and dies there in front of his wife from a massive coronary infarction.

This happens so suddenly that Joan thinks it must be a joke at first and waits for her husband to open his eyes. When John doesn't move, she shrieks at him; then she's running toward the phone, dialing 911, holding his head in her lap, opening the door for the paramedics, watching them beat his chest with their paddles, following them with an overnight bag to the service elevator, then into the ambulance, where she rests John's cold hand on her lap and stares at traffic out the back window.

At the memorial service three weeks later, Joan watches their daughter, Quintana, deliver the eulogy, not knowing that in twenty months' time she will be attending this same child's funeral. Joan sits there, a sylph in oversized sunglasses, hazing in and out of her church seat, her mind unhinged by the suddenness of it, the unreality of the coffin. She feels as if a tectonic shift has split her former life in two, and during the spectral months to follow, pacing the ghost-lined apartment halls, able to eat nothing but soup broth, fixated, restless, somnambulant, she obsessively records the events of that night on paper, minute by minute, as if the creation of a precise time line will magically return John to her.

Life changes fast.
Life changes in the instant.
You sit down to dinner and life as you know it ends.
The question of self-pity.

These four lines, written during that twilight period, will become the footprints Joan follows back into the story of her own life. During this process the detail-crazy mind she's relied on for work and sanity turns flagrantly magical on her (she can't move John's shoes from the doormat in case he should "need them if he comes home"), telling her stories she knows can't be true.

"It was extraordinary," Joan Didion tells me now. We're alone in her large Upper East Side apartment on a December day three years after the ordeal, the windowpanes once again crusted with snow. This literary heroine from my undergrad days is dressed like a prep school ingénue in a baggy lavender sweater, flower print skirt, black tights, and knee-high mukluks. Joan speaks in a sort of gunslinger's drawl punctuated with frequent, lilting laughter and is cordial without being ingratiating, generous in her responses without wasting a word.

"I'd been around people who had psychotic breaks," she tells me, fixing me with her grayish eyes. "But I had never imagined that someone who didn't appear to be raving mad could be so crazy." Joan arranges her skirt across her knee. "I had lived, you see, an entirely conventional, bourgeois life. An orderly life. This broke into my golden mean."

Cut loose from any fixed idea she ever had "about death, about illness . . . about marriage and children and memory . . . about the shallowness of sanity, about life itself," as she later wrote, Joan spent the year following her husband's death wading shoulder-high through grief, untangling the loops of her delusional thoughts, tracing her way back to solid ground. "I've learned that you don't actually get over things," she says. "You incorporate them. They become part of everything you are. I don't mean that you walk about crying all the time. But you change."

"How did you change?" I ask. Having read her books, I'm already aware of Joan's tempestuous mood swings.

"I'm far less patient in certain ways." She uncrosses her legs and slouches forward. "Not that I was ever one of life's most patient people." Joan lets out a childish laugh. "But I do value love more."

Hadn't she always valued love? It had seemed to me that love was one of the few things Didion did trust. Feelings seemed to be everything to this writer. "A poster girl for anomie wearing a migraine and a bikini to every volcanic eruption of the post-war zeitgeist," as *Rolling Stone* described her. Red-hot emotions in ice-perfect prose, that was Didion's legacy. Love had always seemed sacred to her. Was that not the case?

She gracefully ducks the question. "When I think of the moments that are wasted in all of our lives," she tells me. "It is different after you lose someone. These moments become particularly precious to you when you can't replicate them." In *The Year of Magical Thinking*, the memoir she wrote about this vastation, Joan describes the intricate, difficult bond she shared with her husband, the unvarnished truth of their marriage, the diurnal shifts, silences, arguments, the conjugal saga of rising and falling and sticking together anyway. At one time Mr. and Mrs. John Gregory Dunne were the most famous literary couple in America. She was arch and glamorous; he was blue-blooded, devoted, depressive. Together they constructed a legend, the outcome of which she is now living alone. For the most part, she is sane again, though.

"For about six months after John died, I'd get cross when I heard couples bickering," Joan says. "I'd tell them they didn't have enough time." She looks at the ribbons on the dining room table. "We both knew that John had a heart condition. But what would have happened if I'd believed all the time that he was likely to die? There's no way of staying alive if you believe that you're gonna lose someone or yourself any second. What good would that have done?"

"It is hard to live that way."

"I realized that I was berating myself for not being able to control these uncontrollable events. I've learned that thinking you should be able to control things is the worst kind of grandiosity. I used to be such a control freak."

"Used to be?"

"I'm better now. I really am a bit more accepting. Part of anticipating the worst is believing that if you expect it, the terrible thing can't possibly happen." Joan laughs again. "Then when the worst finally does happen, you stop anticipating. I used to be quite fearful, but very little can happen to me now."

"You're fearless?" I ask.

"Oh, God no. I'm not saying that when something terrible is going on, I don't deny every bit of it. In the emergency room, I had to have known that John was already dead, but I was still trying to figure out how to get him home from the hospital. As if I could somehow improve the situation! It doesn't sink in."

"Denial is there for a reason," I say.

"I don't know how people function without it. Of course, we all need to look at things as they are, but if where they are is untenable at the moment, we have to find another way to get through the day."

"Or the year."

"I never quite know what people mean when they talk about being strong," Joan says with some annoyance. "I didn't die. My life has to go on. What's the choice? I had a sick child. I didn't have an option." She did have a choice about whether or not to put her ordeal to some good use, however. By dissecting her own demented time, Joan realized that her story might help others fumbling their way through what she calls "the American way of grief"—namely, "evasiveness posing as courage." "It was something that nobody talked about," she tells me. "The actual physical and mental effects of loss are manifold, but nobody ever admits they're happening. It seemed to me that it could conceivably be a good thing if we started saying, 'Look, you're going to go a little crazy; it's normal, don't panic.'"

One of trauma's more puzzling side effects is its trick-mirror effect on time, how time-as-we-know-it seems to pause and fast-forward simultaneously, throwing you out of the flow of things. This distortion contributes to magical thinking. "What I've learned is that marriage is not only [about] time," she admits. "It is also, paradoxically, about the denial of time. For forty years, I saw myself through John's eyes. I did not age."

I tell her how wonderful she's looking (it's true). My hostess accepts the compliment grudgingly. "I am getting better," she allows. Just the other day, Joan even managed to clear some shelves in John's old office without giving it a second thought. "That was a first," she sighs. When I broach the subject of Quintana's death, however, Joan's poker face lets me know that this is a subject too raw to be touched. "The relationship with a child is a whole different level of loss, at once more fundamental and less intimate" is all that she has said on this subject.

The living room has darkened. Joan looks tired. Still, there's one more thing I'd like to ask, but I fear it may seem tacky. Joan stretches her legs and moves toward the front door. The top of her head barely reaches my chin. I finally get the question out.

"Can you imagine falling in love again?" I say.

Joan stops and looks me straight in the eye. For a second, I think she's going to slap me. Then I realize she's amused. "I wouldn't get married again, I don't think," she tells me in her cow-girl drawl, standing inside her doorway. "But fall in love?" she says, lowering her chin. "Absolutely."

THE ROAR OF FREEDOM

There's a beautiful Sufi story I've always loved. A group of tigers in a forest leaves a cub behind by mistake. The tiger cub is reared by sheep. The sheep teach it how to act like a sheep. It walks like a sheep and baas like a sheep and eats grass.

Many years later a tiger happens to be passing and sees this ludicrous spectacle of a half-grown tiger behaving like a sheep. It is appalled and amused and drags the tiger to a pool in the forest. There, it shows the young tiger its own reflection, and the tiger begins to wake up to what it really is.

The older tiger teaches the younger tiger how to roar. At first all it can do is make bleating sounds. But slowly the tiger roar begins in its throat, and then after weeks of practice, it comes up to its master and gives the great roar of freedom.

This is what survivors do. As domesticated beings, we're fleeced into believing we are safe and special. Then the tiger comes out of the forest. The truth is savage, but in its eyes—in the aftermath of the long tussle—we see that we are wild, too. We only imagined that we were so timid.

It's uncanny what happens when people wake up. Their wattage increases. Their hearts amplify. You see the juju in their eyes. That's why we're so drawn to oppressed people who prevail. One sweltering afternoon in 1988, I'm alone in a third-class train compartment in Florence station, waiting for the departure whistle, when the doors fly open and in marches one of the strangest-looking creatures I have ever seen in my life. Moist and brown as a greased potato, big-bottomed, and sporting a blue jean ensemble (blue denim tennis shoes, overalls, belt, shoulder bag, and pimp cap), this high-voltage creature has chintzy, taped-up luggage swinging from every appendage and is squealing like a girl—"*Che stronzo!*"—at the heat. Finally, he manages to negotiate himself into my quiet cabin and plops down on the seat across from mine.

"*Ay, papi!*" he gasps, fanning himself with one hand, clutching a cannoli in the other, smiling, his yellow teeth smeared with cake. "*Che giorno!* What a day!" He's dressed like a slutty, overweight mall girl, in camel-toe jeans and rhinestone jacket, mucky lipstick, smeared mascara, the top of his forehead sprinkled with tiny, shiny pimples.

"It is hot," I say.

He extends his hand and purrs, "Mario."

Now and then things happen to us in life that truly deserve to be called uncanny. This overnight trip to Paris is such a surprise. Bouncing up and down in his seat, so happy he seems ready to pop, Mario is not what he appears to be—a tranny hooker or maid half in drag, say—but is, in fact, one of a handful of naturally born "sopranists" alive in the world today. Sopranists are males born with female vocal cords. They're the golden-egged geese of the opera world (where boys were once castrated to sing these roles), lusted after by aficionados for their unique sound, as

Mario now explains to me. "They cut off the privates," he says, patting himself. "But not me!"

As if the unlikelihood of this weren't enough, my companion is on his way this very night to make his "day-boo" at the Paris Opera. Describing Mario's pitch as excitement would not do his hysteria justice. He's over the moon, beside himself, ready to burst out—I mean *burst* out—in song. Though he's performed here and there over the years, tomorrow will be Mario's official coming out. His singing teacher, Signora Cowell, has insisted that he prepare a full eight years before premiering his rare instrument on a world-class opera stage. Mario has done *piccolini* parts, nothing roles, in the provinces for fun, he says, curling the top off a tin of lasagna, but tomorrow will be the great debut of his life.

"Signora wanted me to save," he says, tugging at the blue jean scarf on his neck. "I work for her since sixteen years old. Now," Mario, tells me, digging into the noodles, "I am ready!"

I am speechless.

"My patron find me," he claims. "He introduce me to the signora. This is how I come to Italy."

"Found you where?"

"Oh, baby, you do not *want* to go there," Mario protests, in the protesting way of people who can't wait to spill the beans. I assure him that very little shocks me, digging into my bag for a tape recorder. Then, with the Tuscan plains making way for the Appenines, and Mario wolfing down one high-calorie treat after another, he proceeds to relate the far-fetched saga of how he came to be sitting here in this Italian train on his way to—here Mario crosses himself—superstardom.

He came from a jungle town near Salvador, in the northeast corner of Brazil, one of ten children born to an illiterate farmer and his peasant wife. "Dirt poor," Mario tells me, slowly chewing. No school, no medicine, no electricity, he says. Once a month the family ate meat. Five of his siblings did not survive.

"Half of your brothers and sisters died?"

"La misère," Mario says, meaning disease or malnourishment, I guess. "I was always different. I always sing sing sing, everywhere I go. I am always *maricon*, you see—big, fat sissy boy. I am always with the fat." Mario tugs at his love handles, laughs, gouges out a hunk of lasagna. "But nothing matters to me. Nothing but the beauty. I need the beauty," my companion says, laying a manicured hand on his heart. *"Papi,* I grew up in the paradise. *Il giardino di Eden."*

One day when Mario was fourteen, he was drawing water from the well with his sisters, singing his heart out as usual, when a white man and woman came driving by in a Jeep. They asked the local children for a glass of water and were stunned when Mario sang his reply like Maria Callas. The memory still delights him. "These strangers, they tell me to talk normal." Mario chuckles. "I tell them this *is* normal. My sisters tell them this is normal. They come to my house to talk to my parents. This man says that he knows a teacher who would love to get her hands on me. At first this scare my poor mama. She thinks they are trying to buy me as slave. The Italians say, no, this lady is opera teacher. They leave us a card with their telephone number."

I cannot hide my skepticism. "As God my witness," Mario swears, crossing himself again. Then he produces a photo album with several press clippings ("Jungle Boy Breaks the Sound Barrier" etc.) announcing his "discovery," along with a tacky publicity shot of himself in a tuxedo looking less butch than your average lipstick lesbian. I apologize for not quite believing him.

"Nobody believe me," Mario says. "I go to my friend in town who has a telephone and call this number. The man is in São Paulo. He ask me to come to São Paulo to sing for his friend, Signora Cowell, when she comes from Firenze for visit. They send for me taxi from São Paulo—I have never been in a regular car before. I meet this wonderful lady. She tells me that I am a rare bird. That is what she says. *Rara avis.* I tell her I have always known this. Six months later, she is sending the man a ticket for me to come and study with a famous teacher in Italy!"

"That's unbelievable, Mario."

"God is great," he says, and kisses his crucifix. "I have no money, so Signora Cowell find me job in the house of an old contessa. Once, she was a very grand lady. Now she is all alone. I learn many things in the contessa's house. She is so sad, so drunk and lonely. I am alone with her from day until night, doing everything but the cooking all by myself," he tells me. "She is abandoned, this rich old lady—no children, no husband. Her friends only want her money, she says. The contessa tells me I am her only true friend. So much money and I have never seen anyone so unhappy! This old lady tells me her secrets. I listen but—" Mario zips his mouth with a finger. "*Niente. Mai.* I never tell nothing. I only tell you this one thing because you are so nice." He squinches up his nose at me.

"The contessa is having these dinner parties. The villa is *estupenda,* one of the oldest on Corso dei Tintori, near Piazza Santa Croce," he goes on. "Many people are coming. She is sitting at the head of her table in a beautiful dress, with jewels, and piles of food, and laughing—everyone is always laughing—and under the table—" Mario covers his mouth.

"What?"

"Under the table, she is peeing."

What?

"She is sitting there, with all fancy people, and she is peeing on her chair," Mario says, making a face. "She is so drunk she cannot stand up for the toilet. But nobody notices. They are eating and drinking. The contessa is all alone. I am standing in the corner helping with the drinks. She sees me looking and is crying inside." Mario pauses. "In this moment, I understand."

"What did you understand?"

"*La miseria,*" he tells me. "I see that there is *la miseria* of the rich and *la miseria* of the poor."

Equating a lonely alcoholic aristocrat with five dead toddlers? This sounds more like opera than fact to me.

"I have seen this with my own eyes," Mario says, wiping dripped pasta off his chin. "Let me tell you a story. Where I come from it is a miracle if you're alive. When I was small there was a four-year-old girl who lived nearby. I used to hear her all night long, saying, 'Hungry. Hungry.' One day this girl saw some bugs in the well and ate them. Nobody knew till her stomach swelled up." Mario pats his belly like a pregnant woman. "The doctors purge her. I see them. The vermin start crawling out from her mouth."

He is acting this out with hand gestures.

"This little girl choked and they couldn't save her. I see her die with my own eyes. But was this little girl more *misere* than *la contessa*? There are many ways to die, gringo."

"Sure. But, Mario—"

"I have seen both sides of the misery," he stops me. "And still life is beautiful!" Then Mario pulls himself to his feet with some effort, shimmies his jeans into place, and grinds his hips in an impromptu samba, snapping his fingers with one hand, the other perched on his belly. "I love to dance!" He spins around, grin-

ning, surprisingly graceful. "You must never forget to dance."
Mario throws back his head. "And you know what else Italy's
good for?" He punches an open palm with a fist. "*Chiavare.* The
best place in the world for fucking. The men, ooh, I love the ma-
chos."

"And they must love you."

"You know they do! Any way that they can get me!" Mario falls
back down on his seat in laughter. "But people like you don't know
how to live," he says, breathlessly.

"What do you mean? People like me?"

"You gringos. Always so serious! You do not know how to live.
All the time so *nervous.* Too much of the stress. And you look at
the world with—" He clenches his arms up like someone protect-
ing himself from the cold.

"That's not fair—"

"Cold inside," Mario teases me. "Like the ice. The contessa is
cold like the ice inside. She tells me she has no feelings. When she
cries, it is nothing but water, she says. When no one is there to see
them, tears are only water, she tell me. This is tragedy. More sad
than in my country."

I don't bother debating this.

"We have the life," Mario says, making fists with both hands.
"We love the life."

"So do we," I say. "And it's hard sometimes."

"But there is also the beauty!" Mario leans forward and touches
my knee. "*Viva amore.*"

I don't know what to say.

"This is what I tell the contessa. Who cares if life is hard! She
tells me that I am better than her own son, who ignores her. She
says that I am her *soffio d'aria fresca,* her breath of fresh air. She is

not too old to get better, I tell her. We are in the world more than to suffer! Sometimes I sing to make her happy," he says.

"Maybe you will sing for me?" I ask, taking his cue.

"I think that you are never asking!" Mario laughs. Then he straightens his shoulders, closes his eyes, clears his throat, opens his mouth, and begins to sing the aria "Un Bel Di" from *Madama Butterfly* in a high, pure voice. I'm floored by the beauty of Mario's tone—to say nothing of the stupendous volume, which brings the conductor running to see which of us is blasting the stereo. The train official stops in the doorway and stands there listening to Mario sing this incandescent song about love that will come again, one fine day. As he sings, Mario's eyes well up with tears, his throat quivering, hands clasped across his middle. Eventually the conductor slips away, and when Mario finishes, he tightens the scarf around his neck again and zips his finger across his mouth to let me know the show is over. Mario must rest his instrument. Tomorrow, he will step out onto the stage where Callas became a legend. He will offer his voice into "that great darkness," he tells me with awe in his voice, this peasant boy who might never have seen the lights of a city if he hadn't been singing that day by the well.

In the morning, we hug on the platform. "Wish me luck," Mario says, kissing me on both cheeks.

"You definitely will not need it," I tell him.

"Everybody needs it, gringo," he insists. Then he picks up his bags, turns on his heel, and sashays into the morning hubbub cramming into the Gare du Nord.

THE DAY OF LAUGHTER

Self-realization is not for sissies. Transformation comes at a cost. We may be shattered and freed by hardship, eventually, but the process requires a stomach for change. "A condition of complete simplicity (Costing not less than everything)" was T. S. Eliot's way of describing this stripping. Because the process is a spiritual one, it requires a mental turnaround ("conversion"), whose trials may seem counterintuitive, even perverse, to our rational, self-preserving minds. Yet practice teaches us, in spite of ourselves, that even the most destructive forces are harnessable to constructive ends. Pain we would much prefer to avoid can be used as a kind of battering ram for unearthing the true and beautiful. This *yoga*—which comes from the Sanskrit for "yoke" (in the yin-yang sense of yoking opposite forces)—is available to begin immediately.

"What is on the day of laughter is also now," a teacher of mine used to say. This saint had lived for fifty years on a mountain in southern India. "What is on the day of laughter is also now," he would repeat to his students, tossing the words out lightly, rubbing a palm across the gray stubble covering his shaven head.

What did he mean by this? I would wonder. What laughter could he be referring to? In time, his meaning began to dawn on me. He was describing the laugh of a Buddha, the sudden spontaneous guffaw that's said to seize a person when he realizes who and what he really is. Siddhartha, the prince turned Buddha, laughed after discovering his own true nature at last, the story goes. Sometime after his enlightenment, Siddhartha was strolling along a country road when a passerby stopped him to inquire why he was smiling with such quiet joy. Siddhartha did his best to demur.

"Are you a magician, sir?" the traveler asked.

"No," the master answered.

"Are you a god?" the passerby tried again.

"No," Siddhartha assured him.

"Then what, sir, can you *be*?" asked the stranger.

The Buddha replied, "I am awake."

Plato called this *anamnesis*, remembering what and who we are, beneath our lives' shifting camouflage, beyond what can be taken away. "The look of your face before you were born," as a Zen koan describes this hidden self, the essence, the nub of you that transcends your changing circumstances. We are not what we appear to be, they tell us: This is the lesson sages have expounded since the days of the earliest seers and shamans. When we glimpse our true identities, apparently it does inspire laughter. Derek Wolcott describes this recognition in one of his most beautiful poems.

The time will come
when, with elation,
you will greet yourself arriving

at your own door, in your own mirror,
and each will smile at the other's welcome,

and say, sit here. Eat.
You will love again the stranger who was your self.
Give wine. Give bread. Give back your heart
to itself, to the stranger who has loved you

all your life, whom you ignored
for another, who knows you by heart.
Take down the love letters from the bookshelf,

the photographs, the desperate notes,
peel your own image from the mirror.
Sit. Feast on your life.

When I visited India for the first time, I was a wreck, a refugee from the New York publishing life I'd coveted yet grown to dread. I was working at *Interview* magazine, as I've said, in the looming fame-shadow of Andy Warhol. To this day, Andy remains the loneliest person I've ever known, an unquestionable genius but also an alien personage on this planet. Several times a day, Andy would waft through my office, saying almost nothing yet trailing this vacuous atmosphere. Years before, he had admitted that after he was shot in the gut by a crazed fan, Valerie Solanas, his emotional life had been shot out, too, leaving Andy to peer out at the flesh-and-blood world as if through the screen of a TV set. My ex-boss infused the magazine offices somehow with this same dead chill of alienation.

On my last Christmas at *Interview*, Andy distributed presents to the staff. Weirdly, my gift from him was a white silk scarf painted with a black pyramid and lotus-seated figure, the words THE ONLY WAY OUT IS IN scrawled underneath in inked capital letters. Fourteen months later, Andy was dead following complications from gallbladder surgery. He was only fifty-nine.

I was already in India by then, traveling with Andrew Harvey, an eccentric British friend, who had been born in the twilight of the Raj near Connaught Circus in Delhi, where we were now sitting one evening after dinner.

A harvest moon hung low in the sky. The air was dusty, sweet, and warm. We'd been smoking hash, which made it sweeter, and Andrew—a brilliant professor and poet—was now holding forth in his stentorian way on the subject that most compelled him: the loss of sacredness in the world. "Until people realize that *all* of this—" Andrew held out his hands to encompass the great, entropic, swirling mass of humanity, rickshaws, cows, and sirens surrounding us on all sides—"that *all* of this is divine, every last inch of it, even the ugliest parts—till they get past the immature notion that a sacred world would be a world without suffering, a big Disneyland where everyone gets in for free, they will not truly understand that suffering is here for a purpose," Andrew declaimed.

"And what, oh wizard, might that be?"

My friend ignored me. "We spin and spin in our little cages without looking outside of them or even more deeply within," he went on. "But if people took the time to look more deeply, if they dared to look underneath their masks, they would discover something that could change their lives forever."

"Please tell me what you're talking about!"

"They would discover their real face in the mirror."

What real face? I thought to myself. Till that moment I had never considered that there might be a different "face" to things of which I was wholly unaware, some secret, even more bona fide visage. But what if Andrew was right? I wondered, influenced by the smoke and the moonlight. My companion was hyperbolic but also wise on subjects spiritual and mysterious. What if this thing we called ordinary life really was, at least in part, a case of mistaken identity? Something in his words struck a chord of truth, tintinnabulating inside me.

As the years went on, I came to learn that spiritual traditions all put forth some version or other of this same strange realization: that we do not, in essence, know ourselves; that our worldly masks are a mere façade. During times of crisis in years to come, to my great surprise, I found myself increasingly aware of this other face peering out at me through my physical eyes, seeing through my own mask, penetrating with questions. It was impossible not to notice that this new awareness emerged in direct proportion to assaults on my struggling ego.

This must be why the Buddha laughed: because nothing more could be taken from him. He recognized his own true face. He was liberated from craving and fear. He saw the freedom of self-surrender, the hidden reward of not looking backward. This freedom came at a price, of course; it comes at a cost for all of us. But considering the dividends—in joy, self-knowledge, and un-shakable strength—as I would learn on my own roller coaster, only a fool would refuse to pay it.

OM MANI PADME HUM

Andrew and I had flown from Delhi to Srinigar, spent the night on a houseboat on Dal Lake, then boarded a comic-strip bus for Ladakh. Ladakh is India's northernmost province, a lunar, breath-sucking, desolate place at eighteen thousand feet, surrounded by gargantuan Himalayan peaks. The streets of the capital town of Leh are a dusty, fetid confluence of Muslim Kashmiris and Ti-betan Buddhists, handbag-faced women with knee-length hair braided to the waist, draped in coarse maroon clothing and carry-ing their rosary *malas* everywhere they go, chanting, "*Om Mani Padme Hum.*" This Sanskrit mantra is etched like graffiti onto walls and stones (even restaurant menus), like "Jesus Lives" in the American Bible Belt.

There is no simple translation of this ubiquitous Buddhist prayer. An oversimplification might be "Compassion cooks up cosmic juju." The ancient mantra's power does seem to pervade the atmosphere of this otherworldly region. For three weeks Andrew and I hunkered down in a farmhouse pension outfitted with glass-sided rooms and straw mattresses. Our quarters looked onto a sunflower-and-vegetable garden where a prehistoric grandma twirled her rosary and toiled day after day, a donkey no bigger than a Labrador retriever nipping at the heels of her embroidered slippers. A mastiff-sized cow made its nest near the gate. A vast panorama of mountain peaks spread 180 degrees across our window view, dotted with tiny monasteries, each one a five-mile climb straight up. I learned this the hard way during a morning's trek to Gotsang, where Andrew and I were greeted at the temple's gate by a pair of monks who later offered us bowls of yak-butter tea. They slapped their sides and laughed as we struggled to choke the disgusting stuff down, ogling us as if we were escapees from the primate wing of a foreign zoo.

After returning to the States, Andrew began work with a lama named Sogyal Rinpoche on a book they decided to call *The Tibetan Book of Living and Dying*. It was to be an updated, accessible version of *The Tibetan Book of the Dead*, which had caused such a stir when it first appeared in English in 1939. Every so often a book appears that delivers a whiplash to the mainstream zeitgeist. *The Tibetan Book of the Dead* had been such a volume. While we in the West were busy with the Crusades, the Renaissance, and the Industrial Revolution, the isolated mountain masters of Tibet were hard at work formulating a theory (based, they believe, on evidence) of death and reincarnation. Their self-proclaimed grasp of the nuts and bolts of rebirth enabled the Tibetans to devise a complex system for tracking their masters from one body to the next, enabling them to hone and protect their wisdom tradition down through the ages.

I'm agnostic on the subject of reincarnation, persuadable but unconvinced. I agree with Voltaire that being born twice isn't that much more far-fetched than being born once. In any case, Sogyal

Rinpoche asked me to help with the book. Sogyal is a small, powerfully built man with a schoolboy laugh and a stubborn streak. Trained classically in the Tibetan tradition, this *rinpoche* (an honorific meaning "teacher") had survived the Chinese invasion, escaped through the Himalayas to India, then went on to study philosophy at Trinity College, Cambridge, where he worked as an assistant to the visiting Dalai Lama. Today, Sogyal is a rock star in the Buddhist world and keeps the same kind of hectic touring schedule.

One afternoon we were sitting on a patio overlooking a fir-lined palisade in Aptos, California, having a meeting. Sogyal was fielding cell phone calls from Dharmsala, Buenos Aires, and Paris. We got to talking about a perplexing thing that had recently happened to the Dalai Lama. During a talk in New York someone had asked His Holiness a question about self-loathing—how Buddhism handles the common American problem of autophobia—when all of a sudden the talk stopped. There's no word for self-hatred in Tibetan. The translator was stumped. The Dalai Lama himself was puzzled.

"This is something almost unheard of in my country," Sogyal explained to me between calls.

"The trance of unworthiness?" I asked. This is how a therapist friend describes the popular American pastime of disliking ourselves. Whether we blame this destructive habit on the doctrine of original sin or merely inverted narcissism (of the privileged, first world variety), the upshot is the same: too much time spent hating who we are.

"We emphasize the *preciousness* of human birth," Sogyal went on. "The Buddha was a human like us. Our true nature is to be enlightened. You must remember that your Buddha nature is as good as any Buddha's Buddha nature." The lama chuckled over his own cheesy joke.

"But what about evil?" I asked. What about destructive folks who wouldn't know their own Buddha nature if it hit them in the face?

Sogyal swatted my caveats away. "The teachings say that when the world is full of evil, all misfortune should be transformed to the path of goodness."

"Okay," I said. "But these are hard times—"

"It is not the times that are bad, it's the people," he corrected me, quoting a popular Tibetan saint.

"I thought you didn't believe people could be bad," I kidded Sogyal back.

"That depends on the day." He laughed.

Intrigued by this so-called Buddha nature, I make my way to Washington, D.C., to meet a Tibetan nun named Nawang Sangdrol. This twenty-six-year-old Buddhist devotee had been arrested by the Chinese at the age of thirteen and spent eleven years in the infamous Drapchi prison (the Abu Ghraib of Tibet), becoming her country's longest-serving female political prisoner. In a fluorescent-lit conference room, I meet Nawang Sangdrol and take a seat across the table from where she's sitting, flanked by an overly protective Tibetan translator duded out in a cashmere jacket.

For a minute she hardly looks at me. Her scarred hands are clasped on the table before her. Nawang looks twenty years older than her age. Her black braid appears bluish against the worn-out fleece of her plum-colored sweater. She's wearing a red string bodhisattva bracelet around her wrist along with three strands of tiny ivory beads.

When I attempt to break the ice with small talk—her English is close to nonexistent—the metrosexual translator steers me away. "Nawang is too shy," he says.

"Will she tell me her story?"

Nawang nods without being asked and for the next half an hour recites the details of her ordeal. I study the young woman as she speaks, her eyes never widening, her voice never piercing a whisper. She seems so fragile she could blow away.

On August 21, 1990, Nawang was a thirteen-year-old Buddhist nun living in Lhasa. "My family was religious, but I also had the desire to join the nunnery," she tells me. One afternoon she and a group of sister nuns attended a festival at Norbulingka, the former summer palace of the Dalai Lama. Inspired by love for their leader, the nuns felt the urge to move to the center of the large crowd to avoid attention and shout "Free Tibet! Long live His Holiness the Dalai Lama!" along with the rest of the crowd.

Almost immediately, uniformed Chinese police dragged the girls by their hair into trucks and shipped them off to a detention camp outside Lhasa. Following a severe beating, they were thrown together into a cell and kept there for nine months.

Nawang pauses to sip her water. I can't quite bridge the gap between her punishment and her offense. Jailing a thirteen-year-old girl for chanting the equivalent of "Long live the Queen"? Torture sessions began immediately, Nawang tells me. "They called us 'splittists' and counterrevolutionaries. We were beaten with iron pipes and electric cattle prods." Nawang makes a claw with her hand to show the shape of the red-hot instrument. "They would tie us up and take turns beating us, and also attach live electric wires to our tongues." When her captors were feeling especially aggressive, they put prisoners into what they called the airplane position—hung from the ceiling with their hands roped around their backs.

"You were a child," I say in disbelief.

"They didn't care how young we were or whether we were female—they tortured children the same way they tortured adults." Once, while being assaulted with electric shocks to her neck, Nawang instinctively ripped the wire off and threw it to the ground. "A guard pointed a gun to my head and said, 'Now you are going to die.' Then he laughed."

This was only the beginning. Eventually released from prison, Nawang returned home to the news that her mother had died, while her father and brother had both been arrested. Refusing to collaborate with the Chinese, the patriotic girl continued to protest against the destruction of her country. Four months after leaving one cell, she was arrested again (for chanting at a public protest) and sent this time to Drapchi, where she would spend the next eleven years.

"I was put in solitary confinement," Nawang tells me, our eyes meeting for the first time. "It was winter, very cold in Tibet. I was in my cell with only one shirt, no sweater. Because this was my second arrest, they wanted to make an example of me to other splittists. I was forced to stand outside in the courtyard in the snow. If I slumped a little bit, the guards would beat me."

"How did you get through?" I inquire.

"By inwardly protesting for freedom," she replies. "The cell was very small, with the ceiling ripped off so the guards could watch me. It was just like being in a cage. They kept the lights on to prevent me from sleeping. They wanted to mentally and physically break me. My health began to deteriorate. There were spiders. Sometimes the rats would bite me." Nawang turns her head to show me a pair of vampiric puncture wounds. My face must be betraying my unspoken question. "I will tell you," Nawang says, reading my mind. "I did this for His Holiness. For my people. For my country." There's no trace of martyrdom in her voice, no righteousness, no detectable self-congratulation. This woman is an enigma to me. Agape is an uncanny thing, generosity given without self-interest. I am not suggesting that Nawang Sangdrol is a saint, but she is, by any ethical measure, a most highly evolved human being.

"We must never give up this fight," she says. "People must remain true to goodness." Nawang fingers the *mala* around her wrist and holds it out for me to see. "I wove this from the threads of my shirt," she says. The letters read, "*Om Mani Padme Hum.*"

"Hatred does not end by hatred," Nawang says. These words are from one of the Buddha's sermons. Then she makes the *namaste* sign and lowers her eyes. The translator excuses her—the nun's adoptive family is waiting for her outside. Nawang had finally gained amnesty through an international relief organization. Now she is going to school to try to learn English. "Very bad," she apologizes, getting up.

"Do you feel free now?" I ask her. "In America? No Chinese soldiers?"

Nawang tilts her head back and forth in the Indian way that means so-so. In fact, she intends to return to Tibet as soon as possible in spite of the risks. This is baffling to me, I admit.

"There are many like me," Nawang says in English.

"She's a modest girl," the translator says. For the first time, I see the young nun's crooked smile.

Nawang's freedom rests, it seems, in her ability not to hate. Her self-worth does not depend on aggrandizing herself but is simply her birthright as a human being. Nawang will not keep fighting because she is brave—although, of course, she is—I think to myself afterward, but because she has taken a bodhisattva vow, as a Buddhist nun, to help end suffering wherever she finds it. This promise appears to have set her free.

With nothing to lose, she's wealthier and more liberated than most of us. *Om Mani Padme Hum*: the road to freedom is lit with compassion. Then, when the impossible happens, we meet it with an opened heart, knowing the enemy cannot destroy us. Love is stronger than fear, we see clearly. Knowing this opens a different door.

DRAGONS AT THE GATE

Summertime on Southampton Beach in Long Island, July 1970. Two months before their scheduled wedding, Jack Willis and his fiancée, Mary Pleshette, are hitting the surf for one last swim of the afternoon. They are a golden couple—Jack an award-winning, thirty-six-year-old documentary film director; Mary a reporter for *Newsweek* and twelve years his junior. Jack, who'd been an excellent swimmer all his life, throws himself into an average-size wave. A minute passes. Mary sees no trace of him. Suddenly Jack's head bobs up out of the surf, and he cries out to his fiancée for help.

"I'd been bodysurfing since I was a kid and knew I shouldn't have taken that wave," Jack is telling me now. We're in the Willises' living room near Central Park in Manhattan. Jack, now seventy-three, is sitting in an armchair across from me, while Mary putters in the other room. Aside from the tilt in his slender shoulders and the metal walker at Jack's side, you'd never know that he is disabled. Bright-eyed, white-haired, and quick with a joke, Jack's the kind of raconteur you'd expect to meet in an Irish pub, talking blarney with a corncob pipe in his mouth (if he weren't really a Jew from L.A.).

"Suddenly I looked down and saw nothing but sand," Jack says, eyes brightening. "I tried to somersault out of it, but instead I hit the back of my head and was instantly paralyzed from the neck down. I saw flashes of red and realized I had to stay awake or I was going to die."

Mary, a sexy, auburn-haired woman wearing jeans and a black turtleneck sweater, sets glasses of water in front of us and takes her seat on the opposite couch. "My next thought was 'It's okay to die,'" Jack tells me. "It's the clearest that I have ever been about anything in my entire life. There was a genuine feeling of absolute peace. Then my next thought was 'You have to try to get out of this somehow.'"

"What did you do?" I say, turning to Mary.

"I tried to run toward him," she remembers, "but it felt like an anxiety dream where you try to run but can't move your legs. Thank God for the people on the beach. I could never have pulled Jack out by myself."

"They got me out of the water and laid me on the beach," he continues. "I couldn't move anything. Luckily the paramedics who finally came had been in Vietnam. They recognized immediately that I'd broken my neck and knew better than to try to move me."

The Willises are a formidable team, one of those rare true-love partnerships that tolerate—even thrive upon—a soupçon of healthy friction. They adore each other, clearly, challenge each other, disagree, and push the memory envelope in some directions the other might prefer to avoid. It comes as no surprise when Jack tells me that Mary has been integral to his emotional and physical survival. Their symbiosis is poignant and glaring.

"That moment of peace may have come out of shock," Jack backtracks, describing his near-death experience. "But I'm truly not afraid to die now. I just know it's going to be extraordinarily peaceful."

"For you, maybe." Mary arches a brow.

"No big white light," Jack says. "Just a feeling. And the next thing I thought was *Try to live.*"

In the days following the accident, Jack claims to have experienced surprisingly little fear. His real dread came during the twenty-one days of waiting to hear whether his spinal cord had been severed. "I was in traction for six weeks," he says, shaking his head slowly. "The physical pain was terrorizing. The drugs they were giving me caused the most horrible nightmares. I'd dream I was skiing downhill and would hit a tree, then my neck would snap, over and over again." Jack's waking reality wasn't much better. "I couldn't talk about my fear of being quadriplegic with Mary," he admits.

This is Mary's cue to leave the room.

"Would I kill myself?" Jack says in a low voice. "What happens if I'm in a wheelchair? I'm a filmmaker. What am I going to do with my life?" His doctor's bedside manner only made things worse. "One of them said, 'If this happened to me, I don't know what I'd do. I'm a doctor. I need my hands.' I said, 'Fuck you, what do you think I am? A piece of meat?' Luckily Mary brought me a tape recorder I could talk into, which kept me from losing my mind completely. I could say things I absolutely needed to say. Things I couldn't reveal to another soul. Not even Mary."

Trapped in agonizing pain, Jack wrestled hour by hour against horrendous, mounting despair. Denial was his only ally. "In a moment of hopelessness, it's helpful to be lied to," he says.

"It's true," I agree.

"My morale was declining too fast for anything else," Jack tells me. Family and friends, including Mary, colluded with him in the fantasy that everything would eventually be all right. But these assurances didn't always help. "The better I got, the worse I felt emotionally," he admits. "It seemed an incredible paradox—"

"What do you mean?"

"The less physical pain I had, the more subject I was to fits of depression, to feeling trapped," Jack explains. "When I tried to sleep, I'd wake up in a panic of being imprisoned. I remember seeing a picture of Gulliver tied down by thousands of tiny ropes, his arms at his side, his neck stretched out. That's exactly how I felt."

Each small improvement during this waiting period brought with it an onslaught of paranoid predictions about the future. "Once I started to get movement and feeling back, I was worried about my bladder and bowels and libido. My fiancée and I were about to be married, for Christ's sake!" Jack slaps the arm of his chair. "Would I kill myself? I didn't know how much I could bear but decided not to do anything until those twenty-one days were up."

With the news that his spinal cord was intact, Jack Willis got a portion of his future back. In spite of medical assurances that he would never walk again, Jack was back on his feet within a year. He and Mary were married soon afterward, and the couple managed to rebound remarkably well at first. Determined to ignore his frailty, to pick up life where he'd left off, Jack worked at building a firewall of denial between himself and his loss, with Mary's wholehearted blessing.

"I was far less introspective back then," he admits. "Far more alpha male. I didn't want to be treated like a cripple. My own survival demanded that I separate myself from people in my condition." That's why Jack refused to continue rehab: The sight of others like him was too depressing. In business he piled on the machismo. "I was aware in corporate life that I was at a disadvantage." He chuckles at the understatement. "At meetings all these suits would be hustling, and I'm shlepping along. But the minute we sat down we were all equal."

He refused to be stopped by self-consciousness. "Mary and I just denied that there were problems, but there were enormous problems." The buried despair and repressed fury in their home only deepened after the birth of their two daughters, Sarah and Kate. "Our daughters started having issues, but we didn't put two and two together," he says. "We just weren't dealing."

When Jack excuses himself to use the bathroom, Mary stays to keep me company. "Did you ever think of leaving him?" I ask.

"Never," Mary says, not missing a beat. "I was just so in love with him. I was only twenty-four years old when it happened, but I knew I'd found the person I wanted to be with. The options were clear when I played them out." Mary ticks the choices off on her fingers. "Could I live with Jack being paralyzed? Yes. It wouldn't be easy, but we'd manage somehow. Could I live without him—or, God forbid, see him get better and marry somebody else? No way in hell. That was unacceptable. The choice wasn't as hard as it looked."

"So you've never regretted it?"

"Oh, please!" Mary laughs. "Nobody forced me to stay. I'm here because I love my husband. There are plenty of things that we can't do—the hardest thing is not being able to take a walk together—but we really have had a terrific life." (And yes, the Willises do have sex.) "Jack has never lived like he was crippled."

The denial did have to stop, however. In 1990 Jack reached a low point. Having taken a job in Minnesota as the head of Twin Cities Public Television, he became tremendously depressed, overwhelmed by a wave of held-back despair he could no longer manage with make-believe. "It was a bit like what they call post-polio syndrome, where decades after surviving the disease, people's muscles start to atrophy and they end up in a wheelchair," Jack tells me when he's back.

"A midlife thing?" I ask.

"Who knows? But I started feeling very sorry for myself," he says. "What's my life about? That kind of thing. Did I really survive this accident and get this far only to be pulled back down again?"

"In many ways it was worse than the initial crisis," Mary says.

Having refused to use a cane, Jack began taking falls and generally neglecting his health. Mary was beside herself. "She was very angry with me," Jack admits. "We had terrific fights. Mary wanted me to go on a walker, but I was terribly insulted. I'd managed to walk on my own till then, albeit like a drunk on a boat with one leg bent. I threw the walker across the room."

"He was a son of a bitch," she says without mincing words.

"I had too much pride," Jack tells me. "Mary had stayed with me through everything, but I realized that I might lose her. I began, with the help of a shrink, to deal with the denial."

Around this time, a family friend gave Jack a copy of Reynolds

Price's memoir, *A Whole New Life*, in which the novelist, who was paralyzed by spinal cancer, describes how hypnosis helped rid him of chronic pain in spite of his own skepticism. Jack jumped on this lifeboat of borrowed wisdom and began to explore the mind-body connection. He located a hypnotist, who taught him how to work with his own pain in order to function at a more comfortable level. Jack describes how this breakthrough led him to meditation and a passionate interest in what he calls the inner life.

"This has been extraordinary for me," he says. "I was not the kind of guy you could see meditating! But it truly did become my lifeline." The far-reaching effects of sitting quietly twice a day for thirty minutes still amaze him. "My behavior vis-à-vis the rest of the world is so much different than before. I'm working as hard as I used to, but not integrating the daily stress in the same way. I'm able to deal with things a lot more objectively, not taking things personally—internalizing—the way I used to."

"It's true," says Mary, who also meditates.

"It's about having a calmer foundation from which to act, and finding that when I act that way with other people, they respond much better to me as well. I'm less concerned with how I appear to the world, less attached to the physical. But I'm in much better shape than I was ten years ago, because I'm taking much better care of myself."

Jack is able to "unhook" more skillfully from onslaughts by his inner terrorists. "It's a beautiful thing," he marvels. "There's a kind of wisdom that doesn't come from the head, an impulse to do something that isn't influenced by thought. Suddenly you say something really smart that you didn't mean to say, that kind of thing. I can drop the mind, unhook awareness from the thought or emotion. Not all the time, but sometimes I can do it. Right now I'm working on lower-back pain. The process continues."

Jack is also angling to retire. "I've done it," he says, meaning his television career. "There are other horizons." Mary is freelancing for the *New York Times* and working on a second novel. Their marriage remains passionate; from the way Mary hangs on the arm of his chair, you can tell she'd rather be sitting on his lap. Their relationship with the girls is steadily improving. On a recent trip to Paris, Jack even agreed to use his wheelchair.

"At any given moment, you're doing the best you can," he says. "The question is always, what's the logical next step?"

Mary smiles lovingly.

"I try not to worry until I have to. Living with this"—Jack gazes down at his self-described scrawniness—"I've seen that we keep finding tools, all of us, no matter the problem. To help us get where we want to go, even if we're not conscious of where we're going."

"What do you do when you get scared?" I ask.

"Our fears are like dragons at the gate," Jack Willis tells me. "We just have to face them and walk through."

SUPERMAN'S GHOST

"Every journey has a secret destination of which the traveler is unaware," philosopher Martin Buber wrote. The image of life as a labyrinth is ancient and true, each pathway we follow digressing, recircling, occluding, delivering us, unexpectedly, to unsuspected crossroads and brinks. You leave the house to buy a quart of milk and meet your true love near the frozen foods. Your blood tests come back not as you'd hoped, so you experiment with acupuncture, enjoy the needles, take up studies yourself, quit your job at the bank, and wind up living in Chinatown with a Pekingese dog, a new hairdo, and your once-overwhelming condition in retreat.

We watch our destinations change with every loop of the maze. What mattered yesterday seems absurd; today's resolution is already passing. We're severely aware of our lack of control. "Take your hands off the wheel," says a teacher of mine, "and you'll see what's really driving!" He's right, I'm sure, but this requires a difficult faith in the power of life to actually guide you. Such trust is part of the secret, it seems, to finding your way to the place you're going.

Just take the case of Jim MacLaren. A superjock from San Diego, California, the bionic six-foot-five-inch, three-hundred-pound, blue-eyed all-rounder went to Yale on lacrosse and football scholarships, took up acting, moved to New York, and was just leaving a late-night rehearsal on his motorcycle when he was broadsided by a forty-thousand-pound city bus, flew eighty-nine feet in the air, and was pronounced DOA at the hospital.

After eighteen hours in the operating room, doctors managed to stabilize Jim's condition but were forced to amputate the comatose patient's left leg below the knee. Jim hopped, then skipped, then ran his way back to full mobility like a champ, returned to school, took up swimming, then became interested in triathlons. The very unlikelihood of his being able to compete pumped Jim's inner competitor to do it against the odds. Within three years Jim had set records in the New York City Marathon as well as the Ironman Triathlon in Hawaii, where he competed with able-bodied opponents.

Then on June 6, 1993, his true descent into the maze began. Riding his bike near his home in Mission Viejo, California, the amputee was plowed into by a van mistakenly waved through by a traffic marshal. The collision broke Jim's neck at the C5 vertebra and left him paralyzed from the neck down. Defeated, the ex–All Star withdrew to Honolulu and spent most of the next few years becoming a drunk and a cocaine addict, hurling just as much gusto into booze and blow as he had into the long jump and javelin.

Grueling as his previous ordeals had been, it was here, during Jim's dark night of the soul, that his most shattering insights began to occur. Having interrupted his substance abuse, he became aware that his greatest suffering was not actually coming from the accidents but from a source beyond his crippled body. Physical rehab had been a kind of smoke screen; now Jim was meeting his true nemesis head-on: overcoming the depression and addictions that now threatened to kill him. Alcoholism has been likened to a misplaced prayer; certainly, addicts are individuals who appear to have lost their inner compass. With Jack Daniel's and cocaine no longer working, Jim was forced to pull his own mask aside and take a good hard look.

"The first thing I had to do was identify my absolute deepest fear about all this," Jim told the writer Elizabeth Gilbert. What was the worst thing about having to spend life as a quadriplegic? he asked himself. Was it fear of death? Not really. He had had two near-death experiences already, "with the white light and the tunnel and the whole deal," amazing encounters that had virtually removed his fears of dying.

Was he afraid of losing his sexuality? No, Jim said again. "I knew as long as I had taste and smell and sensation, I could lead a sensual life." Was he afraid of helplessness? Not really. "Managing on my own is a drag, but it's just logistics." Was he afraid of pain? No, he knew how to deal with pain. "So what was I afraid of?" Jim wondered aloud. "The answer was pretty clear," he said. "I was afraid of being alone with myself, with my mind, with the dark things that lived in there. The doubt, loneliness, and confusion. I was afraid of metaphysical pain."

Looking inward, Jim came to understand that his greatest pain arose from a damaged sense of wholeness. This is a common refrain among survivors I've spoken to; material difficulties aside, it's the imagined loss of wholeness, of feeling intact, that wounds many of us most deeply. But what is wholeness, really? Jim was forced to ask himself now. What did it mean to lead a full life? What were his actual obstacles? After he had delved into these questions a long time, a new awareness arose in him. Jim realized that as frustrated as he was with his handicap (and envious of the able-bodied), if he could get up out of his wheelchair and walk across the room, that wouldn't really get him to the place he most wanted to go in his life. Because if he was honest, the other side of the room was not his ultimate destination. His ultimate destination was self-knowledge and enlightenment. Did he have to get there on foot? Or could he find some other path?

Eventually Jim did get sober. Today he travels the world in his wheelchair, giving lecture-sermons, kicking butt, still handsome and blue-eyed with his big, burly shoulders. He shows people that it can be done, helps them to navigate their own labyrinths—even take their hands off the wheel when they can—en route to their secret destinations. It's not the life that he had planned for himself—never in a million years. But Jim insists that it led him, however circuitously—and doubters had better believe him— precisely where he needed to be.

HOME IN THE WORLD

We learn to live heroically, though we may not always feel like heroes, watching people like Jim MacLaren wrestling strength from such vicious hardship. The spectacle of dignity wrought from despair is always elevating to behold. The Greeks had a word for this, of course: *catharsis* (literally "to cleanse")—that rousing, purging renewal of spirit that comes from witnessing heroic acts through a humbling mirror of terror and pity. In 1889 Robert Louis Stevenson voyaged to the infamous Kalawao leper colony on the Hawaiian island of Molokai, a place filled with mind-boggling pain and injustice. Though Hansen's disease is not especially contagious, lepers had been stigmatized and imprisoned since ancient times. The residents of Molokai, for no medical reason whatsoever, had been taken from their families and forced into these plague-style encampments in paradise. Stevenson, whose life had been relatively sheltered till then, wrote in awe of it to his brother: "I have seen sights that cannot be told and heard stories that cannot be repeated," marveled the author of *Treasure Island*.

"Yet I never admired my poor race so much nor (strange as it may seem) loved life more than in the settlement."

Like all forms of beauty, heroism alters us when we see it. Indeed, we are taught that we must love something more than we fear death in order for our lives to have meaning, as Martin Luther King believed. Sometimes this reaching requires us to go far out on a limb before we can taste the fruit waiting there. I've yet to meet a post-catastrophe person who doesn't remember realizing, in a panicked moment, that his familiar context is gone (severely changed at the very least), his safety net exploded, leaving him exposed to the elements. Major change nearly always brings with it a wrenching sense of homelessness, feelings of bitter dislocation. This emotional uprooting forces us to adapt; in time we learn to pack up more quickly, even to carry our metaphorical homes inside ourselves, the place where we feel that we belong, which cannot be taken away from us. We're taught by this homeless feeling that *home* means more than four walls and a ceiling. Home is where we find our balance, the pivoting point that connects us to the earth. Sociologists studying the homeless have examined this phenomenon. "It is of more than semantic significance that we call these people 'homeless' instead of 'houseless' or 'shelterless,'" I read somewhere. "Home has an existential importance that reflects our discomfort at being on the earth in the first place."

Having felt homeless for much of my life, whether I had an address or not, I'm fascinated by the link between home and healing and wonder how people living on the street do cope. In Santa Fe, New Mexico, I stop by the St. Elizabeth Shelter and strike up a conversation with a wrinkled nun named Sister Jane, who's dressed in an Emmylou Harris T-shirt, with glasses on a pearl chain around her neck. "Many of our homeless friends are highly artistic people," Sister Jane tells me cheerfully. "Let me show you some of their work."

I follow her along a corridor hung with dozens of brash, over-sized canvases that, were they signed "Basquiat," might bring in a small fortune in a New York gallery. It's obvious to me now why this wild, untrained school of *art naïf* is called survivor art. "Often the homeless are far more aware of sights and sounds than those of us who are wrapped up in our so-called ordinary lives," Sister Jane tells me when the tour is over, seeing me off at the front door. "We forget to see and hear. They take the time because that's all they have."

"In the noise and the business," Kierkegaard wrote, "we're drawn away from our spirits. But in the stillness, when we're absolutely alone in the world, we can sometimes find a vision of justice and beauty that will ever afterwards infuse our lives with purpose."

Jonathan Kozol, the educator whose book *Rachel and Her Children* explores the crucible of homeless life, believes that homelessness itself can be an art form. "No one seeks out misery, of course," Jonathan says when I reach him by phone at his home near Boston. "But many families I've known have been ennobled by their homelessness. Being removed from their ordinary context becomes a spiritual apotheosis. Women who spent their days watching soap operas are suddenly quoting from the Psalms. They're drawn closer to that intense edge which gives life significance."

"You're not romanticizing misery?" I wonder.

"Not at all," Jonathan assures me. He recalls a recent New Year's Eve at the Martinique Hotel in Manhattan, the infamous way station for the homeless, and one particularly inspiring clan he met there. "This family had become like ministers to the tortured souls around them," he says. "They lit a candle on the mantelpiece of their ugly, filthy room and made an altar. Each of us had a glass of wine and read prayers at midnight. It was more sacred to me than anything I've felt in a church or synagogue."

This is poignant to imagine. "The sense of religious feeling just soared when I was in that building," he tells me. The writer contrasts this display of compassion to then-cardinal John O'-Connor's refusal to allow the homeless to sleep on the steps of St. Patrick's Cathedral at Christmastime—"a betrayal of Christianity," in his opinion. "If we could begin to see the homeless not as deficient human beings," Jonathan says, "but as metaphors of the fragility of life for all of us, as epiphanies . . ." His voice trails off. "Only then will we not be able to drive them away."

Little has been written about homelessness as a metaphor for impermanence and what we can learn from people who face its wilderness daily. To begin with, a single afternoon at a soup kitchen reveals immediately that there is no homogeneous group known as The Homeless. There is only *homelessness*, an archetypal state of transience, isolation, and insecurity everyone senses at one time or another (more intensely in times of crisis). As a population, the homeless are as diverse as the human family itself. From suburban housewives to Ph.D. holders, health-care professionals to dope-smoking teenagers, war vets (there are statistics showing that some 25 percent of the homeless in this country fought in Vietnam) to former heads of companies, we discover all kinds when we look to the streets.

In a park across from San Francisco's Glide Memorial Church, where fifteen hundred free meals are served weekly, I sit down with a thirty-nine-year-old West Indian man named Danny Williams, who's been homeless for the past ten years. Danny came to San Francisco in the late 1970s to attend college but fell into alcoholism after experiencing an emotional crisis. Though he's still drinking, Danny insists to me that he's not lost.

"How do you think homeless people survive?" he asks me. "The ones who got everything, they don't need to pray. I pray every hour. But the only church I go to is in my heart."

"What do you pray for?"

"I just tell God that I'm here!" He chuckles. "I pray that he won't let me lose my dignity. I pray that if I'm paying for all the bad I done, he'll forgive me." Danny looks almost tearful when he says this. His neighbor on the next bench chimes in to help his buddy. "That's how most homeless people live," says this greasy-haired dude with a glass eye and a navy tattoo on his forearm. "You might see scars and our attitude might be bad, but we always got that hope."

"I can sleep right here in the street," Danny tells me. "But he's there with me. I just say a prayer and hit the sack, wake up, find me food, find me a drink, and he's there. I don't even care what happens to me down here, 'cause I know that when I get up there to meet him, I'm gonna be on his right side."

"No matter what happens?" I ask.

"No matter what," Danny says.

A passerby, Tanya, throws in her two cents. "We're all just captive spirits, honey," says this fat black Rasta babe in orange flip-flops, holding a mischievous toddler by the hand. "I don't consider myself homeless even if I'm sleeping in a doorway, 'cause home is where you *is*," Tanya tells me. She does a hand-on-the-hip thing ("you dig?"), then wipes Popsicle goo off her toddler's mouth. "Sometimes I'm more at home nowhere than in my mama's house."

Tanya waves to an old guy on the breadline. William "Terry" Stiles introduces himself and invites me to keep him company while he eats his stale rolls and noodle soup. Terry has been living on and off the street for twenty-five years. He has long, bony hands and a film of glaucoma creeping up the sides of his blue-circled, dark brown eyes.

"God is like the air," offers Terry, chewing his roll, displaying a toothless grin.

"How do you figure?" I ask.

"He's everywhere," the old man tells me, his mind drifting to higher thoughts. "This life has been a great teacher. You know, it's taken me a few doorways and trips to the hospital to know who I am," admits Terry, who was a nurse's aide before descending into clinical depression and losing his job. "This life out here," he says, meaning the street, "it will humble you if it don't break you."

"What keeps you together?"

"I know who I am," Terry explains. To look at him, that seems obvious. "What most of you don't realize is that lots of us on the street are brilliant, well-educated people."

"So why do you stay out here?" I ask.

"I wasn't always who I am now," he replies. "I used to be grandiose and egotistical and left God out of the picture, which is why I fell."

"And now, Terry?"

"I'm hanging out in the park," he chuckles. "Ain't that a bitch?" I follow his eyes across the lawn, where a group of pretty teenage girls are laughing and a family is having a barbecue.

"It is a beautiful day. But this life can't be easy," I say.

"It is hard to trust out here sometimes," says Terry.

"It's hard to trust everywhere," I reply.

The old man chews this one over for a moment. Then he says, "Without my spirit, I'd go insane."

When I shake Terry's hand and walk away, I look back over my shoulder and see him beginning to doze on his bench. Tanya takes my seat and lights a half-smoked cigarette. Her little boy gets to tickling Terry with his Popsicle stick; Terry is laughing and trying to swat him off. Has he found his home in the world? you could ask. Is home a metaphysical thing as much as a nailed-down address and a mailbox? Or is a home like a body, always there when we bother to notice? Are we really always *at home* so long as we remain in the world? But if that's so, I can't help but wonder, why do we feel so often so uprooted inside our own skins? Do we feel so homeless because we've yet to locate the keys to interior castles? Or do we keep looking for somewhere different because we're accustomed to feeling lost?

THE ART OF LOSING

Viktor Frankl was a thirty-seven-year-old psychiatrist on the autumn morning he and his wife were abducted from their Vienna apartment and shipped to Theresienstadt death camp. On the train platform Viktor and Tillie were torn apart; then, for the next three years, Frankl endured the horrors of camp life we know about all too well. A brilliant student of human nature (his specialty was suicidology), Frankl spent his years in the camp observing the behavior of his fellow inmates, from the lowliest of the *Muselmänner*—those "walking dead," who had lost their will to live—to prisoners at the other end of the spectrum, who'd kept some dignity in spite of their cruel surroundings.

For Frankl, such dignity—indeed, his very survival—centered on his love for Tillie and the hope that they would be reunited (in fact, she would die in the camp). Frankl would establish himself in the next few years among Europe's most renowned psychiatrists with a school known as logotherapy. Logotherapy, from *logos*, or "meaning," holds that our ability to live most fully depends on finding meaning in our existence. In *Man's Search for*

Meaning, Frankl's classic study, he described witnessing such hard-won dignity in action:

> We who lived in concentration camps can remember the men who walked through the huts comforting others, giving away their last piece of bread. They may have been few in number, but they offer sufficient proof that everything can be taken from a man but one thing: the last of the human freedoms—to choose one's attitude in any given set of circumstances, to choose one's own way.
>
> . . . Every day, every hour, offered the opportunity to make a decision . . . which determined whether you would or would not submit to those powers which threatened to rob you of your very self, your inner freedom; which determined whether or not you would become a plaything of circumstance, renouncing freedom and dignity . . .
>
> Fundamentally, therefore, any man can, even under such circumstances, decide what shall become of him—mentally and spiritually. He may retain his human dignity even in a concentration camp. Dostoevsky said once, "There is only one thing that I dread: not to be worthy of my sufferings."

This sounds like an odd aspiration at first, being worthy of bad things that happen to us. Yet our very resistance to being broken by evil is what prevents us from becoming playthings of circumstance. Without this dignity, Frankl suggests, we might as well be animals.

This dignity is a form of grace. Even the most courageous need it to come through slaughter without being destroyed.

A seven-year-old boy is sitting in a dusty marketplace near his family's farm in the hinterlands of eastern Sudan during the early harvest days of 1986. His name is Francis Bok, and he is here with two of his sisters to sell peanuts, eggs, and assorted produce from the family's homestead, which is among the most fertile in the valley. As the strongest son of eight, Francis is his father's favorite, the boy he calls *muycharko*—a Dinka word meaning "twelve men"—the offspring his father has chosen to replace him as head of the family after he dies.

The children are spread out on a crimson blanket under their lean-to of burlap and sticks, laughing, surrounded by their wares. The rainy season hasn't started; the air is still hot and dry, brimming with the pungent aromas of fish and fresh tobacco leaves, racks of glistening meat hung from hooks in the close-packed stalls. Business is good; Francis is happy collecting coins in a purse his mother has sewn for him to keep inside his clothes.

All of a sudden, bedlam breaks out. Francis hears gunfire and galloping horses, then crowds scattering in all directions as a band of black-turbaned marauders storms into the marketplace. These are the dreaded *juur*, members of the Arab tribes to the north who've sworn genocide on southern black Christians like Francis and his family. As Francis watches in terror, his five-year-old sister hiding behind him, these *juur* begin to hack down the marketers in their path. Francis's neighbor, a girl of eight, is shot through the head for no reason; when her sister becomes hysterical and refuses to leave the girl's dead body, her leg is hacked off at the hip. Women and babies are bayoneted and left to writhe to their death in the dirt.

Terrified, Francis herds his sisters behind him. Before they can escape, a man is there on horseback, towering over him, pointing a gun at Francis's head and ordering him into the saddle behind him. Then the horse is galloping out past the road to Francis's farm and onto the desert highway leading toward Khartoum. Fourteen hours later Francis and his kidnapper, Giemma Abdullah, arrive at Giemma's farm, where Francis is shackled, locked in a pigsty, and told that he is now an *abeed*—a slave—who will live and eat with the animals. If Francis disobeys in any way or tries to escape, Giemma assures him, he will be killed.

What goes through the mind of a seven-year-old boy kidnapped and thrust into such a nightmare? There's numbness first, then disbelief, an armadillo's self-curling protection when "everything went dead" in him, as Francis will tell me when we meet. Shock is followed by wrenching grief, loneliness, and humiliation. For no reason whatsoever, Giemma's wife pulls Francis into the kitchen one morning, puts a pistol to his head, and says, "I would blow your brains out this very minute if I could," with an evil smile. Giemma's children are invited to beat Francis with rocks and sticks as a game. "I wondered why no one was helping me," Francis will tell me. "People just stood there and watched. Why would they do that to me? I was only seven years old."

Night after night in his pigsty, gazing up through a hole in the roof, Francis began to plot and replot his escape from Giemma's farm. "Better not to live," he decided, "than to live as a slave."

He looks like a Giacometti sculpture dipped in blue-black ink and polished. His body, at six feet seven inches, is impossibly thin, severely chiseled, astoundingly odd in its elongation. I've been led to Francis Bok by an antislavery group in Washington, D.C. Francis, now twenty-four, has invited me to visit him in the town outside Boston where the group helped find him an apartment. He wants to tell me the story of how after ten years of slavery he managed to escape to freedom.

Francis crosses his stiltlike legs and observes me with an expression neither friendly nor disinterested. The little apartment, with its thrift store furniture, basketball posters, and color TV, could belong to any college student (Francis is taking courses at a nearby university). This backdrop seems a universe away from the fields where he and his brother's grew up playing *alweth* (hide-and-seek) near their village of Gourion.

"I reached the point inside of myself that I didn't care what would happen to me," Francis tells me in a whisper. "I didn't care if I lived or died. I only knew that I must try again."

Ten years after his abduction, and after a number of close calls, the seventeen-year-old was finally able to slip off Giemma Abdullah's farm while herding cattle, hitched a ride to a local town, and then, after several detours, found his way to Khartoum (where he was arrested on suspicion of illegal activity) and finally to Cairo. After four months in Egypt, Francis was taken up by a human rights group and granted asylum in the United States, where a foster family supported him long enough for Francis to afford the small apartment where he and I are now sitting.

"Do you like it here?" I ask awkwardly.

Francis doesn't say anything. Though outwardly polite and easygoing, he's markedly inaccessible, too, circled by a moat of caution, his voice remote and difficult to hear. I'm reminded of Nawang Sangdrol, the Tibetan nun, who was comfortable while reporting the terrible facts of her public story but turned dreamy, cagey—the word that comes to mind is "porous"—when invited below the surface.

"How is your life?" I try again.

Francis grins and says, "I am well."

"Really?" I don't mean to sound so surprised. But it's not the an-swer one would expect from a man who was forced to sleep in a pigsty, eating discarded kitchen scraps. "What about what hap-pened to you?"

"I am a Christian," Francis says, as if this were sufficient expla-nation.

"I know a lot of bitter Christians," I say.

Francis takes a slug off his Pepsi. He gazes through the vene-tian blinds at a girl in hot pants walking her dog. "I can tell you this," he says in a voice so low I can hardly hear him. "No matter what happens, I try to take it soft."

"What do you mean by soft?"

"I learned much about life on Giemma's farm."

Just then, Francis's demeanor begins to shift. He leans forward and speaks in a deeper voice. "I have learned that it does not mat-ter how much you are beaten or how much you are despised," he says, suddenly sounding like a man. "There is one thing they can never take from you."

"What, Francis?"

He sits up straight. "They can never steal your idea of who you are," he says. "They can never take control of your mind. They can never take away your self-love." It's suddenly easy to imagine him preaching at a pulpit. "They cannot take away my forgiveness. They can never silence my heart. No matter what has happened, I see myself as a full person."

This is astonishing. The majority of people I know haven't lived through a fraction of this loss yet do not see themselves as full people. Francis stands to his full height and ducks under the kitchen doorway for more soda.

"How is that possible?" I ask.

He pops our cans open and pours. "If you want to live, you must fight for your freedom," he says to me. As a Christian, Francis has faith in mercy but also believes in the struggle for justice. "When you abandon yourself, you lose. If you are alive in this world, you must fight. But never with a sword." He's back on the couch now, his long fingers occupying themselves with a rubber band. "My people are using machine guns to shoot the Arabs who are slaughtering us. They believe that is the way to freedom, but it is not." I'm stunned when Francis informs me that there are twenty-eight million people currently living as slaves around the world.

"How do you deal with the memories?" I ask him. "How do you balance out what was taken from you?"

Francis thinks about this for a moment. "It is not easy feeling normal."

"You're not normal," I say. "That's a good thing."

"I am very happy that you think so," he says, finally giving me a smile. Then he reaches for a paperback book on the coffee table. It's Dickens's *A Tale of Two Cities*. Francis reads from the first page. "It was the best of times, it was the worst of times," he recites, picking his way through the English letters. "This is what my life has been like," he says, still smiling. "The best. And the worst."

"This is the best part?"

"I have been given a second chance."

"You forgave Giemma?"

Francis closes the book and puts it down. Apparently he hasn't quite made it to sainthood. For a moment he seems to disappear behind the soft-focus screen I noticed at first. Then he looks me straight in the eye and says, almost word for word, what the Tibetan nun told me. "No one can move forward in hatred."

I realize this, I say. But what does he *feel*?

"And dignity does not come from bloodshed." Francis cuts my American-style nit-picking off at the pass. "There must be a way—you must find it—to love."

He is struggling with himself. I can see that.

"There is no other way," Francis tells me. "Otherwise I am just like Giemma."

A QUARTER INCH
FROM HEAVEN

Hakuin was a great seventeenth-century Zen master, a serious, shit-kicking old guy in black robes who would whack his disciples when they slouched and could meditate for days at a time. Hakuin was not afraid of anything.

One day a samurai arrived at the master's mountain *zendo*. The samurai approached Hakuin and bowed. "Sir," he announced, "I wish to understand the difference between heaven and hell."

Hakuin was the picture of disdain, eyeing the samurai from head to toe like yesterday's chop suey. "I would tell you," the old man said, twirling his silver mustache. "But I doubt that you have the keenness of wit to understand."

The samurai's face blazed with wounded pride. He pulled back in astonishment. "Do you know who you are speaking to?" he asked, puffing out his astounding chest.

"No one much." Hakuin shrugged. "I really think you are probably too dull to understand."

"What?" the samurai demanded, unable to believe his own ears. "How can you speak to me in such a tone?"

"Oh, don't be silly," Hakuin mocked him. "Who do you think you are?" The samurai trembled with fury. "And that thing hanging from your waist," the teacher added. "You call that a sword? It's more like a butter knife."

Finally the samurai could take it no longer. With sweaty hands, he drew his sword and raised it over his head to strike.

"Ah," Hakuin said. "That is hell."

The samurai spun around in his own mind. His eyes then shone with recognition as he lowered the sword and sheathed it.

"And that," the old guy told him, "is heaven."

THE GIRL ON THE ROCK

One rainy afternoon in London, under an ominous mackerel sky, I find myself in a back corridor of the Tate Gallery, standing before an eighteenth-century painting I have never seen before. It is an oil-on-canvas portrait of Hope, the allegorical goddess, as depicted in 1886 by George Frederick Watts. This is no triumphant, trumpeting Hope (no hope springs eternal, let's sound the trombones!). Instead, this Hope is a waifish thing stranded on a lonely cliff, barefoot, tempest torn, eyes concealed behind a blindfold as she reaches her empty hand out toward a harp with only one string.

I'm mesmerized by this mysterious picture, the supplicating pose of the girl whose face is almost hidden from view, fingers straining toward an instrument that offers her only chance of music, yet has only one string still intact, as likely to snap as it is to play. This is how life feels at times, isn't it? You've been blindfolded and left in the dark, knowing that even as you reach into your next moment, the string may simply snap in your face. But that if you don't reach, you're not really living.

I learned this the hard way myself during a routine visit to my onetime doctor's office. This was years before antiretroviral treatments had been invented. I excitedly showed him a magazine article announcing a new prophylactic drug trial for which I might be eligible. I waited nervously for the doctor's response. He glanced at the clipping and handed it back.

"Listen," this substandard whitecoat told me with a patronizing smirk. "Whatever makes you feel better . . ." He trailed off without bothering to finish, as if he were wasting his breath on a child.

I took the clipping, opened the door, left his office, and never returned. If I was on the verge of croaking, I resolved, it would not be while staring up into those cold, tired, angry eyes. My posse of friends questioned the hasty decision, but I knew it was the right thing. Were I to lose all hope, I would be a goner, whether my body survived or not. Souls survive on hope in the absence of physical evidence. Not the naïve hope that everything will be hunky-dory, exactly as life used to be, but the hope that assures us, when things seem darkest, that although it doesn't look that way now, *something else is also true*, as one survivor put it to me. That there is a hidden face to this moment. Such hope serves the same survival function as faith and denial, preserving a space in the shrinking mind for all that has yet to be revealed, leaving a chink for the mysteries. "The function of intelligence *in extremis* is not to judge one's chances, which [may be] nearly zero, but to make it through that day . . . without thinking too much about tomorrow," as one veteran from World War II said. Even when we lose hope for a particular outcome, we may find ourselves experiencing a more general faith in the power of life itself.

Hope is a metaphysical power, the breeze stirring in the darkness. Stan Rice described this mysterious force in a poem. "I was lost," he begins,

> and sang my broken down songs in the hell of the hour.
> Then in my heart moved an oar,
> and I was found by a breeze from a door in the sea of forms
> And was rowed to the cherry trees on the shore.
> *Selah Selah*

When I left Dr. G.'s harbor of doom, the sails of my boat filled again and got me to Dr. Bellman's office.

Fixated hope is a problem, though. When we attach ourselves to a single outcome, it's easy to become hope's hostage, to imprison ourselves in optimism, entrap ourselves through inflexible craving for a premeditated result. Hope of this kind brings sure disappointment. We risk spending our time consumed by longing, obsessed with all the things we don't have and unhappy with what life has chosen to give us.

Buddhists have a word for this gap between fixated hope and its fulfillment: *dukkha*, a far-reaching term encompassing the absence of ultimate satisfaction in an imperfect world where all things must come to an end. Knowing how stubborn the human mind can be—how it wants what it wants *now*—Buddhism warns against too much clinging to desired outcomes we cannot control. Having practiced for decades to release such hope, a teacher such as American-born master Pema Chodron can say something like "If hope and fear are two sides of the same coin, then so are hopelessness and confidence" with a measure of credibility. Pema assures us that suffering is inevitable as long as we believe that things last. Only by discovering "ease with uncertainty, poise amidst shakiness," by learning to stay with "the broken heart and rumbling stomach" and achieving some détente with hopelessness, can we be truly happy, she says. "In the world of hope and fear," writes Pema, "we always have to change [what is]. But when we allow ourselves to feel uncertainty, disappointment, shock, embarrassment, we discover a mind that is clear, unbiased, and fresh."

I'm sure this is true. But for the vast majority of us, hope within reason, like denial within reason, is a form of adaptive genius. Our spirits are kept unsealed by the very breath of hope. Spirit ascends; soul is earthbound; their intersection is human life. The contradictory mess of caring, hoping, and letting go appears to be our curriculum here. Many years ago, a number of meditation teachers I know went to Thailand, where they visited the hermitage of a teacher named Achaan Chah. In Thailand people tend to use the Buddhist abbots and monks the way people in this country use therapists or astrologers. One day a father from the town came to Achaan Chah's monastery, extremely upset, to ask the master how he could possibly live with not being able to protect his children in such a violent world. How could this man, this father, hope to survive his kids' tragedies, the thousand blows that life would deal them? Achaan Chah lifted a lovely crystal goblet from his side table and held it up to the sun.

"I like this glass," the master said, delighting in the diamond light patterns shining through its thousand facets. "I find this glass very beautiful. When the sun shines through it, there are rainbows. When you test it, it gives a wonderful ring. But I know that this glass is already broken."

The worried father did not understand.

"Each time I sip from this glass, I enjoy it," the master continued. "And yet, when a strong wind tips it over or I knock this glass with my elbow and it shatters into a thousand pieces, I will say, 'Ah so, it was already broken.'"

Achaan Chah seemed to be suggesting to the father that were he to love his children in this way, each moment he spent with them would be so direct, and so precious, that there would be no room for regret, no necessity for hope. Acceptance would trump hopelessness.

I wonder if this is true, and what it would mean to the girl on the rock. Whether this lesson would strip off her blindfold, stop her from reaching, seeing that her harp was already broken. Or whether the girl would still want to play because playing itself is in her nature, knowing that one string can be enough, and that if that last string breaks, she can always sing.

GOING TO TAHITI
(OR RAISING HEAVEN)

Psychologists agree that transcendental experience is as necessary to emotional health as family, friendship, sex, and work. Religions are born from this hunger for transcendence, of course, as is the taste for mind-expanding substances, which have been enjoyed by human beings, both ritualistically and recreationally, since recorded history began. From at least the year 5000 B.C. onward, our ancestors have employed a vast number of psychotropic plants to heal themselves physically, to enhance insight, and to ease suffering from what a Huichol shaman describes as "loss of spirit" (what we might call the blues). The Rig Veda, the most ancient of Hindu texts, speaks of ecstasy derived from a plant known as soma, which Aldous Huxley later introduced into mainstream awareness with his 1932 novel, *Brave New World*. (In fact, diagnosed with cancer at age sixty-nine, Huxley requested that a tab of LSD be administered to him on the day of his death.)

Huxley was a firm believer in better living through chemistry. "If we could sniff or swallow something that would, for five or six hours a day, abolish our solitude as individuals, attune us with our fellows in a flowing exaltation of affection and make life in all its aspects seem not only worth living but divinely beautiful and significant, then it seems to me all our problems would be wholly solved and earth would become a paradise," wrote the futuristic author.

He'd never been to a Grateful Dead concert, I guess. Not that I'm against getting high. I like an occasional jazz cigarette. I've been smoking weed on and off since high school and have yet to bury a spike in my arm or hear Son of Sam voices inside my head. I did lose control for a couple of years in my teens, but learned my delinquent lesson the day I ate too many quaaludes, totaled three cars, attacked the cop trying to help me after my head smashed through the windshield, and got thrown into jail for the third time that year. When my poor mother came to bail me out, seeing my bloody, wasted self, she just shook her head and said, "You're gonna end up in Alcatraz."

She was right, which is why I cleaned up my act and drew the line at occasional reefer. When Ecstasy became popular in the 1980s, I wasn't even vaguely tempted. That is why, after receiving two horse-sized capsules of pure MDMA (Ecstasy) in the mail from a well-meaning chemist (as "part of your research," his note read) for a piece I was writing about E, my own conflicted reaction surprised me. This package had come to me uninvited. I'd long ago made the firm decision not to voluntarily leave the three-dimensional world again (and not tweaking, for sure, on some stupid narcotic). I'd worked too hard to build a sane life. I had been told E was different, it's true; it wasn't a hallucinogen, but an empathogen, in fact, a "heart-opening" substance, with the reputed power to enable its users to dissolve emotional barricades in themselves—lucidly—in order to free themselves when sober. Until the Feds upgraded MDMA to a Schedule I drug in 1985 (making its use a felony), therapists had used the stuff for the treatment of post-traumatic stress disorder, addiction, and a number of other hard-to-crack maladies. "Our culture is the first ever to have made the search for self-awareness a crime," chemist Alexander Shulgin complained at the time. In a booze-blasted culture like ours, this double standard did seem questionable. And yet, I was far from convinced.

The horse capsules tempted me from their drawer. It wasn't the prospect of getting high that stuck in my craw. It was the drug's self-liberating promise, and what my staunch refusal told me about myself. I was forty-five, my health was great, I was nested and safe and writing and flossing, but feeling a little too settled as well. I used to be so bold, I moaned. I used to want to taste the whole thing, blast through walls, let caution be damned. Now I wouldn't take a hit of E, which a friend of mine actually buys from her rabbi?

A gauntlet had been tossed, it seemed to me. E morphed in my mind from a few hours' buzz into everything that I feared in my life, the seeker in me who'd gone to sleep. Here were these capsules siren-calling from their drawer, offering me a free ticket out of my bourgeois box, an entrée to a carefree zone of envelope pushing, surprise, even bliss. How could I be afraid of that? If Gauguin hadn't taken that boat to Tahiti (miserable wretch though he turned out to be), he would never have painted those brown-breasted women for museum hoppers to ogle down through the ages. I needed to get out of Dodge for a minute. I needed to go to Tahiti.

Coincidentally, around this time I was approached by a publisher looking for an editor to bail them out of an emergency. One of their star authors, Dr. Richard Alpert, aka Ram Dass, had suffered a massive stroke before completing what they believed would be his final bestselling book. A hero of the sixties counterculture, the pilot fish to a generation, Alpert had started out as a Harvard psychology professor before being fired for performing psilocybin experiments on his students (along with his crazy office mate, Timothy Leary). Alpert had dropped out, gone to India, fallen in love with a guru, been rechristened Ram Dass (Servant of God), and been sent back to the States with marching orders to write a book, which became the iconic *Be Here Now*, once the third-bestselling title in the English-speaking world, after Dr. Spock and the King James Bible. Ram Dass had spent the forty years since then as a humanitarian and spiritual teacher.

Now R.D., as he likes to be called, had survived this massive cerebral hemorrhage (against nine-to-one odds) but been left wheelchair bound and severely aphasic, unable to dress or feed himself, much less finish a book. R.D. desperately needed someone to help extract his mots justes and ventriloquize this stuff onto paper. I caught a flight to San Francisco a few days later to see if the two of us would hit it off.

The first time I catch sight of R.D., he's cramped into a wheelchair on the porch of his Victorian home in Marin, smoking a joint and chuckling, unruly white hair haloed around his head like a cartoon scientist's. I'm taken aback by the dramatic difference between Ram Dass as the world knows him and this overweight senior with Kleenex stuck to the side of his face and a fey Filipino nurse fussing at him from inside the house that it's time to take his nap—please!

Our chemistry seems to work (even without additives), so over the course of the next six months, I spend many long days with

R.D., picking through his haphazard pages, struggling to draw what he's trying to say from the tangled web of his halting brain. With one arm strapped to the chair, barely able to speak, he alternates between crankiness and serenity, distraction and discomfort (R.D.'s arm hurts a lot), assailing me with grunts and half sentences, annoyed when I can't help interrupting him, and eager for this last book of his—which he's calling *Still Here*—to be a faithful account of what he has learned through this physical ordeal. R.D. wants the "fierce grace" of "being stroked" to infuse this manuscript about conscious aging. As he helped lead the flower power crowd toward higher consciousness, he now wants to teach these same baby boomers how to face aging creatively and with a measure of grace.

Every few weeks, I fly out to Marin, where R.D. and I labor together on his book, a photo of his smiling, tom-tom-bellied guru lolling on a plaid blanket always nearby. In exchange for my grammar and patience, R.D. offers me an intimate tutorial on fierce grace.

Now and then I bring up a personal question. "Someone sent me some Ecstasy," I tell him one day while we're having lunch in his shambles of a kitchen.

"Lucky you." R.D. smiles. His blue eyes haven't lost their twinkle.

"I doubt that I'll take it," I admit.

He twirls an index finger slowly next to his head.

"You think I'm crazy?"

"Scared," he says, struggling to get the food to his mouth without spilling. "That is reason to try." I'm well aware that R.D. credits psychedelics with opening his own eyes to "the big picture." Recently he told an interviewer, "My entire adult life has been an attempt to grow into what I saw at that [first] moment of cosmic unity on LSD, to incorporate the immensity of that experience into my being." "Anything less extreme would have been unlikely to break through my mind-set," R.D. suggested.

"I've gotten so middle-aged," I say.

He nods in agreement and makes me feel worse.

"I used to be such a hell-raiser—" I say.

R.D. chuckles and struggles to find a word.

"What?" I lean forward, trying to read his lips.

"Raise," he stammers, "heaven."

At the time of his stroke a year ago, Ram Dass was a vigorous, sixty-six-year-old, golf-playing, sports-car-driving bachelor traveling the world incessantly, reveling in his role as a lionized sage to a generation of middle-aged seekers like me. As the heir to an affluent Connecticut Jewish family (his father founded the New Haven and Hartford Railroad), he was a pampered child, and later Ivy League academic, who threw it all in for the consciousness game. R.D.'s unique appeal as a teacher had always been his self-deprecating lack of holiness, his willingness to present himself as a work in progress, "a poor shlub just like anyone else trying to lead an enlightened life." Richard Alpert the psychologist had thought that Ram Dass the seeker was doing a pretty good job, until his own near-death experience in 1997 showed him how far he still had to go.

"I wasn't cooked yet," R.D. tells me straight off. This is how he describes the night of the stroke (I've smoothed out R.D.'s speech to spare the reader's nerves): "There I was lying in my bed, trying to imagine how to finish this book about aging," he says, "having this fantasy of what it would be like to be a very, *very* old man, when I heard the phone ring." R.D. can recall getting out of bed to answer; his next memory is of a group of firemen "staring into this old man's face—but the old man was me and I wasn't dreaming." (Fortunately, an assistant had arrived on the scene in time to call 911; a half hour later and he would have been dead.) Like many near-death-experience survivors, he describes watching himself being resuscitated "as if from a doorway on the sides of the scene," an out-of-body vantage point that followed him into the ambulance and to the hospital.

"I was sort of fascinated by what was happening," he admits.

"You must have been frightened," I insist.

R.D. denies this. "I never thought that I was dying. There was no flashing white light," or anything else that a lifetime of spiritual practice had prepared him to expect at the moment of death. "That's when I realized that I had a lot more work to do before the end."

His uncooked parts centered on body and pride, the humiliation of allowing himself to be cared for after a lifetime of giving service. Overnight, R.D. went from being the guy on the white horse, visiting sickbeds, heading philanthropic organizations, ministering to thousands of students, to not being able to pee alone or make himself a tuna sandwich. This was more humbling than any *seva* (service) he'd ever performed in so-called spiritual life, he assures me. "I'd distanced myself from my body as merely a vehicle for the soul."

This reminds me of a line from one of James Joyce's short stories: "Mr. Duffy lived a short distance from his body." R.D. chuckles. "I had ignored my body as much as possible," he admits. "I'd tried to 'spiritualize' it away. Calling it detachment when actually it was fear." His body denial may, in fact, have helped to cause the stroke, since he neglected to take his blood pressure medications. Now here he was, trapped, at the mercy of others, wrestling daily with his suppressed vanity in the messy limits of his all-too-human body. This self-reckoning brought down walls in R.D. that he had never before dared to acknowledge.

"The stroke was like a samurai sword," he explains. "The 'I' that I am now is not experiencing things the way the old 'I' would have. It's pushed me up to a higher level."

"Higher in what way?" I ask.

"When there's genuine surrender between people, the boundaries between power and powerlessness, healer and helped, begin to dissolve," R.D. tells me. "It is the dissolving of boundaries between us and the mystery that loosens the hold of the ego. Allows the soul to be revealed."

This soul perspective has been key to his negotiation of physical losses. "You can't work with pain when you are stuck in fear," he tells me. "Watching ourselves through the soul's eye allows us the distance to distinguish between who we really are, spiritual beings having a physical experience, and our suffering at the level of body and mind."

R.D.'s nurse enters the room and slips a straw from a glass of orange juice between his lips. After swallowing, he continues. "The minute you look at a fearful thought you've run from, it changes. Rather than being some awful Goliath, your fears become like little shmoos."

"Shmoos?"

Little nuisances, he means. "Every time you notice a fear, you learn to come closer to it. Fear of paralysis. Fear of dying." R.D.

ticks off the usual suspects. "Each time you do this, you're a little more able to take a deep breath and say, 'Ah, so. Big surprise.' And move forward without being swamped."

"Confronting the fear shrinks it down to size?"

"Absolutely," R.D. assures me. "It's as if the trapdoors of the self have been opened and we can finally step outside and enjoy the view," he says, recalling the famous line from William Blake: "If the doors of perception were cleansed, everything would appear to man as it is, infinite."

R.D. wants people to know that soul perception is our ace in the hole, the ability to widen our subjective lens to take in the full 360. Once we've tasted soul awareness, he believes, it almost doesn't matter whether we've got all our marbles or not. A student of R.D.'s was taking care of an elderly mother with Alzheimer's disease. "This old lady was perfectly happy being gaga, but her daughter simply couldn't let go of the mother she'd known," he says. "She kept pushing her mother to regain her memory. But this eighty-year-old woman didn't seem to care much about losing her mind. When I was able to work with the daughter to let go, the mother's life became much more peaceful."

He has met similar resistance among his own well-meaning caretakers. "The people around me think that I should fight to walk again," he says, raising his eyebrows. "But I don't know if I *want* to walk. I'm sitting. That's where I am." He pats the arm of his chair with his good hand. "I've come to love my wheelchair—I call it my swan boat. I'm peaceful like this and grateful to the people who care for me. Why is this wrong?"

"Maybe it's not."

"It's important not to get dragged into other people's drama," he says. "It's too easy to become your illness, to lose yourself on your 'bed of woes-es.' It is an ongoing practice to stay free of pity and fear. I may be confined by my stroke, but I don't want to be trapped in the roles that people project onto me—of invalid, victim, hero, whatever. I'm truly content the way I am."

I look at him askance. R.D. chides me with a wagging finger. "In other cultures it's a symbol of honor and power to be carried and wheeled around," he insists. "You know, it's really not at all important to be what the culture calls optimal. Healing does not mean going back to the way things were before. It means allowing what is now to move us closer to God," he explains. "The secret is that our limits actually become our strengths if we use them skillfully. The ego's attachment to power is linked inextricably to fear of losing that power. But there is a kind of power that doesn't give rise to fear."

"Spiritual power?"

"Exactly," R.D. answers. "Behind the machinations of our brilliant, undependable minds is an essence that is not conditional," he says. "A being that aging does not alter, to which nothing can be added and from which nothing can be taken away."

The face behind the mask, I think. "How we feel about the future comes down to how we feel about mystery," he tells me. "I've gone through the worst, and it really wasn't so bad after all."

When the manuscript is finally finished, we celebrate with a meal and a smoke. R.D. thanks me for my time. I thank him for his sage advice.

"Did you ever take that E?" he asks.

Oddly enough, the capsules have slipped my mind completely. Being with Ram Dass has left me so high, I've forgotten the need to go to Tahiti. I confess that the capsules are still in their drawer.

"I guess I really am middle-aged," I say.

He spins a finger around his temple once more. "Speak for yourself, my boy."

The last time I see him, R.D. is sitting bare-legged on a single bed, clutching his mattress with taped-up fingers, Indian *kirtans* playing in the background, his nurse slowly peeling socks down over his swollen ankles, the warm, still air of late afternoon falling in shadows across his small bedroom. His blue eyes follow me toward the door. The last sentence we wrote together still resonates in my head.

"While everything else falls away," R.D. told me slowly, extracting the words one painful syllable at a time, "wisdom alone remains."

THE NET OF INDRA

Years ago while volunteering at a hospital, I spent time with a man named Jack, who'd worked fifty years on an oil rig, had arms like a wrestler, and was now, at seventy-five, battling a tumor in his lung. Jack's physical pain was being managed with a morphine pump, his nursing care was impeccable, yet he seemed racked with metaphysical pain, as Jim MacLaren would call it, an isolation so profound that no number of visitors, narcotics, or games of five-card rummy with me were able to alleviate it. The first rule of volunteer training is never to presume to understand how the patient feels, as in "I've been there, I understand." You haven't and you don't. The second rule is to check your cheerleader self at the door and resist the overwhelming urge to do something—anything—to raise their spirits or help them smile. You're there to listen, to be empathic, to put yourself aside sufficiently to be a container— in the therapeutic sense—for whatever a patient might need to express.

So I struggled not to cheer Jack up, dealt the cards, didn't ask any questions, avoided his forlorn expression as much as possible. One day while I was in his room, the hospital chaplain poked her head in. Sister Loretta weighed three hundred pounds and looked a lot like Rosie O'Donnell. "How's my favorite hunk?" she asked Jack, scraping a chair across the floor to sit at his bedside.

"Lousy, Sister."

"Loretta's here," she told him, signaling for me to get lost. I backed into the doorway and listened. From where I stood, I saw Sister Loretta take Jack's hand. At first the old guy didn't say anything. Loretta waited. Then I heard him starting to sniffle. "Talk to me," Loretta said.

"My father never loved me," said Jack. At this his tears broke into sobs. I was stunned to hear this coming from him, amazed that in the midst of a physical crisis, at a time when his health remained uncertain, the ghost of his father's absent love should be the thing that pained this tough guy the most.

Such glaring disconnects are common among survivors of all kinds, the gaps between what ought to be wrong and what really is: The homeless guy who wants conversation more than he wants pennies or food. The ex-POW who needs to belong somewhere more than he needs hosannas or financial aid. The individual surrounded by love who complains about not feeling "cosmic connection," because God, she believes, left her high and dry the day she lost her beloved child.

We spend our lives in a kind of amnesia, sensing disconnection that doesn't exist. Einstein called this an "optical delusion," imagining ourselves to be separate beings, cut off at the root from the rest of creation. "A human being ... experiences himself, his thoughts and feelings as something separated from the rest," wrote the father of relativity.

This delusion is a kind of prison for us, restricting us to our personal desires and to affection for a few persons nearest to us. Our task must be to free ourselves from this prison by widening our circle of compassion to embrace all living creatures and the whole of nature in its beauty.

We sequester ourselves inside our own minds, then project this awful abyss around us, picturing ourselves to be fenced-off, abandoned citizens of a private, bullying universe. This imaginary chasm seems only to widen during times of pain. Yet even under the worst conditions, strength in numbers continues to prevail. As one Holocaust survivor put it, "Lone dogs died first." Mary Robinson, the ex-president of Ireland, observed this principle at work during the troubles in her country. "It is in each other's shadow that we flourish," Robinson insisted to me when we spoke.

This is not sentimental pabulum. In a universe where boundaries do not actually exist, where waves and particles, protons and neutrons are indivisibly strung together, such baseline connection is obvious. In Indian philosophy this glistening, intergalactic jewel-work of matter (and antimatter) is known as the Net of Indra. This web is so tightly strung that "the flap of a butterfly's wings on earth can be felt on the planet of Betteljers," as a physicist observed. If a full moon can make women menstruate, it's not so much of a stretch to realize that individuals in our lives are ricocheting off of us at every moment, creating positive or negative charges depending on their own chemistry.

"We're wired to connect," science writer Daniel Goleman tells me over lunch at his favorite Tibetan restaurant in Northampton, Massachusetts. Ten years ago Dan became a culture hero with

Emotional Intelligence, a seminal book that helped redefine what it means to be smart in our IQ-obsessed culture. Recently Dan has turned his eye to the workings of what he calls social intelligence, which includes the contagiousness of common emotions (think of giggles, yawning, tears, and screams) as well as the pharmaceutical value of keeping good company.

"The brain itself is social," Dan tells me over a plate of yak sausage. "That's the most exciting finding in the past ten years." His gentle mien and thoughtful diction reflect his own thirty-year meditation practice (he was posted in India while doing his Harvard Ph.D. fieldwork). "One person's inner state affects and drives the other person. We're forming brain-to-brain bridges—a two-way traffic system—all the time. We actually catch each other's emotions like a cold."

"Is that really true?" I ask.

"If we're in distressing, toxic relationships with people who are constantly putting us down, this has actual physical conse-quences," Dan assures me. Stress produces cortisol, a chemical that hinders cell health. (He cites a study done on women caring for husbands with Alzheimer's, which found that their actual cell life diminished at an accelerated rate.) Conversely, positive inter-actions cause the body to secrete oxytocin, the chemical released during lovemaking, nursing, and delivery, which lowers stress hor-mones and amplifies the immune system.

"I have this experience often with my two-year-old grand-daughter," Dan tells me. "She's like a vitamin for me. Being with her actually feels like a kind of elixir. The most important people in our lives are actually our biological allies."

Indeed, neuroplasticity, the discovery that the brain is always growing (not diminishing, as our grandparents believed), has revolutionized our understanding of how people evolve over the course of a lifetime. "Stem cells manufacture one hundred thousand brain cells every day till you die," Dan explains. "This defies what used to be the dogma. In fact, the brain continually reshapes itself throughout life with ongoing experience. It's where the maxim 'use it or lose it' comes from in neuroscience. The more you challenge it, the more the brain seems to rise to the occasion, and social interaction helps neurogenesis."

Take something called mirror neurons, whose sole function is to reflect (in us) the things we see in the world around us. "There are neurons whose only job is to recognize a smile and make you smile in return," he explains. "The same goes with frowning." I'm reminded of the Michelangelo effect, in which long-term partners come to resemble each other over time through facial muscle mimicry. Such mirroring on a mob scale helps to create creepy-sounding things called memes, those oversized cultural ideas (Democracy! Hygiene! Infidels!) that spread through populations like viruses. "By mimicking what another person does or feels, we bring the outside inside us," Dan tells me, speaking literally, not figuratively. "To understand one another we actually become like the other a little bit."

Dan describes two kinds of relationships—the I-IT and the I-YOU (first described by the philosopher Martin Buber)—which have antithetical effects on our social lives. I-IT relationships happen when we treat people as objects or functionaries because we want something from them (in the way, perhaps, that Jack's father might have treated him when all the boy wanted was an I-YOU pat on the back). "In I-YOU relationships, there's a human connection. There's feedback, a loop, because who the other person is, and what they have to say, matters." Unfortunately, the "inexorable technocreep" of our culture conspires against such intimacy, Dan believes. As T. S. Eliot presciently observed of our first major cultural social wedge, the TV set, back in the early sixties, television "permits millions of people to listen to the same joke at the same time, and yet remain lonesome." Not only is constant digital connectivity stressful, science has discovered, but also, Dan says, "to the extent that technology absorbs people in virtual reality, it deadens them to those who are actually around them."

Since "empathy is the prime inhibitor of human cruelty," as he reminds me, such alienation can have disastrous results. "Withholding the natural inclination to feel with another allows us to treat the other as It—as Them," Dan says. "The more Thems we have, the more dangerous the world becomes." But how can it possibly be true that human beings are essentially altruistic or that "the human brain is preset for kindness," as he has written? What about the newspaper headlines? "Remember," the ex–*New York Times* reporter tells me, "if it bleeds it leads. We pay more attention to human cruelty. But it's an aberration to be cruel."

The famous Yale University Milgram experiment was not the last word on human nature, he assures me. Despite their reputation for being selfish savages, even young children demonstrate altruism from an early age, apparently. In one study, infants reportedly cried when they saw or heard another baby crying but rarely when they heard their own distress. Monkeys have been known to starve themselves after realizing that grabbing food delivers an electrical shock to their cage-mate. Dan makes reference to the philosopher Mencius's assertion that any conscious adult would automatically jump down a well to save a drowning child. Yes, I say, but do they cheat on their wives? "We may not always be hooked up," he says, laughing, "but that doesn't mean that the wiring's no good."

The link between kindness, survival, and social intelligence seems obvious. As a Harvard post-doc studying meditation in India, Dan noticed that seasoned practitioners tended to exude what he calls "a special quality, magnetic in a quiet sense." Contrary to stereotype, these spiritual types did not seem otherworldly at all, but were "lively and engaged, extremely present, involved in the moment, often funny, yet profoundly at peace—equanimous in disturbing situations," as he describes it. What's more, this quality was *communicable*. "You always felt better than before you'd spent time with them, and this feeling lasted."

Physicists and mystics agree on this point. The components of altruistic energy appear to be as measurable as photons and electrons; they are also more palpable than a skeptic might imagine, as San Francisco psychologist Paul Ekman reports to me after spending a week in Dharmsala with the Dalai Lama. "At the airport afterward, my wife looked at me and said, 'You're not the man I married!'" says Ekman, who is not a Buddhist, laughing. "I was acting like somebody who's in love." The foremost authority on the physiology of emotion, Ekman detected four characteristics common to people with this contagious power: A "palpable goodness," first of all, that went far beyond some "warm and fuzzy aura" and seemed to arise from genuine integrity. Next, an impression of selflessness—a lack of concern with status, fame, and ego—a "transparency between their personal and public lives that set them apart from those with charisma, who are often one thing on the outside, another when you look under the surface." Third,

Ekman observed that this expansive, compassionate energy nurtured others. Finally, he was struck by the "amazing powers of attentiveness" displayed by these individuals, and the feeling he had of being seen in the round, wholly acknowledged by someone with open eyes.

If these qualities were unique to spiritual masters, they wouldn't be nearly as compelling. What inspired Ekman the scientist was the evidence that such energy is available to the rest of us. "It wasn't luck or culture or genes that created this qualitative difference," he tells me. "These people have resculpted their brains through practice." Survivors with no knowledge of brain science often experience this phenomenon for themselves—the way in which when we stretch past our limits, stretching becomes our second nature. Pushing the envelope seems to actually rewire our brains, adding a new repertoire of thoughts and emotions. When writer Andrew Solomon speaks in a later chapter of becoming more compassionate after his recovery from depression, for instance, this is more than Prozac speaking. It is an actual realignment of self through shifts in chemistry and neural conditioning.

In a laboratory outside Raleigh-Durham, North Carolina, a monk was monitored a few years back while meditating on compassion. Among other findings, scientists reported a dramatic increase in gamma waves (sparked in the part of the brain associated with positive emotions) while the monk focused on maintaining an open heart. Gamma-bumping like this requires ongoing practice. As a healer named Maxine Gaudio told me, "Everybody can draw, but not everybody's a Picasso." Unfortunately, we can't even pick up the brush sometimes, much less locate the canvas. Such forgetting is our nemesis, teachers maintain. "It is our daily dilemma," as Benedictine monk David Steindl-Rast tells me from his hermitage in Upstate New York. "A spiritual energy flows through the universe, a super-aliveness—an active *yes*," says the eighty-year-old hermit. "Yet even though our greatest happiness comes from feeling this eternal connection, there's a tendency in all of us to close off from it. Those who counteract the tendency through practice deepen their sense of belonging and free this latent energy." Brother David recommends such remembrance practice to his students. "When we say, 'Count your blessings,' this is a very profound teaching," he stresses. "A stream of energy—of blessing—is flowing from the universal source as blood pulsates from the heart. Knowing this, I'm energized and pass the blessing along to my brother so it flows again to its source." In this way, Brother David believes, "we create a network of grateful living."

The Net of Indra, shimmering. Remembering our indissoluble connection might actually bring more love into our lives. "It is love," Brother David assures me. "The love which passes understanding." I've sensed this love myself in the company of genuine masters: a great, unstoppable, pulsating love that draws you toward its own radiance. This force could radically change the world, melt away borders, give hope for increased happiness. Another great Christian, Pierre Teilhard de Chardin, articulated this hope for all time. "Someday after we have mastered the winds, the waves, the tides, and gravity, we shall harness . . . the energies of love," the French paleontologist-priest wrote. "Then for the second time in the history of the world, man will have discovered fire."

REINVENTING YOUR WIFE

An eminent New York psychologist named Henry Grayson was seeing a patient named John who claimed to be married to the world's biggest shrew. As analysands often do, John appeared to want commiseration from his loyal shrink, but Grayson isn't that kind of doctor. "What are you willing to do?" he asked the unhappy husband.

"Anything," John assured him. Dr. Grayson's instructions were oddly simple. The next time John became anxious over his wife's behavior, Grayson said, he should focus on his own upsetting thoughts and replace his inner, wife-hating voice (*she's ruining my life!*) with a tender memory of the woman he had married. At first John couldn't recall such a woman. Eventually, a happy memory oozed up from the distant past. He promised the doctor to give it a try.

John seemed confused at his next appointment. His wife had been strangely subdued that weekend. "She must be coming down with something," he said.

Grayson told him to try the experiment again.

This time John appeared downright suspicious. He and his wife had spent their first tirade-free weekend at home in as long as he could remember. Maybe she'd started seeing a therapist secretly, John wondered out loud, still failing to connect the dots. It would take yet another session for John to realize that the shift in his internal monologue had actually helped manifest his wife's improvement.

"Behavior stemming from our own thoughts may manifest in the people around us," Grayson explains to me when we meet. He resembles a more dashing Mr. Rogers in khaki pants and a paisley tie. Like many of his peers in the field of transpersonal psychology, Grayson came to his insights by way of hard science. It was while he was attending a lecture in physics, in fact, that his work as a psychologist began to shift. "This physicist helped me understand that the reality we perceive is a tiny fraction of the universe as it really exists," Grayson tells me. He began utilizing the Heisenberg principle, wherein objects change when they are perceived, on the interpersonal level. "We are connected not only as human beings but as energy, mind, and matter," he says. "We are interacting in profound, intimate ways we are rarely aware of."

"What about John and his wife?" I ask.

Henry Grayson smiles. "Let's just say they're playing a whole new ball game."

MAN THINKS, GOD LAUGHS

Irony can save a life. No survivor escapes without it. Often the irony is cruel, unbearably so if you can't laugh. "What fresh hell is this?" asked the ever-cheerful Dorothy Parker, sharpening her bitch nails on grief, lining up her exit options—rivers are damp, drugs cause cramp, guns aren't lawful, nooses give—concluding, as she once had in a poem, that "you might as well live." At other times, fate plays the joke on you. Think of the great British psychologist Wilfred Bion, awarded the Victoria Cross during World War II and later noting, "The only difference between getting that medal and being shot for treason was which direction I chose to run."

Our most serious eventualities arise from the most ridiculous chance. Moments. Twists. Split-second decisions. Telephone calls that might have saved lives. Strokes of luck that bring surprise mishaps, accidents that carry you forward, encounters out of the blue that alter your life irreversibly, hesitations that prove disastrous, then morph into windows opening. Pinballing along in this way, we're reminded of how little we control, how little we know of what good or bad luck is, the way things should or should not be, what we deserve and what we don't, at any given moment in time. We only know that we do not know, and never will, and tough petunias. *Menschen tracht und Gott Lacht*, my grandma Bella used to say in Yiddish. Man thinks, and God laughs. Your best-laid plans are really a punch line. Life is one insult after another. The bottom will drop; you will lose what you love; then you'll lose some more, hit your head on a rock, and sink into the lap of contentment—till you fall again. If you fail to find the humor in this, you might as well just leave the theater. Or sell the farm, better yet, if that's your idea of real estate.

Take the story of the farmer and his horse. Parables are annoying, I know, but irritation is the path to wisdom. One day a farmer lost his favorite horse. After the animal ran away, his neighbor appeared at his doorstep to offer condolences. "I'm so sorry for your loss," said the yenta neighbor, glad that it had not happened to him.

"You never know," the farmer replied.

The very next day, his horse reappeared with a beautiful wild mare alongside him. Again the neighbor stuck in his two cents. "That's wonderful!" he offered. "What a stroke of good luck!"

"You never know," said the farmer, wanting him to go away.

A few days later the farmer's son was trying to break in the wild mare, got thrown to the ground, and broke his leg. Immediately the neighbor appeared to comment again.

"You never know," the farmer repeated, now becoming a little annoyed.

Not long after the accident, the Cossack army came through the village in search of young men to fight in the war. Since the farmer's son was injured, he was allowed to stay at home. "Are you not a fortunate man!" exclaimed the neighbor.

You know what the farmer murmured.

Horace Walpole, the eighteenth-century English writer, was the first to invent a term for this bipolar phenomenon: serendipity (from a tale about the peregrinations of the three sons of the king of Serendip). Doubleness is the way of things, which is why narrow, cycloptic minds are so funny. The human condition, somebody said, is to be a fragment and a fool (pretending not to be a fragment). We couldn't be more ridiculous; this is also the good news. You have to be a trickster to trick up fate and turn it into destiny. Jim MacLaren's inspirational mission, Joan Didion's solvent book, Samuel Beckett's invention of the Theater of the Absurd after being stabbed randomly in a Paris street where his attacker shrugged after being asked why he'd done it. "*Mais, je ne sais pas, monsieur,*" he said. Serendipitous sproutings and lemonade twisters that come from laughing along with God (fate for atheists) instead of stomping your feet and pouting.

"Here's the thing about fate versus destiny," Jim Curtan tells me, bottom-line style, sounding like the Hollywood big shot he was before prostate cancer (and actors) made him start hating show business. "Fate is what happens to you. Destiny is how you respond."

Jim and I have been friends for thirty-five years. During the 1970s he was a personal manager for movie stars, spending his days appeasing, massaging, uplifting his clients' fragile, photogenic egos, which turned his life into a Sturm-und-Drang-fest. Stressed beyond reason, Jim was more than ready—before his diagnosis—to throw in his Tinseltown credentials and get his sense of humor back. But his spirits had sunk lower than even he realized.

"I got to a point where I thought more than once that it might just be wonderful not to wake up in the morning," Jim admits, sounding uncharacteristically downbeat. He's a towering ex–Jesuit novice with a cowboy preacher's head of hair (in spite of having just turned sixty-five). A trip to the doctor's office ten years ago revealed a midstage tumor in Jim's prostate. With grander exits to worry about, the decision to quit his job was a no-brainer. "I was terrified," he tells me. "You heard cancer, you thought, 'Oh well, maybe a year.'" A theater addict since childhood, Jim remembers thinking each time he saw a Broadway show after his diagnosis, "'Maybe this is the last play I'll ever see.' Or 'This could be the last time I ever see Paris.' Or whatever." Oddly, however, Jim has not been depressed a single day since getting his unwanted news from his doctor.

"I'm passionate about my life now," he tells me. "Hardly a day goes by that something doesn't happen—sometimes big, sometimes tiny—that I don't say, 'I love my life.' I'm aware of it now and grateful." This joy had escaped him in the midst of his career. "Before, I didn't live a life with gratitude," he says. "As a good Catholic, I knew that I was *supposed* to be grateful. I said all my prayers. But now I began to realize that if life actually is a gift, then the right response is 'thank you.'"

"It sounds obvious when you put it like that."

"You have to be like a prospector in your own life," he explains. "You have to look for the gift."

"How do you do that?" I want to know.

"If this is the last time I go to Paris, then I'm going to do everything and see everything I can in Paris, damn it!" he says. "I don't want any of me left over for a yard sale. I'm not saving my life anymore. I'm spending it." Jim realizes that this might sound a bit glib. "Of course, my smart-ass side said, 'I wanted a pony, why did

I get a winter coat?'" he admits. "We all ask for certain gifts. When you're a grown-up, you understand why your parents gave you a winter coat, but as a kid you're really pissed off about no pony. Cancer was like getting a winter coat."

"And it wasn't a mink."

"It wasn't even fucking nutria! You know how Auntie Mame says that life is a banquet and most poor sons of bitches are starving to death?" Jim asks. "But what she doesn't say is that sometimes you're the guest, sometimes you're the chef, and sometimes you're the main course."

"That's comforting."

"But true," Jim tells me. "And it actually works in your favor. Things become less provisional, less insecure, the more grateful you are. I don't have to earn my life anymore. It was given to me to cherish as I would a precious gift from someone who loves me and whom I love."

Serendipity came when Jim was led to a workshop given by a healer named Carolyn Myss. "I'd gone for my cancer, but something else happened," he says. "During the weekend, Carolyn remarked that many people in crisis seek out therapists when what they really need is spiritual direction. I had started out wanting to be a Jesuit priest before Hollywood got to me. Ministering to people was my passion. When Carolyn said that, I knew why I'd really gone to that workshop. I'd gone there to be healed but came out with a vocation."

This vocation announced itself with a voice Jim believes came from his creator. "I heard God say, 'Your job is joy.'" Jim realizes that this may sound insane. "At first I resisted. I said, 'But everybody wants that job!' God said, 'You'd be surprised. No one wants your job.'"

My old friend laughs. "God said my job was joy. But joy is not just about being happy. Joy is a rigorous spiritual practice of saying yes to life on life's terms," he says, reminding me of David Steindl-Rast's suggestion. "I never said, why is this happening to me, which a lot of people do. It was more like, okay, I'm perfectly happy to learn all the lessons of this. But I want to graduate—meaning, I don't want to live the rest of my life as a cancer patient, even if I have cancer."

How can people not blessed with a hotline to God get their marching orders? I wonder. "It has nothing to do with religion, first of all," Jim says. "Religion is for people who are afraid of hell, and spirituality is for people who've been there. Winston Churchill said, 'If you find you're going through hell, keep going.' The road to heaven—to peace of mind—leads through hell. Nobody's built a bypass."

During his training as a spiritual counselor, Jim learned more about these survival instructions from the Sorbonne-educated African teacher Malidoma Somé. Somé described his own attempt to explain life insurance to his village elders. "One of them asked, 'Do you mean people get paid for their catastrophes?'" Somé told Jim. "'Then how do they ever learn anything?'"

Today this grateful show-business refugee ministers to two dozen clients a week, talking soul survival instead of box office grosses. He advises his clients to live as if their lives actually depended on it. He tells them the story of the medieval monk who was watering his garden one morning when a passerby asked him, "Father, if you knew you were dying tonight, what would you do?" The monk thought a moment before replying. He said, "These flowers would still need watering." Jim looks at me. "I want to live my life in such a way that I wouldn't have to stop, or change, what I was doing—or being—if I was going to die to-night," he says.

Then Jim arches an eyebrow in Mame's campy way. "But I'm not."

PRAYING

According to a recent poll, 70 percent of Americans over eighteen claim to pray at least once a week and receive "great satisfaction" from doing so. I found this statistic confusing when I read it. I'd never felt better in the least after my own sporadic attempts to pray. Never had I, to my knowledge, received a single divine response to any particular *crise du jour*. Maybe this was because I've never believed in a God who'd care about my day-to-day life (being busy with dwarf stars, black holes, and quarks). When it came to prayer, I felt like the cliché orphan pressing his face to the window of a room in which God was nuzzling his own true children beside a roaring fire. The miscreant infidel (me) could only watch them from outside the window, slumped in a stupor of self-pity.

"You're not focused," my Christian friend John used to say.

"Nothing ever happens," I told him.

"It has to come from the heart," John said, as if I were trying to phone my prayers in. Sincerity is a private thing, as everyone knows, so I didn't try convincing him. I'm also from Missouri on all matters concerning interior experience. I need to see or feel

something in order to draw any sort of conclusion. I need for
there to not be parochial rules. If there is a God, I've always
thought, it wouldn't require credulity, protocol, or leaps of the
imagination. What God would want, I could only guess, were self-
reliance, love of the truth, and a little trust that if it does exist—
having spawned the Andromeda Nebula—it knows what I'm
thinking anyway.

One afternoon I opened my mailbox and found a postcard from
John with a quote from the late Trappist monk Thomas Merton
printed in bold capitals on the reverse side. It read:

TRUE PRAYER AND LOVE ARE LEARNED IN THE MOMENT
WHEN PRAYER BECOMES IMPOSSIBLE AND THE HEART HAS
TURNED TO STONE.

John knew that this would get under my skin. I couldn't vouch
for the prayer part, but the bit about love being impossible sometimes I was too well acquainted with. Daunting experience had
forced me to acknowledge the power of staying, abiding, enduring
(with lovers, books, uppity friends) through moments when I most
wanted to run. The Buddhists call this "practicing against the
grain," and I had the splinters to show for it. I'd found that when it
came to questions of self-evolution, the rougher the timber, the
stronger the floor. Testing the truth only made faith stronger.
Doubting Thomas, I'd always thought, was probably one of
Christ's favorite disciples.

But the act of prayer, as I understood it—as wish fulfillment,
solace, entreaty; as hook, line, and sinker for reeling God's voice
from the depths of inner (or outer) space—struck me as delusional. Till one day I found myself walking alone on a forest path

in Germany. It was the dead of winter in the village of Thalheim, twenty kilometers from Cologne, and I was feeling despicable. I was living with an Indian teacher who'd mysteriously planted her home there among the garden gnomes and Hessian Catholics, a stone's throw from the hospital where Josef Mengele did his experiments on Jewish children during the war. The snow was heavy on the ground; dark evergreens stood outlined, chiaroscuro, against a bleached, indifferent sky. I don't think my spirits could have been lower; nor could I have found a more Bergmanesque setting for laying my bald head down in the snow and blowing my fucked-up brains out.

I was hating myself for everything. I truly believed that I should be stronger. I stood there in the forest, freezing my ass off, blasting the trees, berating myself for a million things, including the fact that I couldn't pray. I found a clearing in the forest and let it rip, ranting at the whole damn thing—and what was I supposed to do *now*—when the obvious point descended like bird poop. "You're goddamn fucking praying, you asshole," the nurturing voice in my head informed me. The power that kept a person ranting, fist to the sky, whining at fate, was the heart and guts of prayer itself. The same longing for response, reunion, relief from pain that I equated with self-pity was actually the blood and limbs of prayer. Believing that prayer was meant to be a polite entreaty by the pure of heart, I'd missed the obvious point till that moment. "Struggle is the highest form of song," the proverb goes. It was also, I saw now, the backbone of prayer. I hadn't been frozen, ignorant, muzzled, or shut outside the walls of the holy, but offering prayers in my own screwed-up way for as far back as I could remember.

Back at the house, I spoke to my teacher, who was dressed in a sari and shoveling snow from the spot that months from then would be her garden. Her dark face was spotty, her hair a mess, her red plastic rain boots splattered with gunk. I told her what had happened. She said almost nothing, as usual, just smiled and nodded and sent me along like a slow kid checking in with an indulgent aunt. Years later I came across a commentary from the book of Job that reminded me of that walk in the forest. "By the end, Job's suffering has erased all formality and he speaks to God directly, challengingly, intimately, just the way God speaks to him," it read. Job was transformed by dissolving the distance he dreamed between himself and God. Both humbled and enlightened by pain, the prophet finally understood the miraculous proximity of radiance, the commonality of his language with the divine's, the truth that emerges when we speak plain. Believers are welcome to call interlocution of this kind prayer; nonbelievers can call it truth-telling. Either way, we are changed, it seems, by the speaking itself. Telling—not the response—is the secret that links us to a source beyond our own minds, which rarely see past their own distress. When I came to see prayer as a periscope—a means of peering through the surface—instead of a phone call that never got answered, it finally became real for me.

DEMON LOVERS

Carl Jung called addiction a "prayer gone awry." Desperate for transcendence, solace, communion, addicts turn to booze and blow, casinos and cutting, anonymous sex, bulimia, binge shopping, even domestic violence—some compulsion to spoon in the void—to substitute for higher or deeper connection. Yet cosmic loneliness prevails, especially in the addict's world. This is why Jung advised Bill W., the founder of Alcoholics Anonymous, that without a spiritual component the program could never work. Addicts require a higher power (even one that nonbelievers claim to be making up for themselves) to recover from such hunger and the deadly, doomed behaviors it causes.

Like many addicts-to-be, Michael Klein grew up in a house where spiritual hunger and the threat of abandonment were ever-present facts of life. Night after night he and his twin brother, Kevin, would watch their mother slip into a barbiturate haze in the glow of the family TV set. A sensitive kid, Michael would study Kathryn's face as she disappeared behind her narcotic cloud, wondering what he and his brother had done to make her go away like that. Why did his mother, whom he adored, seem so angry at her twins (though she loved them as well) for needing her to stick around? Her own mother hadn't stuck around; at forty-three Kathryn's mother had gotten drunk and jumped to her death from her balcony on Fifth Avenue. Kathryn was abandoned herself; now she imagined doing the same to her children. This shame seemed to be yet another reason for going through with it.

You learn the world from your mother's face. You learn about God from the way she moves, how she loves or doesn't love, how she smells, what she says in words and silence. You learn about creation from the way your parents love each other, the story they tell you about how they came together to make you. These details create your idea of who you are and where you came from; the color, texture, depth, or shallowness of your universe; the particular tangle of roots that brought you out of the ground. The grief in his mother's eyes seemed to prove to Michael that the world was a very cruel place, that no one would be there to save him, that he would always be alone.

By the time he was twelve, Michael was drinking. We're talking at a Midtown Manhattan deli, with corned-beef-balancing waitresses rushing around and yelling. A muscular two-by-four of a guy with blondish hair, insane sense of humor, and thrashed-gravel voice like Harvey Fierstein's, Michael is a teacher and award-winning poet who's been sober now for twenty-two years. But back then he was a lost boy, grasping at strangers with one hand, drinking himself to death with the other, pulled down by an emptiness he didn't understand, sucking down liquor like mother's milk, trying to feel at home in the world.

"I was drunk every day for ten years at least," Michael tells me, squirting relish on his burger. Kathryn, his mother, had died when he was twenty-two—from natural causes or an overdose, no one seems to be quite sure. Kevin, his twin, was leading an isolated alcoholic's life by then; Michael could feel him slipping away. Introduced to the horse-racing world when he was twenty, Michael got himself a job at Belmont grooming thoroughbreds (at one time he tended the champion Swale). It was a gin-soaked, unstable stable life on the road, stumbling from track to bar to anonymous bed in the endless, insatiable search for connection. "I started drinking to make passion easier," Michael wrote in a memoir, *Track Conditions.* "I could fall into a stranger's sheets when I was drunk. It was desire without fear."

"That's what everyone wants," I say, "desire without fear."

In her own wonderful book *Witness to the Fire: Creativity and the Veil of Addiction*, Jungian analyst Linda Schierse Leonard recounts her own recovery from alcoholism and explains how obsession reduces the addict to thinghood. "Addiction leads to monomania," she writes, "a narrowing of life and vision, reducing the addict to the status of an object defined by its craving."

Michael's craving was to be touched. He was torn between two lovers, he tells me: art and death. Every addict has two *daimons*, Leonard explains, one destructive and the other creative. Michael had both in spades. Already, he was writing poetry in earnest—but his life was out of control. "The creative person *chooses* to go down into that unknown realm," Leonard reminds us. "Even though the choice may feel destined. But the addict is pulled down, often without a choice, and is held hostage (by his disease)." Michael was starting to bottom out. Around thirty, his reckoning came to him cold. "I was really tired. My life was a shambles. But I wasn't dead yet," he says simply.

"You lost me," I say.

"I started drinking because I wanted to die," Michael tells me. "But it wasn't killing me fast enough. If I was going to live and be an addict, I realized that I would rather just live."

"Just like that?" I ask.

"Just like that."

Checking himself into detox, he found the physical part relatively easy. "I had the shakes on and off for three months," he says with a shrug. "I couldn't stay awake for more than seven or eight hours a day."

"What about your mind?"

Michael compares his psychic rebirth to "a crash victim coming out of a coma. That *this* was the world I remembered before the accident, and I wanted to live here again."

"Like the man who fell to earth," I tell him. "I know that feeling."

"I realized again that the world was in color!" he says, digging into his fries. "The world went from two- to three-dimensional. Everything was heightened. I had an amazing amount of energy. I could remember my dreams!"

"You make it sound like you rose from the grave."

"It was like that. You *know* everything is there when you're drinking. But you can't see it and you don't care. As an addict, you're totally unteachable. You lose the desire to learn *anything*. I remember being struck by the fact that people are interesting!" The decibel level of Michael's laugh startles our neighbors at the next table. "I didn't *love* anybody," he admits. "I didn't even like anything before, except sex. When you're drinking," he says, waving down a waitress for our check, "you're able to become your worst self. The difference is that you really don't care."

Outside, Michael lights a cigarette as we make our way down Lexington Avenue. His twin brother died last year, he tells me, after an alcohol-induced heart attack. Michael is still confused by this loss. Unlike Kevin, Michael wrestled with his childhood demons in order to stay sober. "Two or three years into sobriety, reality hits and you realize you need therapy," he says. "There are big parts of you missing, whole chunks of what makes a person whole."

"What about this higher power thing?" I ask.

He reminds me that the program's first step is admitting that you are powerless against your disease. "This step gives you tremendous power," he says, aware that it sounds paradoxical. "But the strength you find isn't in your ego. In recovery everything gets reversed. Many things you thought were signs of strength simply aren't."

"Such as?"

"Self-absorption. Self-pity. Self-destruction." Michael is being facetious. "You start to see the big picture. To not take things quite so personally. You become part of the collective consciousness—a worker among workers," he says, using Marxist lingo. "This gives you equanimity and a sense of connection to the essence. You and your disease are not the epicenter of the universe."

"Powerless before what? God?"

"Maybe." Michael shrugs. "You can't have strength without spiritual awareness, however you define it. If I had to pick a synonym for what strength is, it would have to be self-realization."

In the thirteenth century the German mystic Mechthild of Magdeburg described being able to finally connect her own misplaced prayer to the arms of a lover she could trust, the one she wanted to begin with. "Whoever is sore wounded by love will never be made whole unless she embrace the very same love which wounded her," the abbess wrote. Mechthild was speaking of her divine love for Jesus, but the same can be said of an addict like Michael who is wounded early by loss of parental love and only treatable through surrender to a primal source. Today he's a transformed man, Michael tells me, publishing books, teaching writing, happily in love with a long-term partner, taking yoga, almost cigarette free.

"I never thought I'd see my thirtieth birthday," says this softhearted, gruff-sounding man at the top of the subway stairs. "Every single day I'm alive after getting sober is gravy!" Michael Klein's voice reaches a crescendo that threatens to stop oncoming traffic. "Gravy, gravy, gravy!"

But what about the secondhand casualties? How do those spouses, children, lovers, friends, struggling to save their own lives around addicts they love—and cannot leave—find their way through?

Kathleen grew up in a fatherless house in Fresno, the middle daughter of three. Her parents divorced when she was in second grade; her father, a trucker, moved to Ohio, where he started a second family and left Kathleen's mother, Geraldine, to raise the girls on her own. Her family was under constant threat of eviction, since Geraldine, a sort of Irish princess, didn't like being imposed upon to work. She gravitated toward migraines and serially abusive men instead. Kathleen and her sisters ran the house, found odd jobs, put food on the table, catered to their mother's mood swings.

"I guess you'd say that I never got to be a kid," Kathleen tells me. We're having lunch in Pike's Market in Seattle. Kathleen is a big-boned, redheaded woman who wears her hair long, like Wynonna Judd. "We never got to be kids," she says. "Me and my sisters had to grow up too fast."

A brilliant student, Kathleen managed to get a scholarship to

UCLA, where she felt happy for the first time. A theater major, she acted, directed, even tried her hand at playwriting, which proved to be her gift. "Big surprise—I was the queen of make-believe," she says, chuckling. "I had been scripting my own imaginary life since I was a little girl." As a director, Kathleen was out of her depth, though, which is why one April evening she put an ad up on the university job board, needing someone to direct her first play, and came to meet an ex–theater student turned out-of-work director named Andre.

"He was everything I fantasized about in a man," Kathleen tells me. "That should have been enough to scare me."

At six foot three, with amber eyes, a tenor's voice, a wardrobe out of *L'Uomo Vogue*, and the "most luscious" lips she'd ever seen on a man, Andre was the kind of hunk who caused testosterone whiplash in public. "If they could've thrown their panties at him, like Engelbert Humperdinck, they would've," Kathleen says. She hired him to direct her play, then allowed Andre to spend the night after the second curtain call. In bed afterward, he took Kathleen in his lap and said, "You're the kind of girl I want to take care of."

Kathleen still can't believe she fell for it. "I actually believed it," she says, shaking her head. "After that it was like 'open sesame.' I went into a kind of trance." Andre's dashing appearance aside, Kathleen was attracted to what appeared to be Andre's beautiful soul. Failing to mention the woman he lived with (or the child of his she was carrying), Andre wooed Kathleen and, when the time was right, invited himself to move in. On the night that the other woman showed up on her doorstep, Kathleen took Andre's word that this previous relationship was over. He promised to look for work. One day Andre showed up with a pair of his-and-hers engagement rings (although he hadn't bothered to pop the question). The word ROOTS was inscribed on the underside of Kathleen's ring (Andre's read WINGS). "That's all I'd ever wanted was roots," she tells me now. "Andre had this sixth sense when he wanted something. He always knew people's weak spots. Like killers know."

In retrospect, Kathleen can trace the web. But back then she was happier than she'd ever been. She found a job as a dramaturge that paid enough for them to buy a modest house in Berkeley. Andre played the stay-at-home, freelancing husband while she limned Chekhov for first-time directors. On weekends they planted, mowed, cooked soup. Their sex life was supercharged, though Andre could be a little too rough. "A guy like that gets away with murder," Kathleen tells me. Not a day went by without her noticing some alarming flirtation with her husband, who protested too much, as philanderers do, against having the slightest interest in anyone but his own wife.

Ten years passed. Two children were born. Andre now worked as a personal coach. Kathleen had been happily surprised, all things considered, by how well their marriage was turning out. She'd finally put down the roots she craved, established a home, even if it came at a cost. Andre had grown moodier with age. Sex stopped. Then cuddling stopped. But at least they had an understanding, she thought. It was still, she told herself, a marriage. And at least she wasn't alone, Kathleen would catch herself thinking, watching her handsome husband sleep.

Then this picture imploded. One ordinary weeknight around eleven o'clock, Andre did something he'd never done before in a decade of marriage: He rose from bed after he was undressed and left the house. He claimed to have things on his mind. After a couple of hours Kathleen grew anxious, drove to town, found Andre's car outside the dry cleaning store—then saw her husband making out with a blond teenager behind the counter. "Here's the really sick part," Kathleen tells me, lighting a cigarette. "I decided that I could let it pass. I wasn't going to make a big deal out of a peccadillo. He's a gorgeous man. It was bound to happen. I even thought maybe it was my fault for not trying harder to keep him interested."

Prepared to forgive if not to forget, Kathleen was less prepared for what happened when Andre finally did get home. "He appeared at the house all upset, sweating, shaking," she tells me. "He wanted me to sit down, he had something important to tell me. Now I'm really getting scared. I'm getting that something is really wrong."

It wasn't the kind of other woman Kathleen expected. Andre had fallen in love with "Tina," the street name for crystal meth. Apparently a gym buddy had given him a bump of T one night to help him get through his workout. Now, Andre told Kathleen, showing her the track marks on his arms, he had been shooting Tina every day for the past three months.

"I froze. I just went dead inside," she says. In a zombielike voice, Andre proceeded to confess the rest of his sordid tale: the party girls he'd met on the Internet, the secret hookups, an entire meth subculture Kathleen knew nothing about, where Andre was cheating under her nose at times when he was supposed to be playing golf or working out at the gym.

"It was the worst moment of my life," Kathleen tells me. "Like watching a mask snap off my husband's face." She looks scared remembering it. "I saw who he was. I saw who he wasn't. I didn't know my own husband. Andre was a complete impostor."

"So you kicked him out?"

"No, that's what a sane person would have done." Instead, Kathleen put Andre to bed, told him he was forgiven, and took care of him while he tried to kick the drug on his own. He was sick in bed for a week, alternating between crying jags, rage, and puking. "Have you ever had to spoon-feed someone you wanted to kill?"

Unfortunately, I have.

"Wipe their ass when you want to strangle them?"

Ditto.

"I had never felt so violated or disrespected in my life," she says. "But I was still scared he would disappear."

"You don't stop loving someone just because they ruin your life," I say.

"I wanted to hurt him, but I couldn't stop loving him," she admits. "So I did what I thought was the right thing to do." Kathleen the caretaker found Andre a rehab (and paid for it), kissed him good-bye in the hospital lobby, and promised to be there when he got out three weeks later. "I believed every lie that came out of his mouth," she tells me. "I wanted to believe it was still my Andre. That he was going to change. For me. For our kids. That the whole drug thing had been a mistake."

It seemed as if rehab had worked at first. "When he got out of the hospital, he was like the man I fell in love with—no, he was better than that," Kathleen says. "He was the Andre I used to dream was there, underneath the macho bullshit, the vanity."

"It's called rehab afterglow," I remind her.

"I was so happy!" She shakes her head. "We had a couple of honeymoon weeks. Andre seemed so raw. So humble and real. He went to meetings every day. Then I found a hypodermic needle in his sock drawer." Kathleen turns to the view out the window. "He'd been shooting up since the day he got out. Another lie inside of a lie. This time I got rid of him. I called the cops and everything. There wasn't enough evidence to hold him, so Andre was out of jail the next day. And that's when the fun really started."

Kathleen sold the house, moved from Berkeley to Seattle, changed her telephone number, and placed a restraining order against her husband in case he ever showed up. But as the weeks went by without a word, Kathleen couldn't get Andre out of her mind. "I started having panic attacks," she says. Scary tidbits of news reached her through the grapevine, friends who'd seen him here or there looking terrible. Even worse, their dog, Sadie (kidnapped by Andre), appeared to have been neglected. "It was the dog that really got me," Kathleen says now. "He was devoted to Sadie. If she was being neglected, I couldn't imagine what kind of hell he was in." Swamped by nightmare scenarios of Andre starving to death on the street with their dog, Kathleen caved in. "It was just like being possessed. This demon wouldn't let go of me. I could almost hear him calling me, like he was pulling me down into this dark place with him."

She did the only thing she could. "I called. I told him I wanted to see him. I left the kids here and flew down to Berkeley. He was sick in bed, hadn't been out of the house in six days. Sadie was skinny." Kathleen cleaned the place, gave Andre back rubs, sat beside him on the bed as he moaned about being hooked, never meaning to hurt her, wanting to die. Not wanting to.

"I never knew anything could hurt so much," she says now. "I felt so trapped. Like your worst dream happening with you inside it." Still, Kathleen allowed Andre to stay in touch. "I let him call me. It was harder than not knowing how he was." This went on for close to a year. "He'd call at all hours of the night. Howl on the phone. Beg me to help him. Sometimes he'd blame me for the breakup."

"You?"

"He's an addict. I told myself to forgive him because he was sick. But I couldn't keep the demons out." Soon Kathleen was so guilt-ridden and depressed that she considered checking herself into some kind of a rehab. She was unable to cut the cord between them. "*That's* when I got it," she says. "I realized that there were two addicts here. I was addicted to saving him from his disease. His addiction had become my sickness. I realized that he was going down and it was either him or me. And no way was this man going to kill me."

Kathleen changed her telephone number—again—and cut off all contact with her children's father. Three times a week for close to a year, she found kindred spirits at Al-Anon meetings. "I always made fun of the twelve-step thing before," she confesses. "The slogans. The victim mentality. But that was just my arrogance talking. These people weren't victims—they were major survivors." Listening to tales so like her own, however varied the details, Kathleen got to know her own disease—the savior complex, the fixer obsession, the codependent impulse to rescue someone in order that she herself could be saved.

She gazes out at the boats in the harbor. "People don't get how insidious codependency really is," she says. "What it means is that you—the caretaker—actually *disappear* behind the addict's pain. You cease to exist when they need something. When Andre got sick, I felt like it was me who was dying."

"I know how that feels, exactly."

"He wanted me to sit there and watch him kill himself. But I would have probably died before he did. I had to save my life—it was him or me. Not just for me but for our kids."

The hardest part of healing from her own addiction, Kathleen found, was admitting that there was absolutely nothing she could do to help this person she loved. "Getting it through your head that there is nothing—period—that you can do that will change a thing."

"The rational mind doesn't get it," I say.

"It goes against every natural instinct. Because addiction turns everything around. What feels like love in normal life is 'enabling' when you're talking about an addict. Tender loving care is actually harmful. Tough love, which feels like neglect, is the only thing that might actually help. I've never felt more powerless over anything in my life. Or more honest."

She looks directly at me. "I had to accept the fact that Andre might actually die from this. And I could do nothing at all to stop it."

Three months after our interview, I receive an e-mail from Kathleen with the news that after asking his own parents for help, Andre is now in his second bout of rehab. Kathleen will not visit him there; she has, however, given Andre's therapist permission to convey messages. Kathleen also got custody of Sadie. If her ex-husband ever does get sober, she tells me in her note, she may consider giving him visiting rights. "The kids could use a father."

"What about you?" I write back.

She responds with the news that she's almost ready to start dating again. Kathleen is considering using an online matchup service so she can start learning how to set boundaries. "No beauties," she makes clear. "And they have to be short. Without any muscles."

"No muscles?" I tease her.

"And no hair!" she responds.

"A daddy thing?" I ask her in an instant message.

"Touché," Kathleen writes back, ending her note with one of these: ☺

QUESTIONING
(OR THE SPHINX)

It seems perverse that authenticity should stem from loss. The outline cracks, you split apart, half of you is left stranded on an iceberg floating into the chilly distance. You're suspended in partiality, cut off from who you thought you were. This is when questioning starts, that's the truth—when you can't put yourself back together again, when the old parts don't fit and the new ones have yet to arrive. You stand there looking into the mirror, wondering, What in God's name is that? This lopsided mess of an unglued creature leering back at what used to be me? How can I live with this alien changeling? Where's the rest of my ensemble?

You haven't yet heard of the hidden face. You haven't quite learned that losing what you thought could never be lost is precisely what shows you who you really are. "The art of losing isn't hard to master," wrote Elizabeth Bishop, tongue in her cheek. "So many things seem filled with the intent / to be lost that their loss is no disaster." We step through one loss after another, look down to find our feet still on the ground, and get the Buddhist joke of it all: that we're not that stuff we feared leaving behind, "filled with the intent to be lost," not that persona attached to its world, but the thing that's left standing when that starts to go, the self who's watching and asking the questions. Each time this happens, the spring in our step is a bit more pronounced, as if we've lost ballast, been bounced and made lighter.

Questioning is an art form in itself. Inquiring, who are you to-day, for starters—and what is it that you want most intensely? Where is intuition leading? Questions till the ground of "begin-ner's mind," plow fresh road, scrap outdated agendas, help us to reimagine our way.

In a refrigerated convention hall in Chicago, I find myself waiting with two hundred other workshop participants for the arrival of the queen of questions, Byron Katie. Named one of *Time* magazine's "Spiritual Innovators for the 21st Century," Katie, as she likes to be called, is a self-taught, sixty-four-year-old teacher, who, as a result of a nervous breakdown she barely survived twenty years ago, has developed a technique she calls The Work.

This assault on self-delusion consists of posing four direct questions and what Katie calls a "turnaround." (We'll enumerate these in a moment.) What I know on arriving in Chicago is only that this respected woman fully believes that her technique can re-lieve the pain caused by any situation, save physical torture. I'm skeptical but interested. A respected therapist friend returned from his weekend with Byron Katie describing it as "psychological shock and awe." Even Katie's hardheaded husband, scholar and translator Stephen Mitchell, claims that The Work is a bona fide path to what the Buddha called "the cessation of suffering," a ve-hicle for navigating the turbulent mind into calmer waters.

The crowd is beginning to fidget in their folding chairs. A technician sound-checks the mike and jumps offstage. My new best friend, Peggy, an overweight prison chaplain with a white Lulu hairdo and close-set eyes, offers me a Velamint.

At the stroke of nine, Byron Katie struts onstage in a chocolate silk pants ensemble, a shawl thrown dramatically over the shoulder, Doris Day pretty, perfectly coiffed, self-assured as a lion tamer. Stephen Mitchell takes a seat stage right, scholarly in his beard and tweed jacket. Without introduction Katie begins.

"Our most intimate relationship is the one we have with our own minds," she says. "I was in a very dark place for a long time. Then one day I realized a simple thing."

Peggy's pen is poised on her notebook.

"When I believed my own thoughts, I suffered," says Katie. "When I didn't believe them, I didn't suffer. Everything changed for me after that day."

A man behind me clears his throat. "You see, thoughts are like children," Katie continues, moving downstage. "They're gonna scream and scream till we pay attention to them. When we do this and begin the work of questioning, things we've believed our whole lives—forty, fifty, sixty years—our most stressful, self-defeating thoughts are brought to an end."

Peggy elbows me and raises her eyebrows.

"It isn't easy," Katie assures us. "It takes a lot of courage. But isn't it time to get real, my honeys?" She scatters endearments like bonbons to children. "Haven't we been conning ourselves for long enough?"

"We sure have!" shouts a goateed therapist named Mick (we're all wearing name tags).

"All right, then. This is your shame worksheet," Katie tells us, holding up a purple folder. She instructs us to make a list of our darkest, most aggravating, shameful beliefs—the poisonous, top-secret, horrible judgments we reveal to no one—then choose the greatest shame of all and apply the four questions and turnaround. "Be brutal!" Katie exhorts the crowd. "This is your chance to see what's really going on in your mind. If we don't question what we believe, we are destined to live it out."

The Work consists of a series of four questions that sound almost too simple to be effective:

1. Is it true?
2. Can you absolutely know that it's true?
3. How do you react when you think that thought?
4. Who would you be without that thought?

Once these questions have been asked, the student is instructed to invert the original thought and give three examples of why this "turnaround" is as true as, or truer than, the original belief. "My mother doesn't love me" might become "My mother does love me, and here are three reasons why." According to Katie, any painful thought subjected to this inquiry loses its power to hurt us, since most of what goes on between our ears is a pack of lies.

These questions are said to have come to her spontaneously after a nervous collapse in the mid-1980s. Born Byron Kathleen Reid on December 6, 1942, she was the second daughter of an engineer for the Santa Fe Railroad and a typical fifties housewife in the dusty town of Barstow, California. After a shotgun wedding at nineteen, Katie spent the sixties, and most of the seventies, raising her three kids and making a name for herself as a local real estate mini-tycoon.

What happened next turned her life upside down. During a period of domestic turmoil (her marriage ended when she was thirty-three), Katie grew paranoid and suicidally depressed. Morbidly obese, she was also agoraphobic and barely left her own bedroom for two years, often unable to bathe or brush her teeth, much less take care of her children. This crisis was exacerbated by the absence of visible cause. "I had plenty of money, a beautiful home, three kids who were healthy," Katie will tell me when we meet. "Being depressed was even more shameful with no cause to point my finger at. I felt ungrateful and confused. I was dying."

In fear that their mother might hurt herself, Katie's children located a halfway-house-like facility near Los Angeles where Katie could be kept safe—and the family could be away from her tirades. Relegated to the attic, Katie fell asleep on the night of October 16, 1986, not knowing that when she woke up the next morning an insight would occur to her that would snap her depressed mind in two. Had this spontaneous awakening not been witnessed by those around Katie, it would seem too miraculous to believe. But her family corroborates what happened. "She seemed completely at peace," Katie's daughter says now. "I couldn't believe it was really my mother."

"I woke up to reality" is how Katie explains it. "I realized that my thoughts were creating my suffering." Gradually, she began to share her "work" with locals in Barstow who wanted to know why their formerly crazy neighbor was suddenly smiling. Over time Katie received invitations to speak from around the country—then from other nations. She made no effort to promote herself. The last thing on Katie's mind was becoming the queen of questions.

Asked if she was enlightened—or what?—she has consistently waved such nonsense aside. "I'm just someone who knows the difference between what hurts and what doesn't."

Once the allotted time is up for completing our shame worksheets, Katie opens the room to volunteers. I have no intention of sharing, but the exercise has been illuminating. My number one shame (pertaining to a relationship failure) readily revealed its own flimsiness when I tested it against these questions. Not only did the "fact" I'd been using to flagellate myself reveal itself to be bogus, it flipped over like a harpooned fish when I stuck it with Katie's turnaround. In fact, the opposite of what I had believed was far truer than my self-defeating thought. The exercise leaves me feeling unsettled.

Katie fields the crowd of waving hands. A middle-aged Latino man steps up to the microphone. "My wife cheated on me," he whispers. "But that doesn't mean I'm less of a man."

"Thank you, precious," Katie replies.

"I think I might be gay," mumbles a teenage kid in an Axl Rose T-shirt, his eyes darting nervously around the room.

"I'm glad you're here, sweetheart," she assures him. My white-haired neighbor timidly raises her hand. "I'm too fat," Peggy whispers into the mike, hiding her belly with the purple folder. In fact, Peggy is portly but hardly obese.

"Is that true?" Katie asks, planting a hand on her hip. All eyes in the room are on my shy comrade. "How many of you would rather get a hug from Peggy than, say, a supermodel?" Katie asks. Nearly every hand in the room goes up. "You see that, honey?" Katie smiles at her. Peggy is visibly trembling. "Remember, it's what we think or say or do that hurts us." Peggy covers her mouth and sits down.

"Anybody else?" Katie surveys the audience. Finally, a well-dressed, fiftyish guy stands up and waits for the monitor to reach him with the mike. He mumbles, "I hate my life. I don't want to be here."

"Can you be more specific, honey?" asks Katie, stepping to the apron of the stage, fixing him with her steady gaze.

"Sometimes I want to die," the man says.

"Very good," Katie assures him, oddly. "Now let's do The Work," she says. "Is that true?"

"Yes," he answers.

"Can you absolutely know it's true?" asks Katie, unfazed by his visible pain.

"What do you mean?" he responds.

"Can you know with absolute certainty that you want to die, precious?" she asks very slowly.

"That's how it feels," he says.

"Of course it does. Now, how do you react when you think that thought, sweetheart?"

The expression on his face shifts from slack misery to minor annoyance. "How do you think it makes me feel?" he asks irritably. Katie has been down this road many times before. Gently but firmly, she requests that the volunteer simply answer the questions as directly as possible, "in order for The Work to work."

"Okay," he says. "It makes me feel like a friggin' loser."

"Thank you, sweetie. That's excellent. Now," Katie asks, leaving the stage and approaching him down the aisle. "Who would you be without that thought?"

"A liar," he tells her straight out.

"Honey," she asks. "Do you want to be happy?"

"Why do you think I'm here?"

"So who would you be?" Katie inquires again.

"I have no idea," he says.

"Bingo!" she tells him. The man looks puzzled. "Without the thought 'I want to die' you don't know who you would be."

The room gets quiet. "I don't understand," he says.

"That's okay," Katie assures him. "Now, can you turn it around?"

Once again he seems annoyed. It's revealing to watch his anger increase with each benign question that further rattles his story. He reaches for his jacket to leave. Then he puts it down again. "I'm not enjoying this game," he mumbles.

"Then why did you volunteer, sweetness?" she asks. Peggy elbows me, nodding her head—it's checkmate and the poor guy knows it. "Just try to answer the question," says Katie. "What turnarounds can you imagine to the thought 'I want to die'?"

"What?" he answers. "You mean, 'I don't want to die'?"

"Any other turnarounds?" she asks.

He shrugs and says, " 'I want to live'?"

But Katie isn't finished yet. "Now," she says, "give me three reasons why this turnaround—'I want to live'—is as true or more true than your original thought."

He now appears more lost than irate. "All right. Can it be purely vindictive?"

"Whatever's true for you," she says, chuckling.

"I want to live to divorce my bitch of a wife and see her face when I walk out the door. Does that count?"

Katie hoots out loud with the rest of us. "That sounds like a pretty strong reason to me. Any others?"

"Well, I'm crazy about my kids. I'd like to be here to see them grow up."

"Good. Now, can you give me one more reason?"

Pausing for a good long time, he finally says in a wobbly voice, "I think I'm a pretty good man."

With these words the last blush of anger drains from his face. He sinks back into his folding chair as Katie returns to the stage. "And we wonder," she says to the room, "why a mind being deluged with angry thoughts would be telling us that we would rather be dead. Remember, the mind is a child. It believes whatever we tell it."

"A retarded child," Peggy whispers.

"Whatever I am convinced of *creates my world* until I question it," Katie says, stressing these three words. "Our unquestioned thoughts only turn into nightmares. We carry this suffering to our graves. But we each have the power to stop the deception, stop abusing ourselves. Someone hits you. Wham! It's over. That's grace."

I'm struck by the severity of her logic.

"But the mind keeps re-creating the pain. There's so much courage in these rooms," Byron Katie says, steepling her fingers under her chin. "It always amazes me."

While there's nothing new in the notion that how we think is how we live—think of Buddha, Descartes, Dr. Phil McGraw—Katie has succeeded in articulating this ancient wisdom in a modern, effective, dogma-free way. Rejecting the role of guru or seer, she insists that nobody needs her (or any teacher, for that matter) to reap the benefits of self-inquiry. As evidence that The Work functions on its own steam, at least six hundred independent "inquiry circles" (where peers ask these questions together) have cropped up around the world, from Helsinki to Hong Kong to Houston.

During the lunch break, I speak to several veterans of Katie's work who claim to have made greater progress in their lives by applying these four questions than they've made through years of recycling childhood trauma in pricey therapists' offices. "The beauty is that people can do this for themselves without having to go through analysis or doing expensive processes," says one consultant in her forties, who recently came through a bout of breast cancer. "One of the gifts of getting older is that although change may be more difficult, you're forced by the facts of life to work with destructive thoughts in a positive way or go down with the ship."

Our blue-eyed, goateed neighbor, Mick, a fifty-two-year-old social worker, agrees. "This is almost like a non-therapy," Mick explains. "Most people are addicted to a dangerous level of emotional pain. They might want to improve things, but only a little bit. This work is most effective for people who are genuinely sick of their stories and ready to drop them 'cause they're too damned painful. But if I was looking for a reason to stay stuck, a lot of what Katie says would sound like bullshit."

Indeed, this teacher's radically positive, tough-love message rubs many of her peers the wrong way. A Los Angeles–based psychologist I spoke to had some serious qualms after watching Katie apply her process to an especially traumatized person. "It's a creative extension of some preexisting cognitive behavioral therapies," he tells me, sounding a little snooty. "For people in the normal neurotic range, it might be useful," this therapist allows, "but as a template for whatever ails us?" He harrumphs. "To assume that simply by asking four questions, then turning the thought around, you can address the complexity and seriousness of issues such as rape or incest, for example—well, that is just narrow and naïve, psychologically unsophisticated."

Katie's cruel-to-be-kind approach, her categorical rejection of victimhood as a legitimate position, is indeed what rankles her critics most. A meditation teacher who asked to remain anonymous went so far as to suggest that The Work "has no heart in it." Yet observing Katie carefully, I never doubt for a moment the full involvement of her heart. While it's true that she does not coddle whiners, and uses the fierce road to compassion, her toughness seems to come from an unwillingness to watch people torture themselves—as she nearly tortured herself to death—without challenging them to cut the crap.

When I meet with Katie and her husband a few days later in New York, she elaborates on this contentious point. She and Stephen are facing me in high-backed chairs in their Midtown Manhattan hotel room.

"Empathy is terrific," Katie says, looking glamorous in another flowing silk ensemble. "But when a person is struggling to survive, pity is not their friend. It does more harm than good. If someone we care about is hurt, then I feel hurt because *they're* hurt—'Oh, you poor thing, I'm so sorry for you!'—now there are two of us hurt. What good am I?"

Again, this simple logic is hard to dispute. Pragmatism is what matters most when you've sunk to the bottom, Katie believes, and drama's a luxury you can't afford. This ruthlessness in the realm of self-knowledge reminds me of the goddess Kali in Hindu lore, a metaphor for the fierce feminine, severing chains of delusion with the sword of self-knowledge; or of a Zen master I used to practice with who took great pleasure in whacking meditators across the shoulder blades when they fell asleep, with a shrieking "Wake up!"; or of a triage surgeon in the field inflicting pain on the wounded to save their lives. Like every authentic teacher I've met, however friendly their exterior, Byron Katie is as tough as nails inside and passionate about helping people free themselves from suffering.

"People spend their lives in dread," she says, pouring me a cup of tea.

"It's self-inflicted torture," Stephen agrees.

Katie takes his hand. "The mind that has questioned itself looks forward to life," she tells me. "We can't stop life from happening, honey, so we might as well look forward, right? Can you imagine what we might be capable of if the bulk of our energy were not being taken up with stress? Can you imagine?"

She's preaching to the choir, I assure her.

"But the question we need to ask ourselves is, do we choose to live the most fulfilling life we possibly can? Or would we rather prove to the rest of the world that life is all about suffering? And that we are the primo example of that?"

This reminds me of Saul Bellow's description of his fellow Jews in the novel *Seize the Day*: "If they quit suffering they're afraid they'll have nothing."

Katie continues. "But what are we teaching our children?" she asks. "Are we teaching them the possibility that they can be happy no matter what happens?"

"Hardly," her husband says.

"And yet that's the truth of it! Our lives are determined by our thoughts, not by what happens to us. Also, by minding our own business." In the workshop Katie suggested that there are only three kinds of business in the world—"yours, mine, and God's"—

and that most of the trouble we make for ourselves comes from confusing them. "It is up to each of us to take care of our own business, question our minds, set ourselves free. If I'm over there in your business, who's taking care of mine?"

She empties the rest of her tea from the green enamel pot. My time, I realize, is almost up. There are so many questions I'd still like to ask, but one seems unavoidable. How can a person survive his own losses, adapt without bitterness to twists of fate he can't stop wanting to turn back the clock on? "We're human," I say. "We have memories."

Katie hears me out. Then she asks directly, "Do you want to know the truth?"

"That's why I'm here," I tell her.

"All right, then. Whatever suffering we feel over things that have already happened is nothing more than an argument with the past."

An argument with the past?

"You're bringing on your own pain now," she says. "Your father slapped you when you were three years old, but *you've* done it now a million times." She is right, of course. "Nothing can be over till it's over for *us*. On our deathbeds we're still blaming our parents, our spouses, our children, our jobs, our country, our disease, our handicap—whatever it is—for ruining our lives."

"Insane, right?" Stephen asks.

"But we can stop the insanity," Katie says. "Questions can stop the suffering."

Had she not discovered this work herself, healed herself of her own madness, were Byron Katie not sitting here in front of me, radiating palpable joy, I would discount this claim as pie-in-the-sky, smiley-face, New Age hoo-ha. But her survival story is real. The skeptic in me wants to argue, to find fault with her simple teaching, but even as I think these thoughts, my mind inadvertently starts doing The Work: Is it true that her claims are exaggerated? I wonder. That life can be free of suffering? Can I absolutely know it's true?

"Reality is so much kinder than our thoughts about it," Katie says.

JE M'EN FOUTISME

One hectic day on a freelance editing job, the magazine's copy chief shows up in my office looking like he wants to talk. Tom, who's goofy and blond and comes from Indiana, has hardly said a word to me till now, but seems to have gleaned my field of interest and appears to want to tell me his story. "Can you keep a secret?" Tom asks, closing the door behind him. Before I can even tell him I'm writing a book on this subject, he launches into his remarkable tale (and later allows me to include it here).

Two years ago, Tom, who was thirty-two at the time, was getting drunk at a New York publishing party, cracking jokes and slugging beers, when all of a sudden his head flew back and he found himself, as he describes it, "doing an unconscious break dance on the floor of a swanky SoHo ballroom." Tom had rarely been sick a day in his life but appeared to be in the throes of a grand mal seizure. A colleague he had been hoping to date shoved a wallet into his mouth to keep him from biting his tongue. "The end of that relationship," Tom deadpans.

The next thing Tom knew, he was in the back of an ambulance

surrounded by paramedics preparing to rush him to the hospital for tests. At first he refused, climbed off the stretcher against his friends' protests, hailed a taxi, and headed uptown for home. "I figured I was stressed out," Tom explains to me now. "I wanted to go home and sleep it off." Moments later, he was overwhelmed by another seizure, though, and the taxi rushed Tom to an emergency room. This is a very lucky thing. If he'd gotten his way and gone home to bed alone, Tom O'Connell would most certainly have died before morning.

This is what happens, apparently, when the brain tumor you don't know you have has hemorrhaged and filled your head with blood.

Within hours of arriving at the emergency room, after an MRI had identified the blood mass, Tom was rushed into surgery, where his head was cracked open, his face peeled off, and a piece of skull carved out in a procedure called a craniotomy. Tom reaches into an envelope and produces a photograph of himself on the operating table, hair slicked to the skull like a newborn baby's, blood dripping over a closed purple eyelid, a Tampax-like object protruding from his mouth.

"You had no warning signs?" I ask, handing back the gory picture.

"Nothing," Tom says. "Out of the blue." A month after his emergency surgery, Tom's doctors informed him that the tumor was not only malignant, but a grade 3 anaplastic oligodendroglioma—a particularly aggressive cancer—that needed to be removed immediately. In the days before the operation, Tom walked the streets in an existential fog that made day-to-day machinations seem absurd. "I was consumed with thoughts of speech therapy, Pampers, and being spoon-fed," he says. During the two-and-a-half-hour procedure, the surgeon removed a mass "the size of a small can of cat food." Although the surgery was a success, Tom would now be forced to undergo five days of chemo a month for alternating six-month periods—indefinitely.

"How did you take the prognosis?" I ask.

"It wasn't the news I was looking for," Tom shrugs. "Then again, I had a chance."

For someone less feisty than this good ol' boy, scary news of this magnitude might have signaled the end of life as he knew it. In Tom's case it only intensified the desire to figure out what made him happy, physical risks notwithstanding. The French have a term for this brazenness: *je m'en foutisme*, the brave art of not giving a damn. Tom, the carefree Midwestern boy, stopped playing anything safe in his life. He broke off a long-standing engagement to a girl he knew wasn't his soul mate. He ditched his boring publishing job and went back to his precarious-but-stimulating first-choice career as a pop culture journalist. His most daring decision by far, however, was to buy himself a Harley GTE chopper that became his escape route during his off weeks from chemo. Friends and family were worried about him. Were Tom to miss a single dose of his anticonvulsant medications, he could easily have another seizure. Yet this very danger is what kick-started his innate desire to heal, he believes.

"Riding gave me a sense of invincibility," Tom says. "I remember one time riding eight hours in the pouring rain, going like ninety, playing music full blast in my headphones, passing these trucks on the highway, feeling fantastic. Tempting fate is in itself therapeutic."

"You probably realize that this sounds nuts," I tell him.

"What's so great about sanity? I'll take passion." Trusting his biker fantasy, Tom took a solo trip north to Vermont one June afternoon, eight months after his surgery, unaware of what fate had in store for him next. Landing in the town of Montpelier, where a college buddy ran the local bar, Tom was chugging brews with friends when a sexy woman caught his eye. "This seriously hot brunette comes rolling in with a couple of girlfriends," he tells me. "I couldn't take my eyes off of her. She was one of those people you look at and your heart just melts. I watched her for close to an hour."

Before Tom could protest, his half-drunk friend had traversed the room to chat up this group of lonesome females. Without Tom's consent, his bigmouthed pal spilled the beans about Tom's recent surgery, hoping to win the ladies' sympathy. Suddenly, to Tom's amazement, the brunette came charging across the barroom and threw her arms around his neck.

She had a brain tumor, too, she told him.

This is where Tom's story ascends to the incredible. The following weekend, Trisha invited Tom to spend the night in her nearby mountain cabin. "Turns out she's eight years older," he tells me now, an unhappily married ex-professional bicycle racer turned horse masseuse—and a fourteen-year survivor of brain cancer. Tom reports this to me with the undisguised glee of the kid who finds the pony in a pile of shit. Better still, Trisha recently bought herself a Harley so that the two of them can tour around the country together. Her philandering husband doesn't ask questions.

"You've both got brain tumors and you're racing motorcycles around the country?" I ask. This sounds too fantastic to be real.

Then Tom invites me to join him and Trisha for dinner in New York the following weekend.

"I still look at her and can't quite believe I actually get to be with this person," Tom is saying. He's got his arm around Trisha in a booth at John's Pizzeria in the Village. Trisha Stevens rolls her eyes. Wearing tight blue jeans, boots, and a brave streak of premature gray in her auburn hair (which a vainer woman would cover up), Trisha tells me, "I've never cheated on my husband before. But there was something about our connection that I couldn't deny." Tom puts his arm around her. "It's confusing and scary," she admits. "We don't really know where this is going—"

"I'm hoping that Trish will be my wife," Tom says. Trisha looks at me and shrugs. "I didn't plan it."

"Who plans it?" I agree. Trisha seems grateful for my lack of judgment. Raised in a tiny Vermont town, she was a professional long-distance bicycle racer, immersed in winter training in Florida in 1993, when she started having mysterious seizures. "All of a sudden, I'd be sitting there and could hear and see people, but it was like I was behind a curtain and couldn't speak myself," she tells me.

"Just out of the blue?"

"No warning whatsoever." When these episodes started happening three times a day, Trisha set out on a frantic, frustrating search for a doctor who could diagnose her illness.

"They kept calling them panic attacks just because I was a woman," Trisha says, shaking her head. "Do I strike you as a hysterical woman?" What Trisha strikes me as is the kind of ass-kicking mama you'd want watching your back on a grisly episode of *Survivor.* Eventually, an MRI revealed a mass on her parietal lobe.

She was relieved to have an answer at least. "It was like, no shit, Sherlock!" Trisha laughs. The risks involved in opening her skull for a biopsy were potentially catastrophic, however, so she opted for a wait-and-see approach, combined with a daily regimen of anticonvulsants. "I was out-of-my-mind scared, absolutely petrified," Trisha admits. "Just walking around like a zombie. Numb. I couldn't figure out how people were just going through their daily lives."

"Isn't that freaky?" I say.

"Like being in a parallel dimension." As someone who takes comfort in being active, Trisha volunteered to be a poster girl for the Brain Tumor Society and eventually became the number one female cyclist in New England. "I wanted my experience to be good for something," she tells me.

That was fourteen years ago. Since then, Trisha has helped to raise hundreds of thousands of dollars so that other people like her "don't have to wait around ten months for a damn diagnosis." During one thirty-nine-day solo trip from San Francisco to Boston in 1995, she had a seizure while crossing the Rocky Mountains at fourteen thousand feet. But this tough woman shrugs off the danger the same way she has accepted her *Easy Rider* romance with Tom. "I'd rather die like this than fall and hit my head at the grocery store," Trisha says. "Otherwise you're just sitting around waiting to die."

Tom agrees. "I still smoke and drink and carouse," he reminds me. "Tempting fate can be therapeutic, like I said. The people around you are more scared for you than you are for yourself."

"I'm terrified of dying," Trisha admits. "Don't get me wrong,

But before something like this comes down in your life," she says, tapping the side of her head, "it's easy to forget to pay attention. Watch the signs, take the exits. Not miss the thing that life's giving you."

"And *don't* hang out with people who don't make you feel good!" Tom insists. I'm reminded of science writer Dan Goleman's research proving that good company is actually pharmaceutical. "I get nuts seeing people ignore their gifts! For a while after I got sick, I could hardly go out on the sidewalk without getting pissed off!"

"Calm down, honey," Trisha says, patting his hand.

"But people are so oblivious!" he tells her.

"We all get our wake-up calls," I remind him. "Sooner or later." Tom and Trisha now find themselves in a fraught-but-fantastic situation that neither of them could have planned, crazy in love with each other, uncertain about what the future will bring. It's like *The Bridges of Madison County*—with cancer.

"My husband is a good man," she says. "He doesn't beat me. He cares—in his way." Now it's Tom's turn to roll his eyes. "But from the moment Tom opened his mouth, he made me feel like a princess," Trisha tells me.

"You are," Tom says, kissing her forehead.

"I've never had that before," Trisha says. "Never in my life. I wasn't looking to get out of my marriage before we met. But there was something undeniable about our meeting, and having this common bond."

When Tom excuses himself to use the restroom, Trisha confides in me. "He's fine right now," she says in a low voice. "He might be okay for a long time. But that's a very nasty tumor he has. Mine could turn out to be benign." Before I have time to ask

Trisha what effect Tom's prognosis is having on her big decision, he's back. "I'm mad about him," Trisha says quickly, covering up our brief digression.

"And I've never been happier," Tom crows, slipping into the booth beside her.

"What are the chances?" I say.

"Without these tumors," Trisha says, "we would have been just two people in a bar." She pushes a cowlick off his forehead.

"How magical is she?" Tom says, smiling. Trisha seems to glow when he talks about her. For a second, she does remind me of a Cinderella who snuck out of the house and became a princess—if only for a brief stretch of time before the stroke of midnight. Tom orders more beer and starts humming a Counting Crows standard. When he begins an actual off-key serenade, Trisha lays a hand gently across his grinning mouth, for both our sakes.

"We'll just have to wait and see," she says.

THE TERRORISTS WITHIN

A couple of weeks after 9/11, I was walking my dogs around Washington Square, one mile north of Ground Zero, feeling strangely unalarmed. The stench of smoke was still thick in the air. Like everyone else, I'd been horrified on the morning of the Al Qaeda attacks. I'd stood on the corner of Sixth Avenue, along with hundreds of neighbors, watching shell-shocked people in business suits covered in ash as they wandered north from the scene of the crime, knowing that American life had just changed forever. In the days that followed, an eerie quiet had settled over the neighborhood. While this atmosphere of communal shock was unmistakable, though, I was not quite as traumatized, it seemed, as the majority of people around me. Not being devastated made me feel like a hypocrite. Had I grown so hard-hearted, cynical, jaded, I wondered, that mass murder in my own backyard left me feeling less tragic than stoical? Peering down into the empty airspace where the towers had stood at the end of West Broadway, I questioned the absence of more outrage inside me and why—with my neighborhood collapsed in despair—I was walking my dogs feeling so weirdly normal.

Others' lives were changing dramatically. Friends were no longer riding the subway, crossing bridges, risking tunnels, venturing outside walking distance from their kids for more than an hour or two. A girlfriend had already sold her apartment and fled for British Columbia with her husband and two young sons. In those first weeks after the planes struck, every day brought more conversations about rage, depression, post-traumatic stress—along with the chanting refrain that *we were no longer safe.* This is where my mind would snap shut, hearing this apocryphal phrase. No longer safe? When were we safe? Had the facts of life really changed so dramatically on the morning jihad arrived on our shores? Many smart people seemed to think so. They appeared to be responding to 9/11 as if the human condition had just changed; as if life had just shifted from fair to unfair; as if Eden itself had just fallen apart and the garden was suddenly planted with bombs and lunatics eager to explode them; as if these formerly sheltered Americans had been transformed on that terrible morning from innocents to prisoners of war, forced to confront a violent world for which they were unprepared. To face life's demonic forces, terrorists within and without, whose presence till then they'd been able to keep at a distance. A sixty-year-old woman whom I respect, wise in many worldly things, had confessed to me in those aftermath days that she realized how deeply she herself could hate and how easily this rage could lead her to violence.

Americans had been initiated into terror. Having dwelled till then in a bubble of comfort, we were forced to acknowledge the dark side of things—not *over there* but here at home. We were neither invulnerable nor immune, nor was our victimized country a victim. Invited to take deeper stock of how 9/11 had happened to us, many Americans, while in no way condoning terrorist acts, were forced to acknowledge our nation's checkered history (a reckoning intensified by the misdeeds of a warmongering president), to admit that our great country has never been truly innocent. While spreading democracy we have also at times been bullies, imperialists, and provocateurs, manipulating lesser nations' affairs from behind a superpower mask. Forced to become aware of this, Americans began to grow up. Many changed the way they lived. Others used fear to feel even worse. But I don't know many whose lives didn't change somehow (going through airport security alone gave you pause), as sudden citizens of the world rocked awake by this devastation. The arrival of the terrorists reminded them that their own lives were exposed and fleeting. Bodies hurling themselves from windows reminded us that our lives had windows, too.

The ancient Greeks had a word for this progression from naïveté to mortal wisdom: metanoia, *the opposite of paranoia.* Metanoia literally means "turning around," crossing away from fear into the zone of truth. The ancient maps that chart the stages of human life recognize that midway through (though some get butt-kicked earlier), after the shake-up, a process of intense self-examination and reassessment of the world begins in an individual. For this process to bear fruit, metanoia requires acknowledgment not only of the terrorists out there, but of the demons we carry within as well.

This appears to be counterintuitive at first. Why should an attack from outside prompt acquaintance with our own inner killers? We are the victims, some people say. Why should their bloody fatwa be used as a mirror to our buried hatreds? In order to expand the mind, to make use of what otherwise is wasted terror. This is what the enlightened tell us. From Gandhi to the Dalai Lama, even the escaped slave Francis Bok, we hear the paradoxical refrain that only by rejecting false virtue and self-righteousness can we see the truth. "I contain within me the seeds of all possible crimes," claimed the near-saintly philosopher Simone Weil. Without condoning the crimes of others, we use them to examine the criminality latent in ourselves. "I must forgive," Francis Bok had told me. "Otherwise, I am just like Giemma." His kidnapper.

Metanoia, and the emotional strength it brings, demands that we name our own demons. "Devils, Communists, capitalists, terrorists . . . the evil we previously objectified and assigned to exterior agents . . . must be discovered within," in one psychologist's words. At first we're shocked by our own shadow. It's not so easy now to divide the world into black-and-white camps of good and evil. "We have met the enemy and he is us," the comic-strip character Pogo said. Metanoia turns us around. All of a sudden, we're reeling back not only from terrorists' deeds but also from the brutal awareness that these actions were carried out by humans like us. This is what we are capable of in extremis, we think, and the sickening thought burns our righteousness off. For the first time there is no Other. We can never again pretend not to have seen this.

Luckily, we're hardwired for this awakening; body and soul know what to do with terror. Courage is in our genes. "It would be strange, indeed," wrote geneticist C. H. Waddington (in a passage that deserves to be quoted at length),

> with so many millions of years of survival experience packed into our genes, if at some deep involuntary level, we did not possess

capacities specially geared to cope with extreme situations. In the beginning there was nothing but extremity. Nothing but the random rush of life in a touch and go struggle against extinction. Men and women began to notice, as no other animal can, the frightfulness of infinite spaces opening everywhere around them . . . Death awareness is the bitter fruit of man's having risen to the level of consciousness. What began a billion years earlier as neurological response to environmental stimuli, with man came to climax in terror.

Americans were mostly fortunate before 9/11 not to have had to face this harsh fact. But the horror has opened thousands of people's eyes, too. My sixty-year-old friend, for example. She had her own metanoia moment. "I never knew I could hate so much," she told me the other day at dinner. Al Qaeda had ruptured her golden mean, interrupted her trance of cashmered privilege, the comfort zone of the chronically lucky, to whom things like 9/11 don't happen. It brought her face-to-face with her monsters, including the depth of her own fear, which made her look as if she'd been knocked upside the head. My friend seemed gentler and less aggressive. She seemed to listen with more intent.

Perhaps it's a new kind of innocence. Not the fiction of perfection but an openness born of truth-telling, wonder, and awareness of endings. In a novel called *Gilead*, Marilynne Robinson wrote about something she calls a "learned innocence." "There is a learned innocence as much to be valued as the innocence of children," she suggests. This innocence contains the dark. It germinates in the footsteps of monsters.

EARTH ANGEL

"Last night I dreamt I was a butterfly," wrote the Taoist philosopher Chuang Tze. "Now am I a man dreaming I am a butterfly or a butterfly dreaming I am a man?" Swept up in the current of powerful change, spun around by metanoia, we're startled by how changeable our identities turn out to be when our familiar context—the containers we inhabit—is forcibly taken and stirred. We're more protean than we ever imagined. In Greek mythology Proteus is the god of changing forms, the shape-shifting, tricksterish aspect of the self that adapts instantaneously to shifts in the current. He is also the patron deity of survivors. The quicker we change, the stronger we swim; the smoother we morph, the better we surge; the less fear we swallow, the higher we dive and the more deeply we're able to plunge.

This may be why children are often more resilient than their baggaged adult counterparts, and why, as the Bible says, the child can become "father to the man" in emergent times. Children have fewer layers to unpeel, less history to keep them stuck. Only later in life do many children who've endured bad things learn to be afraid.

It's a ball-freezing, dreary-white, midwinter's morning in the exurbs of Chicago and I'm waiting in a strip mall espresso bar to meet a young Bosnian woman named Adisa Krupalija. I've been waiting for years to meet Adisa. In 1994, after returning from a trip to refugee camps in Pakistan, Eve Ensler, an activist friend whose life has been devoted to ending violence against women (including with her play *The Vagina Monologues*), told me about meeting a remarkable twelve-year-old refugee at a camp near Islamabad. Apparently, Adisa was a language whiz, and had been inducted as the camp's official English-language translator in spite of being barely pubescent. For a year it had been Adisa's responsibility to help hundreds of fellow refugees trying to gain asylum in the United States. Eve described seeing her for the first time, a tiny girl in a *shalwar kameez*, rushing around that malarial hellhole in 120-degree weather, translating testimonials, documents, love letters of her desperate compatriots struggling to talk to the outside world. "She seemed selfless to me," Eve told me. The Krupalijas had eventually landed in Chicago to be with relatives; Adisa had gone on to win a scholarship to Northeastern University, where she was now studying for the bar. Although Adisa does not like to talk about the war, she'd agreed to speak to me as a favor to our mutual friend.

Adisa comes rushing into the café a half hour late and locates me in a corner booth. In a movie she'd be played by Natalie Portman—all gazelle neck and brown eyes and bobbed, gamine hair. "I'm so sorry!" Adisa clutches my hand and smiles. Apparently, somebody, somewhere, needed Adisa's help with something and she couldn't bear to tear herself away. I recognize her kind right away; she's the sensible, caretaking, peacekeeping type to whom everyone else turns for help, regardless of what she might need herself, the Rock-of-Gibraltar person who rarely says no, because she mostly feels like the strongest.

I assure Adisa that there is no harm done. A gulag-faced waitress comes lumbering over. Adisa orders the chocolate pancakes. We drink our coffee and talk about Eve. Then this lovely young woman slowly begins to tell me her story.

Once upon a time, in 1992, the Krupalijas were a happy family leading a privileged life in the Yugoslavian town of Trnovo (population four thousand), thirty kilometers from Sarajevo. Adisa's mother grew roses on the terrace and had girlfriends over for tea. Her father was a town official. Beneath the window of their apartment, a nineteenth-century cobblestone square served as a playground for the Krupalija children. Adisa jumped rope there. She was a top student in her fourth-grade class.

One morning the milk lady showed up at their doorstep looking panicked, Adisa tells me now. "She told us that this would be her last time coming. She looked so pale." Soon afterward, barricades were erected around their apartment building to keep out Serbian tanks rolling toward them from Sarajevo. "Explosions began shaking the window. My father said that we must leave right away. But my mother refused."

"Why was that?"

"She was worried about who would water her plants." Adisa's look of strained forbearance tells me all I need to know about her beloved mother.

No longer safe in their apartment, the Krupalijas hid out in the basement for three days, making candles from shoestrings and oil. Adisa was charged with caring for her hysterical infant brother. "It was like hell," she says simply. "As if everything is one big scream and you're caught right in the middle of it. I now know what a rat feels like."

Under cover of night, the family escaped from their underground hideout and set out on a frightening exodus, wading across cold rivers at night without flashlights, hitching rides on trucks, avoiding Serbian snipers' bullets. After several months, and many close calls, the Krupalijas were airlifted to the Pakistani refugee camp. Promised a decent place to stay while they sought U.S. asylum, they arrived to find a filthy, insect-ridden, food-poor compound devoid of hygiene and surrounded by barbed wire, with AK-47-armed policemen posted at the gates.

It was at this point, Adisa tells me, that her father hatched his plan, laying the family's fate on the shoulders of his twelve-year-old daughter. Adisa still doesn't understand how this happened. "All my father said was that unless I learned English, we would never be able to leave that place."

"But you were so young."

"It was all happening so fast," she says, aware that this sounds like a weak explanation. "I don't know why it was up to me. Maybe because I like languages." Something in Adisa's tone suggests that perhaps her parents were too distraught to be more help.

"It worked out best for everyone," she says, excusing them. "It was the best thing that I've ever done in my life. Helping people in the camp is what got me through. I learned to put others before myself."

Her pancakes arrive, looking like a dripping Dalí chocolate still life. "It made me strong," she insists, pushing her breakfast aside for the moment. "I was doing what was necessary, that is all." Inside of two months Adisa had perfected her English enough to begin the family's immigration process and to offer service to other camp-mates. This sudden shape-shifting from preadolescent to refugee caseworker was a wonderful thing, she assures me.

"How did you learn so quickly, Adisa?"

"I've always been independent," she says, shrugging. "No matter what happens, I've always tried to focus on what I could learn from any given situation."

"At twelve?"

"Even then." She smiles. "I was thinking, how can this improve me as a person? I have always been intensely curious, wanting to learn more and more. Curiosity makes life so much more interesting. In the camp, everybody was so despondent about how hot it was. Some got malaria. Some became jaundiced. But all I could think was, 'Wow, I get to learn English. Now I get to see the world outside my little town.'"

"It was your ticket out."

"Exactly. Not that it was so easy, of course not. We saw terrible pain and violence. But I grew up in that refugee camp. When you go through something like this, a part of you is changed forever."

"Which part of you changed?"

"The one that refuses to conform. The part that can never be like other people. You're always pushing yourself to be different, to take the harder path. Challenge yourself to be stronger."

That sounds like a lot of pressure, I say.

"It is, sometimes. But it helps you in the end. It gives you tenacity. A high tolerance for change and hard times. When I look back at my time in Pakistan, there was nothing that brought me down. Nothing. There was nothing that made me doubt that things would be all right."

She almost sounds nostalgic, I notice.

"Not quite." Adisa chuckles. "But I do have many good memories. Sometimes I do miss that little girl," she admits, reaching for the sugary pancakes.

"She's still here. Underneath."

"More some days than others," Adisa tells me. Creating a new life for herself in America has required a difficult new skill set, she says. She compares the process to an artist shifting painting styles in his studio. "At first it's like a Jackson Pollock," she says, alluding to that artist's spontaneous, rainbow-splattered canvases. "You're just getting through. It's all about instinct. You're throwing paint at this canvas and hoping it will become something."

Adisa bites into her gooey breakfast. "Later it's more like Georges Seurat," she says, meaning that Frenchman's micromanaged canvases covered with tiny pinpoint strokes. "That's when you're putting it all back together. You have to do the little dots and at the same time see the big picture. You carefully proceed step-by-step, being patient, focused, precise. You pick a goal and set it high."

"But look at you now," I say. "It worked." Ten years ago Adisa was a Bosnian refugee without a cent in her pocket. Today she's studying for the bar exam and recently accepted a lucrative job with an international corporate law firm. "You did something right."

"I'm doing okay," Adisa says, deflecting the compliment. "But I have to remind myself sometimes of what my twelve-year-old self would have done. When I'm in school, or with my family or boyfriend, I have to remind myself. I used to be so fearless," Adisa says. "I never want to lose that."

"Where would it go?" I ask.

"I know it sounds strange," she says. "But I almost felt more free back then. Life seemed so simple. I just have to keep remembering that."

"And trusting," I tell her.

"And changing," she answers. "I never want to stop changing."

"As if you could," I say.

For a second, Adisa looks as young as she is. Then she says, "Change is everything."

THE END OF SEEKING
(OR DIG IN ONE PLACE)

In the decade after quitting my job at *Interview*, I lived in twenty-eight different locations (not counting extended road trips and short-term squats), camping out in retreat centers, spare bedrooms, house sits, sublets, sport-utility vehicles, anywhere that I could find a cheap bed and a teacher who claimed to have something important to say. From Frankfurt to Philadelphia to Fuengirola, Myrtle Beach to Bubeneshwar, San Francisco to Paris to Pondicherry, then back again to Manhattan, I became a compulsive dharma bum, following my divine impulses wherever they led and my Visa card was accepted. People told me I was crazy for living this way—for *so* long—and they might have been right. But it was good crazy, metamorphosis crazy, crazy for learning and waking up before the fat lady crooned her last.

Spiritual seeking was the most intense love affair I'd ever had. It brimmed with unconsummated desire, the tantra of playing peekaboo with God—the Beloved that no one could ever possess. The divine perfume kept me snout-to-the-ground, self-absorbed as any hopeful romantic. I'd finally found an object of desire that seemed worthy of both the chase and the heartache. Pursuing wisdom instead of money, sex, bylines, or security (which I rejected then as a bourgeois illusion), I felt authentic for the first time. My life had a noble purpose at last. I thought I'd become some kind of hero.

Then my honeymoon with the Holy Grail ended as swiftly as it began. I was minding my own business one afternoon, by a lake at a South Carolina retreat center, meditating on the meaning of light on water and whooping loons munching on Spanish moss, when the Ghost of Christmas Future appeared wearing orange harem pants and a single pink flower stuck into his long gray hair. With no invitation from me, this aging hippie proceeded to tell me the sobering story of his life. He'd been a spiritual seeker since R.D. first proclaimed, "Turn on, tune in, drop out," in the sixties, searched for God (nirvana, he called it) and avoided the trappings of worldly life. Now this poor guy was staring down retirement age with nothing to show for his years on the God trail, he told me sadly, but a P.O. box in Santa Cruz, a plethora of religious moments, and his membership card to the AARP. He was lonely, road weary, wistful, and bitter. His resemblance to who I myself could become (were I to live that long) was too pointed and painful to overlook.

"You wanna know what I ended up with after all that seeking, brother?" the old hippie asked me, tugging one of his many gold earrings. "*Nada*," he said. "Nothing."

But how could that be? I asked in self-defense. He'd chosen a life of surprises and travel, spent his time on the road not taken, expanded his mind with wisdom and awe. "We all make our choices," I said to the guy. Every choice has its pros and cons. Maybe he was just having a crappy day.

The stranger waved my excuses aside, then paused my heart with these frightening words: "Go home while you're still young, buddy boy. *Dig in one place.*"

I felt as if God had sent me a prophet, a sign to ignore at my own peril. The sign pointed straight at the secret suspicion—the one I'd been trying so hard to ignore—that I was metaphysically full of shit. I was running away from my life, not toward it, focused on holiness Casanova-style, mounting the next retreat, teaching, ayurvedic chakra cleanse, for the same reason philanderers can't stop chasing skirts: They're afraid to die. They're secretly scared that if they stop running, they'll be trapped. The trap (or woman) will morph into a grave. The reaper just might spare a moving target. You stick to the edge when the middle's too scary. Promiscuous seeking, I saw, was a ruse.

Next, I had the deflating misfortune of reading a book called *Cutting Through Spiritual Materialism*, which, if you haven't read it, don't—if you want to have an ego left. Fantasy-wise, it was downhill from there. Sages across the board proclaimed against the refuge of the road: "When a thing is everywhere the way is not to travel but to love" (Augustine); "To seek is not to find" (Rumi); "I came to a spot in the road where all paths were one" (Dogen); "Most seekers are just Narcissus in drag" (Da Free John).

The checkmate of this was abhorrent to me, but I did not want to end up with *nada*. Returning to the city for the time being, I rented a cheap apartment downtown. I lined my walls with photos of otherworldly-eyed saints to help relieve me of claustrophobia. This strategy didn't work for long. Soon enough, I was going crazy, the walls were breathing in on me, I couldn't breathe myself, and then came the morbid ideation. This led to moments of genuine, knee-knocking panic. I really didn't want to die. But as winter passed and the leaves returned, the courtyard behind my apartment quite peaceful, I began to get used to staying put. Being still made way for a ghost to appear.

In the bathroom one morning, as I was brushing my teeth, a numinous presence announced itself behind me—not an actual ghost, exactly, more a mounting apparition of dread, a condensation of feeling so thick it appeared to envelop me as I stood there holding my toothbrush. The ghost invited me to have a figurative seat. I paused and listened. The tone of its voice was more poignant than scary. The ghost told me it was a distillation of all my greatest fears. It was the combined essence of all that I dreaded, the dark thing I'd been running away from. This ghost simply wanted me to listen, as if hearing confession from myself, to music sadder than anything I had allowed myself to hear before. It spoke to me in a major chord about the "unfinished symphony," the longings and dreams that could go unfulfilled, the lopped-off, pissed-off refrain that began the day I started expecting to die young. Hearing the ghost's voice touched me. It was not horrifying. So I listened to the ghost in the months to come.

There's a place where beauty and sadness meet—if you've been there yourself, you know this already—where the two become indistinguishable. It's the place where sadness is no longer ugly, where grief begins feeling like soap in a wound, painful but purgative at the same time. Once, in Italy, I watched my host, a restorer of damaged paintings, as he worked on a Renaissance canvas so encrusted by time that the image had been covered up completely. Robi dipped his brush in the lye-smelling liquid and ran it across the grimy surface, revealing an eye, an ear, a cheek, and finally, the face of a curly-haired child gazing up at a pair of wings. It amazed me that something so foul and evil-smelling could uncover such hidden beauty. At home now for the first time in years, I was learning that grief works the same way, poisonous if withheld too long, clarifying upon its release.

This ghost and I became allies that year. Its voice told me what I was afraid of. Today we're still close, but I rarely see him.

There's a story about a beggar who was sitting on the side of a road. The old man had been on the road for years. A stranger approached one afternoon. "Spare some change?" mumbled the beggar, mechanically shaking his tin cup.

"I have nothing to give you," the stranger said. The beggar turned away in disgust. Then the stranger asked, "What is that you're sitting on?"

"Nothing," the beggar told him. "Just an old box. I have been sitting on it for as long as I can remember."

"Ever looked inside?" asked the stranger.

"Why?" the beggar replied. "What's the point? There's nothing in there."

The stranger insisted, "Have a look inside."

The beggar refused at first, then finally decided to pry the lid open. With astonishment, disbelief, and elation, he saw that the box was filled with gold.

Coming home, I had opened the box.

SOMETHING ELSE IS ALSO TRUE

Doubleness comes as a revelation. The realization that every experience has two sides, even seemingly monolithic distress, turns the mind around. There is always a mystery face to experience, including the most painful episodes. We realize this slowly over time as we watch life turn its other cheek, again and again.

Maria Housden, then a New Jersey housewife, learned this countervailing lesson by enduring a mother's worst nightmare. On the morning of January 7, 1993, Maria's two-year-old daughter, Hannah, was diagnosed with a galloping, untreatable rhabdoid cancer of the kidney sure to kill the little girl within the year. The shock of this information plunged Maria from the ordinary world of soccer mom into the parallel zone of nursing a dying child—while her other two children still needed her—without losing her sanity.

"Hannah's diagnosis catapulted me into another reality," Maria explains to me. We're alone on the porch of her rented seaside house in Sea Bright, New Jersey. Maria is six foot two, weighs 120 pounds, and has the glass-green eyes, forward-lurching hips, and classic cheekbones of a runway model. She's like Uma Thurman's basketball-playing supersister, with white pedal pushers up to her knee. It's distracting to walk down the street with Maria. People often point and stare, especially the men, who gaze at her towering beauty with wonder.

Maria lights a Virginia Slim and takes a sip of her margarita. "I had been very good and faithful to what I understood as God all my life," she tells me. "I believed that I could control what happened to me, more or less—minimize my own suffering and certainly that of my children. That was my job as a mother," she says. "But Hannah's diagnosis dissolved all of that."

Her survival response was to keep appearances up as meticulously as possible. "I became very methodical," Maria remembers. "There were so many things that I couldn't control, but there were a few others that I could. If Hannah was going to die, for instance, I wanted to have a say in what that looked like," she explains. "I wanted her to die at home instead of in a hospital, to have family there instead of strange people." Maria stubs out her cigarette. "My job was to do everything possible to help my family through this."

Underneath the mask, however, she was quickly going to pieces. "I had it all under control on the surface. Oh, brother! People kept telling me how amazing I was to be doing what I was doing! I felt like one of those dummies you see in store windows, walking around behind a cardboard cutout of myself." Maria shakes her head. "Behind the façade there was loneliness and turmoil."

"But you couldn't show that to others?"

"I needed to make it feel okay to other people so they would keep showing up for me and for Hannah. Who wants to hang out for a year with someone who is completely in despair, unable to cope with what's happening?" she asks.

I let her know that I've had my own share of friends walking away.

"It's a survival mechanism," Maria agrees. "I made the outside part very intact—you could draw a line around it—but the rest of me was this kind of soup." Her grief over losing Hannah immersed Maria in this muddling void. The wise little girl who insisted on wearing her red Mary Janes during surgery, who refused to speak to doctors unless they told her their first names, became her mother's intimate muse in the year that she died. Maria has detailed this wisdom in her bereavement classic, *Hannah's Gift* (published with the telling subtitle *Lessons from a Life Fully Lived*). Caring for Hannah revealed to Maria truths about her own life she had been avoiding, places where she wasn't telling the truth, parts of herself that were being dishonest.

"I'd poured everything I had into maintaining an illusion of perfection in every aspect of my life," she says now. "I'd forgotten what was right for me." For starters, her marriage was on the rocks long before Hannah got sick. The little girl died a year after her diagnosis, and in subsequent years the weight of accumulated lies became unbearable. Maria slipped into such a deep depression that she decided, against the advice of family and friends, to leave her three children—Will, twelve, Margaret, four, and Madeleine, three—with their father in New Jersey, while she took time to sort herself out. She needed to make a lobster's plunge, to shed one skin and grow a new one before she could enter her next phase of life.

Retreating to a Christian center in the Michigan wilderness, Maria could still hear the mocking voices of those who judged her for what they called running away. Yet she held to her conviction that she needed this solo time in order to heal and absorb the lessons that Hannah's death left with her. "There's no room in deep grief for anything but the truth," Maria says. "You're able to see things in your life, and say things to yourself, that you couldn't at any other time."

"Grief can be distorting, too," I say, thinking of Joan Didion's magical thinking.

"At first it is," Maria agrees. "But I learned that grief has another side to it as well. For example"—she takes a sip of her drink—"something can hurt so badly that you no longer have patience with the fucked-up-ness you might be living in your life. It's that kind of movement. That kind of energy."

"I know what you mean."

"'Grief' shares the same root as 'gravitation,'" Maria reminds me. "It's a force, an energy with momentum. Grief is a power with weight and heft. And the fact that it has weight also suggests that it is something that can be shifted. You can succumb to grief and be buried in it. It can suffocate you and hold you down. Or your perspective can shift and the pain can be used to compel you in a different direction."

The notion of grief as a rerouting force intrigues me. "Where were you on the night of nine-eleven, for instance?" asks Maria. "And did you know then—in a way you may already have forgotten—what matters most to you?" She allows the question to settle for a second. "That's how grief can keep us honest. This is what I learned from Hannah's death. There is always another side to things, a mystery. No matter how great the loss, *something else is also true.*"

This mantra has a haunting quality. Doubleness, I think. The hidden face.

Maria appears to be one of the happiest people that I've ever met. Contrary to what one might expect, talking about Hannah gives her joy. "My daughter taught me to be a whole person," she says.

Thirteen years after Hannah's death, Maria does appear to be thriving. Back in New Jersey with the kids, working on a film version of *Hannah's Gift* with a French director, easing her way into the community, patching up a friendship with her ex-husband, beginning to date, she loves her new life as a writer and is looking forward to what comes next.

"I'm grateful for every day of my life," she says simply. "I never thought I would say that again." Maria takes a copy of *Hannah's Gift* from the shelf and points to a passage near the end of the book. "Hannah had taught me that there is a death more painful than the one that took her body from this world," it reads. "A soul suffocated by fear leaves too many joys unlived."

"That's the truth," I say.

"Hannah was my teacher," she tells me. Then Maria reaches for a photograph of the fair-haired girl sitting on her mother's lap. She studies the picture for several moments. "I used to be afraid of mystery," Maria says, setting the photograph back on the table. "But the unknown doesn't scare me anymore. Instead of drowning in it," she says, pulling her bare knees to her chest, "now I'm swimming."

PAIN PASSES, BUT THE BEAUTY REMAINS

One day a student comes to her guru overwhelmed with pain. She tells the old woman that she isn't sure how to survive her own sadness.

The teacher listens to her distress. I imagine the guru's eyes softening as she hears the disciple's story, suffused with fathomless wisdom gained from having crossed her own wilderness to the powerful place where she now sits.

"I want to end my pain," says the weeping student.

The teacher leans forward with a gentle smile. "You cannot conquer your pain by destroying it," she tells the disciple. "But only by allowing it to be what it is—unbearable poignancy within an infinite nature, which also contains joy. Even bliss."

The visitor does not understand.

"Look into my eyes," the guru says. The sad woman raises her gaze to meet the teacher's steady countenance. "Do you see in my eyes an ignorance of your pain?" the old woman asks.

The student can see that her teacher's eyes contain no ignorance

at all. They are as clear as crystal and shining bright with uncondi-
tional compassion and understanding.

"Do you see that I accept your pain fully?" the teacher asks.

The student can see that this is true.

"What you see," the teacher says, "is that I am not afraid of
your pain. I have conquered the illusion that such terrible pain will
destroy me. The pain is what it is. And I am what I am."

The humbled student bows to this wisdom. How liberating it
must be to know this, she thinks, to know that you are not your
pain even when you cannot see beyond it. To overcome any bitterness that may have arisen because you were not "up to the magnitude of the pain that was entrusted to you," in the words of
another master.

Like the mother of the world who carries the pain of the world
in her heart, each of us is part of her heart and therefore en-
dowed with a certain measure of cosmic pain. You are sharing in
the totality of that pain. You are called upon to meet it in joy instead of self-pity. The secret: offer your heart as a vehicle to
transform cosmic suffering into joy.

The student leaves her guru's house feeling small but happier.

HEDONICS

Being happy, wrote Colette, is one way of being wise. The indomitable French authoress who refused to leave Paris during the Siege, scribbling her erotic novels as war planes dropped bombs near the Arc de Triomphe, was certain about the wisdom of joie de vivre in times when life is roughest.

The burgeoning field of happiness studies, known as hedonics, tells us a lot about why (beyond dumb luck and longevity genes) some people thrive in miserable times while other, more outwardly fortunate souls actually decline rather quickly. Hedonics would not exist, it turns out, if Sigmund Freud had had the last word. Famously declaring happiness to be a quixotic pipe dream, and "the transformation of hysterical misery into common unhappiness" to be the most we poor neurotics could hope for, the father of psychoanalysis was largely responsible for science's formerly paltry understanding of how happiness figures into a human life. Before neuroplasticity demonstrated that the brain is evolving, learning new tricks, forging felicitous pathways till the day we die, psychological research had focused mainly on negative emotional states.

The recent shift from what goes wrong with us to what goes right has brought the positive psychology movement to the cultural table at last.

Subjective well-being (SWB) is the nickname experts in this field give to happiness. Since your hell may be my paradise, subjectivity appears to be the single greatest variable in the happiness equation. Homeless people in Calcutta have been found to be less unhappy than those in California (because they have a stronger sense of community), while Amish folks rarely claim to be bored, though sifting curd might not be your idea of a laugh riot. Each of us is born, it seems, with a happiness "set point," a genetic level, from giddy to grumpy, around which SWB tends to settle, regardless of what happens to us. A now famous study of identical twins reared in different environments suggests that this set point determines approximately 50 percent of our disposition to happiness.

"Happiness is genetically influenced but not genetically fixed," David Lykken, a geneticist at the University of Minnesota, tells me. "The brain's structure can be modified through practice. If you really want to be happier than your grandparents provided for in your genes, you have to learn the kinds of things you can do, day to day, to bounce your set point up and avoid the things that bounce it down." Apparently, there are as many happy-bumping tools as there are people wanting to cheer up. They range from commonsense maintenance such as sleep, exercise, and nurturing relationships to shifts in core beliefs and expectations. This reminds me of Maria Housden's experience after Hannah died. One researcher I speak to recommends taking control of your own time and keeping a "gratitude journal." Another promotes "acting happy," since there seems to be a direct link between facial expression and emotion, as in fake it till you make it.

Happier people seem to be those who rely on familiar shortcuts rather than overthinking every little situation. Happy people tend to forgive; they're also inclined to gravitate toward making commitments. It comes as no surprise to learn that stress is the Darth Vader of contemporary life. Jon Kabat-Zinn, who helps run the Stress Reduction Clinic at the University of Massachusetts, goes so far as to say that "we have a sort of autoimmune disease—chronic stress and discontent—caused by not looking deeply enough into this question of genuine happiness." Kabat-Zinn teaches people seeking stress relief that wellness practices such as meditation make it possible, even in the midst of hardship, to experience simple pleasures. "To know delight, what is right and beautiful with the world," as he puts it. "With mental balance, we develop a keel-like ballast that helps us to remain stable even under extreme conditions." (We will discuss stress specifically in a later chapter.)

Regardless of which particular tools we choose to help lift our own SWB, one thing appears to be certain: We're better off aiming for happiness moment to moment than trying to engineer contentment through long-term planning. This is because, as science now shows us, human beings are fairly hopeless at predicting what will make us happy or how long that happiness will last. Harvard psychologist Daniel Gilbert spends his days exploring the riddle of human self-delusion. He's a pioneer in the field known as affective forecasting, whose researchers measure the distressing gap between what we believe will make us happy and what actually ends up doing so. "We're such strangers to ourselves," Dan insists to me. "Nowhere more than in our pursuit of the Holy Grail of happiness."

"But why?" I'm still puzzled by how this self-blinding happens.

"Because we usually overestimate how things will affect us and rarely underestimate them," he explains. This discrepancy, known as the impact bias, causes a great deal of what Dan calls "miswanting." When post-catastrophe people talk about cleaning house, getting rid of unnecessary crap in their lives, they're talking about the fruits of miswanting.

To confuse things further, the results of our choices are nowhere near as life changing as we think they will be. In a 1978 study of SWB among lottery winners and paraplegics, both groups adjusted paradoxically to their respective changes of fortune: The lottery winners settled back to levels of happiness that did not differ significantly from a control group's. The paraplegics, while less happy, were not as unhappy as expected. In fact, as another study revealed, major events—happy or not—lose their impact on happiness levels *in less than three months*. If we understood how quickly this adaptation process worked, we might choose to invest our hopes in things that could actually last—and deliver.

Money is not one of them. It has been proven beyond a doubt that once our creature comforts are met, having more in the bank account rarely makes people more content. Once middle-class comforts are in place, the line between wealth and survival, Dan Gilbert tells me, is virtually negligible. "The first forty grand makes a dramatic difference," he says, "but after basic needs are met, the next ten million does almost nothing."

I tell him that I'll be the judge of that.

Just as Italians have eight words for love, we need more definitions of happiness, a spectrum wide enough to encompass struggle, loss, and unwanted change. The smiley-face version of happiness simply will not do. Life is too complex, we know too much, there's too much pain to be satisfied with a naïve idea of what it means to be glad for life. Even survivors of the direst experiences attest to this paradox. "Who knows what happiness is?" asked one Holocaust refugee. "Perhaps it is better to talk in more concrete terms of the fullness or intensity of existence," she wrote. "In this sense there may have been something more deeply satisfying in our desperate clinging to life than in what people generally strive for."

Dr. Marty Seligman, the godfather of the positive psychology movement, has created a three-tiered happiness model with direct implications on how we make our life choices. Beyond the first level, which Seligman calls the "Hollywood" view of happiness ("getting as much positive emotion as possible"), a second kind of happiness arises from discovering our "signature strengths," which range in his core list from honesty, kindness, and forgiveness to ingenuity and love of learning. When we use our signature strengths in the service of something beyond ourselves, Seligman believes, we reach the highest tier. Learning to transcend our own needs, to at times sacrifice our immediate desires for the sake of the greater good, not only boosts our happiness level but also promotes the survival of the group. It is never a good idea to take care of others while ignoring one's own needs, of course. We've all known some grim-faced do-gooder who secretly resented those he or she insisted on helping.

"Just look at the Ten Commandments," I'm reminded by New York psychoanalyst Michael Eigen. "To covet is the gateway to pain."

Of course, comparisons are invidious in the best of times. Happiness researchers assure us that the single most powerful variable concerning well-being is how we choose to look at things. The wider the frame, the more vivid the picture. The softer the brush, the more sensuous the light. Colette had one of the most brilliant palettes ever, in both art and life—the ability to soar, crash, and pull herself back up again from the wreckage; to always remain herself somehow; to finish her novels, love her younger men, drink her wine, relish her gossip, even with garrisons outside her window. She knew that happiness wasn't a Popeye grin—no triumphalist horse-ride into the sunset—but a brewing admixture of bitter and sweet. Metanoia made her wise. "Bring it on!" the gout-ridden writer would say, clutching a bulldog to her breast, meaning life with all its colors. *C'est la guerre!*

INVISIBLE FEAST

"Vision and sight are not the same thing."

Photographer John Dugdale is blinking at me through his Coke-bottle lenses, cocking his head and leaning forward, attempting to catch a sliver of my silhouette where I'm sitting less than three feet away. His Seeing Eye dog, Manley, is nuzzling his foot on the floor beside him. John is a strikingly handsome, square-jawed man with a perfect nose and crown of dark hair, recalling a portrait by John Singer Sargent. He is also a human hologram. After three major strokes, five bouts of nearly fatal pneumonia, toxoplasmosis (a brain infection), peripheral neuropathy, Kaposi's sarcoma, and CMV retinitis that robbed him of most of his sight ten years ago, John is hardly the hale-fellow-well-met he appears at first to be. He's more of a walking riddle, in fact.

"Losing my eyesight at the start of my career was the thing I dreaded most of all," he tells me now. "I'd look at the sky, my hands, my face, my mother. I felt like I was disappearing, losing more sight every day." We're alone in John's drafty, top-floor Greenwich Village apartment. The room is filled with copper antiques, oversized cameras, and John's own haunting photographs—blue-tinted images of ghostly trees and naked lovers in dreamlike space. It's hard to believe—nearly impossible—that such beautiful pictures were created with only the fraction of eyesight left to him.

"Everyone told me that my career was over," John tells me. "But I decided that if I was going to lose my eyesight, I wanted to do it in a courageous way, hanging on to my camera tripod . . . not strung up to an IV pole. This was my moment to prove that illness did not have to end my creative life. I've had thirty-eight solo shows internationally since then. And my best work is still to come."

The trajectory of John's life in the past fifteen years is daunting to even imagine. Hospitalized for seven months in 1992, John was slowly preparing himself to die. "My doctor's goal was to get me through the year," he says. "I was struggling violently in my mind. I'd always been a huge overachiever. Everything I touched succeeded. For a long time I thought this couldn't be real, this couldn't possibly be happening to the golden boy. But it was happening. Fast."

Caught in this sudden downward spiral, John reached for the only gifts left him: creative intelligence and obstinacy. "I drove my doctors crazy. I questioned everything they wanted to give me." He smiles. "But you must never let people talk you out of what you want to do. Sometimes they don't even *want* you to get better."

This is sometimes true, strange as it seems.

"They need you to go on the path you're *supposed* to go on," John says. "You're supposed to be here for eighteen months and then die," he mocks. "So don't get off that bed! Don't get out of

WHEN YOU'RE FALLING, DIVE

that box! A nurse once told me I was going to have to take a certain medication for the rest of my life," he tells me in disbelief. "I said who the hell told you that? She kept barraging me with medical propaganda filled with doomsday information. I told her, you put those pamphlets on my bed when I'm sleeping one more time, and I will have you arrested!"

With nothing to lose, John chose his own artistic approach to self-healing. Learning to walk again after his stroke, he refused the hospital staff's equipment. "That walker was like the scarlet letter for me," he says, reminding me of Jack Willis, the paralyzed TV producer who threw his own walker across the room. John chose to rely on his sister's shoulder instead. Recovering from toxoplasmosis, he invented visualization techniques as a way of buoying his spirits. "I tried to come up with the most powerful thing each person in my family could do," John explains. "It's corny, but my mother happens to like doing laundry. So I told her, when you go home to the washing machine at night, imagine you're taking my brain out of my head and putting it in the warm rinse cycle."

John laughs at his homespun solution. "I said, 'Imagine toxo coming out of my brain and going down the drain,'" he says. "'Then take my brain, all clean and fluffy, and picture putting it back into my head.' My sister loves to cook, so I asked her to picture my brain in her lettuce spinner and spin the living daylights out of it! I thought of the purest, most perfect thing I had ever seen and remembered newborn lambs in spring. I pictured them nestling peacefully inside my head."

A week after several violent drug reactions, a flummoxed internist paid John a visit. "He told me that the infection in my brain seemed to be gone," he says, smiling. "The doctor said he didn't get it. It could have been a coincidence. Or maybe it wasn't."

Either way, John was still here.

John realized that his physical and spiritual survival depended now on his ability to keep making art. "I had to become the world's first blind photographer," he says simply. Late one afternoon, at his farm in Upstate New York, he finally found the nerve to pick up his camera and attempt to take a picture with most of his eyesight gone. What happened next, in fact, changed the course of John Dugdale's life.

"I had just gotten out of the hospital," he says, once we've moved to a sofa in the sitting room. "I was out in the pasture, trying to take a photograph using a magnifying glass, struggling to focus, adjusting the backdrop and light meter," John tells me. "I kept tripping over the tripod, getting more and more frustrated. Every time I was just about ready, the sun would move and I'd have to switch the whole thing again."

The idea of a mostly blind photographer in a country pasture, struggling to find the right light for a picture, is too mythopoeic to quite imagine.

"When I was about to go crazy, I finally got the whole thing right—just perfect—and bam!" John says, slapping the table. "In that very moment the sun went down and everything disappeared, went black. That's when I completely snapped." Sensing the distress in his master's voice, Manley searches John's face for trouble.

"I hit the deck in a heap of nothingness," John says. "Just fell down on the ground and covered my head, pushed my face in the dirt, and started to cry in a way that was almost inhuman. There was grass in my teeth, my mouth. My eyes were full of dirt. I just wanted to burrow into the ground and die. I was furious, sad, frustrated, sick of everything," he says. "Bawling my eyes out, asking, why did this have to happen? In a way that was completely out of control—like hiccups when you can't stop."

He strokes Manley's nuzzling head. "I was feeling the full impact of what had happened to me for the first time," John says. "I thought I was having a nervous breakdown. My friend came out of the house to see what was happening. Thank God I wasn't alone! He scooped me up and carried me to the house, sat me on the couch, and held me in his arms like a child. He said, 'Okay, go ahead and cry.' I lay on his lap and bawled until there wasn't another drop of fluid in my body. He didn't try to stop me at all. Finally, I asked him to get me a camera so I could take a picture. I got back in his lap and snapped the shot. It was so beautiful, like a pietà. I called it 'The Descent of Man.'"

This stunning photograph, which resembled nothing in John's previous work, became a centerpiece of Shadows Night Fall, the solo exhibition that catapulted him from the ranks of well-paid shutterbugs to the echelon of world-class artist. Since then, John's unique azure cyanotypes (a nineteenth-century camera process that allows him to enlarge images enough to see them) have earned him comparisons to Julia Margaret Cameron, the Victorian master, and invitations from collectors and museums around the world.

"I never expected this tremendous response," he says with a smile. "I've got this great Cheshire cat feeling. The thing that I thought would be the end, in fact, actually took me somewhere I would never have imagined. I came to New York to be an artist, not a magazine hack, and finally landed in the place I was meant to be when I started. I just took a very different route," he says, reminding me of disabled athlete turned teacher Jim MacLaren.

Creativity in the midst of chaos, the turn toward beauty in ugly times, has been John's lifeline back to health. Yet he learned early on that transformation is only possible when we make peace with the facts of our lives. "Survival doesn't really mean anything without acceptance," John explains. "That's the paradoxical part. You have to take the thing that's wrong and own it. Make it into something that has meaning for you. If you try to hide or negate it, it will just eat you up," he says. "If you're hoping for things to be other than they are—constantly wondering how or why something happened, or how to fix it—you're *lost*. You'll completely miss out on the graceful time you have."

John witnessed this paradoxical truth during his time in the hospital. "The minute they rolled somebody into the room next to me, I could tell if they were going to stay on the planet or leave," he says. "I could hear the resistance to change in their voice."

That quickly? John swears to me that this is true. "The ones who wound up giving up were the people who couldn't imagine themselves except the way they were," he says, while patients who exhibited flexibility prevailed. "The opportunity for transformation when we enter deeply into our experience is absolutely unbridled," John believes. "It's just like nuclear power if you choose to use it properly. But if you can't imagine yourself in a new way, you're just not gonna make it," he insists. "If you think you're gonna be the person you were before tragedy struck—internally or externally—it's impossible. Once you pass through that fire, you've been smelted. You're gonna to come out gold on the other side or you're not gonna come out at all."

Such metamorphoses are sometimes confusing to folks around us. "People often ask me why I don't take happier pictures," John says, chuckling. His famously moody photographs could not be more unlike his peppy commercial work of yesteryear. "People ask me why I don't just see a shrink," he says with raised eyebrows. "To make the complicated feelings go away. I respond by asking what they see in my work, exactly. Is it loss, fear, joy, sadness, sexuality, beauty, tiredness? Because all of that is there. I have just as much joy as I do melancholy."

Kahlil Gibran described this doubleness in a poem.

Your joy is your sorrow unmasked
And the selfsame well from which your laughter rises was
    oftentimes filled with your tears.
And how else can it be?
The deeper that sorrow carves into your being,
The more joy you can contain.

This wisdom has widened John's point of view. "I ask these well-meaning people which part, exactly, they are afraid of. Which part can they not look at? Because loss goes on for all of us. It is authentic to be human and in pain."

At his lowest time in the hospital, John says, he had an epiphany that remained with him. "I was in this tiny, dumpy room at the end of the hallway, with one window onto an airshaft, feeling completely helpless. Nobody was around that day. I was counting the hours, the minutes, the seconds. One thin strand of light was coming down the airshaft. And as I was gazing at it, something began to shift in me," John says. "It was more an awareness than a thought. But as I lay there watching this light, I knew that that was where I was going to. That I would become part of that. It's hard to explain," John acknowledges, "but when I exhaled, a straitjacket fell away and I became very peaceful with the idea of leaving the planet. In *success*, not failure," he makes clear. "There was a transcendental shift in my personality."

He claims now that this transcendent shift is more precious to him than his actual vision. "The light comes from inside," John explains. "Vision and sight are not the same thing," he repeats. "Sometimes I think that if God came down and said I could have my sight back but I'd have to forget everything I've learned, I couldn't do it. Once you've really been forced to let everything go, life becomes much more peaceful."

"It's hard to communicate that without sounding delusional," I say.

"Once you've come home for the tenth time to news that someone you love has died, you start to have this other experience of life that most people aren't familiar with," John agrees. "I have a better grip on mortality than my parents do. My mother, God bless her, always wants to give me her eyes. But I tell her, 'Ma, I have my special eye. No one sees only with their eyes. You just don't realize it until you have to.'"

John's macho father learned this lesson as well. "When my dad thought I was going to die, he came to see me and gave me the first peck on the cheek he'd given me since I was eight years old," John says, his eyes pooling up behind the thick glasses. "It was really awkward. He banged his head on the swing-arm TV." My host wipes his eyes on his sleeve. "But for my father, that kiss was like stepping over a chasm. It would never have come about in any other way. Now, whatever happens, I know deep down in my heart that he loves me. And my father knows that I love him."

In the past few months John has started to lose the fraction of vision left to him. He isn't happy about this, of course. But he doesn't seem especially frightened either. "Loss goes on," he tells me when we meet again. "I don't want to leave the planet. I want to see what's going to happen with my garden this year. I don't want to not see my friends and my family. But when that happens, I'll be forced to accept it."

In recent photographs John has begun inserting himself into the images. A male figure can be seen around the periphery—sometimes a hand, sometimes his face, other times just an arm or a shadow—as if to remind us, his doubting viewers, that he's still here. John Dugdale calls these his spirit pictures. "When I talk about losing my sight these days, I find myself touching my own face," he says now, fingers reaching automatically toward his cheek.

"I haven't finished taking that picture yet."

ORIGINAL BLESSING

We cannot transform what we have not first blessed. Without blessing everything, our harshest parts especially, we cannot be turned around by the *coincidentia oppositorum*—the conjunction of opposites, the sacred marriage, the wisdom that only arises from reconciling yang and yin. Ancient alchemists applied this same principle, adding a pinch of *negresca*, the blackest element, in order to make what they called gold. Our dark parts then become allies, enriching our *prima materia*, the mess that we must learn how to bless if we want to move forward.

The word *blessing* comes from the French verb *blesser*, "to wound," and often arrives through the hands of pain, as Samuel Kirschner, an Israeli bodyworker living in New York, learned when his father was dying. Samuel grew up craving his father's blessing but chose to save his own life instead, fleeing Israel at the age of twenty to become a permanent exile in the United States. His family's grief was too suffocating. Raised by Holocaust survivors (Samuel was conceived in a relocation camp after the war, in fact), the troubled prodigal son went through decades of psychotherapy before learning how to feel happy inside his own skin. Then one day, five years ago, Samuel's mother called from Israel to tell him that his dying father wanted to see him.

"Being with my father at the end of his life changed me completely," Samuel says when we meet at his loft near the East River. A soulful fifty-something man, Samuel is pinching an Indian cigarette between his fingers like a joint, his shaven head silhouetted against the garden window. "My father and I had never been close," he says. "My mother used to tell me when I was a kid that he wasn't fit to be a parent. She may have been right, but how could I tell?" Samuel muses, flicking his ashes into a cup.

"She always kept a wall between him and me, so my father and I were distant strangers. He lived with us, but always apart, like the shell of a father. Then he got sick, and for some weird reason I was the one he wanted close by. I saw how tender my father really was. Sitting with him at his deathbed during those weeks saved my life."

"In what way?"

"It's hard to explain," he tells me. "I realized how much of me was missing as a man. I'd been trying so hard not to be like my father—the image of him that I'd made up—that I had no idea who I really was. I had all this power but no foundation, just this huge hole underneath, where my father should have been."

He sips from his cup of tea. "We like to pretend like we're all grown up—handling it," Samuel says, making air quotes. "What a joke! Sitting with my father, I felt like I was five years old again. I was amazed by how much I still craved his approval after all these years, though I believed I didn't care."

"You never completely stop caring," I say.

"I still wanted him to be proud of me!" Samuel says with

amazement. "He loved to be pampered, so I just sat there next to the bed and touched him. One day my mother asked me to shave him, and when I finished, my father kissed my hand." I'm reminded of John Dugdale's father kissing him in the hospital bed, only in reverse. "He was too sick to talk, but he looked at me and smiled."

This smile helped to heal a painful breach in his adult psyche. "Something shifted in me when he kissed my hand," Samuel explains. "I don't know exactly how to describe it. My father lived through his hands. He was a baker, and in his spare time he liked to garden. My father's soul was in his hands. I know he felt this, too, because he began to trust me."

He lights another *beedi* and continues. "Anything to do with his body, my father asked for me to help him. I changed his catheter every morning. The first time I did it, I was actually shaking," Samuel admits. "Touching him there was so strange, so intimate. It reminded me of the story in the Bible when Isaac dies. The blessing was meant to go to the older son, and whoever got the blessing would thrive. Jacob was younger than Esau, the way I was younger than my brother, but he managed to touch his father's thigh. Touching the father's thigh was the symbol of being blessed. I knew when my father was dying that he was blessing me. No words, but that simple touch was more important than any therapy I had ever gone through before."

In a famous letter to his own absent father, Franz Kafka expressed the depth of such filial longing. "My writing was about you," confessed the author of *The Metamorphosis*. "In it I only poured out the grief I could not sigh at your breast."

Samuel concurs with this feeling. "I finally feel like a whole person," he admits. "It only took me fifty-nine years."

"You're lucky to have had it at all," I say, never having known my own father.

"I think about that all the time," he says.

The value of blessing goes far beyond family bonds, however. Blessing is a metaphysical act that elevates and transforms our view of the earth and our lives here. In fact, it's well worth asking ourselves what protean effect the replacement of original sin with original blessing might have on the way we see things. Brother Matthew Fox, a controversial Catholic priest, was actually silenced by the Holy See after suggesting that a doctrine of original blessing could help to heal a divided church he described as a "dysfunctional patriarchy." What's more, Fox wanted to know, how differently might we approach our own lives if we viewed worldly existence as blessed, not cursed; risen, not fallen; sacred and worthy instead of profane? Shortly after his silence is lifted, Brother Matthew agrees to sit down with me on a sunny morning in Washington Square Park to discuss how this absence of blessing in daily life continues to wound the modern soul.

"I spoke to a young person in Australia," Matthew begins. He's wearing jeans and a sky-blue button-down shirt, his silver hair neatly parted at the side, and is munching contentedly on a bagel. "This young fellow said something surprising," the priest remembers. "He said that it was as if adults had given today's youth a revolver containing six bullets: the hole in the ozone layer, the disappearing rainforests, polluted air and water, joblessness, debt, and the tightening field of education. He said it's as if adults have put this revolver to their heads and said, 'Now be happy,'" Matthew tells me. "Youth are in despair all over the world."

It's hard to believe that this mild-mannered Wisconsinite is the same fire-breathing reformer—one journalist called him the "D. H. Lawrence of theological lit"—who put the blasphemous screws to his Mother Church. "I remember teaching a course to a summer group of a hundred people or so," Matthew says, tossing bagel bits to the pigeons on the lawn. "We began with what is called the *via negativa*," the "school of hard knocks" in layman's terms. "I asked how many people had experienced the dark night of the soul. Every single person's hand went up."

"You were surprised?"

"Maybe not. But the point is that such awareness isn't just something for nuns and monks—we all know about it. What we often fail to realize is what to do with our sufferings."

"A friend of mine used to say that in a materialistic culture, we have no transcendental context for our suffering."

Matthew agrees. "We've been Novocained to death by television, entertainment, alcohol, drugs, school, work—all our addictions," he says. Matthew makes clear that he is not opposed to having fun with shallow, meaningless entertainment; he merely warns against junk culture as a steady diet. "It covers up our capacity for awe. For passion and deep feeling. It sets us up for superficial experience."

He often mentions Jewish philosopher Abraham Heschel in this regard. "People today are shocked by the weakness of our awe, but also by the weakness of our shock," Matthew says, quoting the visionary rabbi. "Heschel says that we've lost the capacity for radical response."

"Blessing is a radical response?" I ask.

"Of course it is. So is creativity. Creativity lies at the heart of freedom from addiction," he tells me. "Otto Rank, my favorite psychologist, says that the resurrection story from the Gospels is the most revolutionary idea that humans have ever come up with. Rank worked exclusively with artists and found that the number one obstacle to creativity is the fear of death. The redemption power of the Jesus story is that death is not the final word, so we don't have to fear it. When we believe in stories like the resurrection, we rediscover our creativity and are not afraid to use it. Imagination gets us into evil, and imagination gets us out."

"Tell that to Kim Jong Il," I say.

He sidesteps the North Korean despot. "Violence is intrinsic to the universe," Matthew says. "Terror and beauty go together. We don't live in a pretty universe, we live in a beautiful one. That's not evil. It's just part of being here."

"We would all like easier answers," I say.

"Yet awe is the thing that wakes us up."

"And awe contains darkness?"

"Always. The demonic and the divine join in the act of creativity," Matthew explains. Blessing counterbalances darkness and helps turn adversity toward the creative. "The cure for evil—the constructive reaction to suffering—is to redirect our imaginations," he says. "To be more conscious that we *have* imagination. And to never turn these imaginations over to the few. If we teach people that their imaginations are not powerful, important, or divine, then something essential begins to atrophy.

"Art, ritual, erotic life, prayer—all of these are a form of blessing," the priest goes on. "They strengthen the heart. They open us to wonder. Take something like a sweat lodge." He chuckles. "My first twenty minutes in one of those things, and I thought for sure I was going to die! I was looking for the fire exit. Then I said, 'I am going to die,' and I yielded. When you yield to the process, you undergo a transformation. Your heart grows."

"In the surrender?"

"In the play." Matthew's watching a group of toddlers attack the jungle gym. "We're here to celebrate with one another," he reminds me. "This ought to be an everyday thing. According to Meister Eckhart [the thirteenth-century mystic], 'For the person who is aware, breakthrough does not happen once a year, once a month, once a day, but many times every day.'"

This is the power that arises from blessing, Matthew Fox believes. We view ourselves, and the world itself, through a sacramental eye—perceiving the holiness in our lives—rather than the sting of damnation.

This radical priest seems to be saying that when we perceive life for what it is—miraculous, fathomless, staggering, brilliant—and view ourselves through this same opened window, blessing automatically occurs. Brushed by extinction, the most cynical person can be rendered childlike, curious, and glad. Bertrand Russell, the cranky British philosopher, almost died from double pneumonia in Peking during the winter of 1920. For several weeks all of the doctors in attendance thought he would be dead before morning. But with the coming of spring, his health—and gladness—returned, as Russell wrote in his autobiography:

Lying in my bed feeling that I was not going to die was surprisingly delightful. I had always imagined until then that I was fundamentally pessimistic and did not greatly value being alive. I discovered that in this I had been completely mistaken, and that life was infinitely sweet to me. Rain in Peking is rare, but during my convalescence there came heavy rains bringing the delicious smell of damp earth through the windows, and I used to think how dreadful it would have been to have never smelt that smell again. I had the same feeling about the light of the sun, and the sound of the wind. Just outside my windows were some very beautiful acacia trees, which came into blossom at the first moment when I was well enough to enjoy them. I have known ever since that at bottom I am glad to be alive.

Russell had finally blessed his own life, understood with both heart and mind, and what he perceived in this way surprised him. We are meant to be surprised by this world, he learned in almost losing it, meant most of all—in hard times, even—to be glad for the chance to have been here at all.

ENOUGH

Satisfaction becomes an art form. Knowing enough to recognize fullness. The wisdom of knowing when to stop is critical to *techne tou biou*, the craft of living. Yet this is not a lesson easily learned in our land of conspicuous plenty. Ours is a culture without sabbath or pause, a theater without an intermission. We measure ourselves by a more-is-more yardstick, drive ourselves beyond our limits, sacrifice life quality for productivity, and often end up feeling so burned out that we can't enjoy the fruits of our own labor through the bitter backwash of exhaustion.

But what if we didn't live this way? What if we practiced satisfaction and the skill of knowing when to stop? What if we engineered into our frantic schedules a weekly day of actual rest, a sundown-to-sundown tradition of stopping, cessation, renewal, and "non-doing," lived "as if we were at home in the universe," as Rabbi Rami Shapiro puts it? "Lived for one day without trying to control the people around you or the situations in which we find ourselves? Reserved one day for a state of acceptance? Not a day without desire, that would not be possible," Shapiro suggests, "but a day not to act on those desires." He believes that creating such a refuge might actually give us "a foretaste of the world to come."

Whether you believe in an afterlife or not, a sabbath does sound heavenly. Imagine your neighborhood stopping for twenty-four hours every week, as if Mother Earth herself were catching her breath after many days of sweat and toil. God worked mightily for six long days before cooling his heels on the seventh, the book of Genesis tells us. "Even the Lord could sit back and be satisfied that nothing more needed to be added to his creation," a Jewish colleague explained. "Even he could stop and say, 'It's good already. Enough!'"

How often does anything feel like enough? When, for more than a random instant, does life appear completely sufficient, with nothing to edit, improve, aspire to, arrange, or nudge forward in some way or other? Isn't there always something more to be done, work to be finished, ground to cover, prospects to investigate? When it came to enough, I had always believed, it would not be my personal fate in this lifetime.

But burnout is an insidious process. You don't know you're choked till you're already smoking. For a long time after my own "alive day," taking a break seemed ungrateful somehow, an affront to the gift of vitality. Living fully meant overdrive. Forced to choose between sanity and productivity, I would gladly have chosen prolifically nuts. But the smell of smoke was in my nostrils. I woke up too many mornings feeling like toast. My calendar was booked, my downtime upbeat, but my life had turned into a run-on sentence. I needed syntax. I needed a sabbath. I needed to figure out how to stop.

For someone like me this was difficult. I was the insecure geek in school who wrote twenty-page papers when five pages were assigned (and even those weren't good enough most times). Double the effort for half the self-esteem, that had been my lifelong motto. My Swiss-cheese ego just wouldn't stop leaking. These cheese holes announced that I was fully deficient and nothing I did could keep them stuffed.

I was living as a hungry ghost. Hungry ghosts are those ravenous figures in Buddhist mythology (metaphors for the insatiable ego) condemned to eternal craving in a world of elusive satisfaction. Nothing is ever enough for these monsters. There exists no end to their craving for more. We all have our ghostly orifices, the places where, if there were just a little more, we could be the people we long to be. But there comes a time, if we're paying attention, when this Pavlovian drool-and-whine charade reveals its own futility. We realize with dismay and shock that nothing will ever suffice as a permanent stopgap between us and our ravening hunger. Still, we can't stop trying to plug the space. We're endlessly dissatisfied, you will agree, driven to feed the unfillable void using things with a snowball's chance in hell of actually lasting.

Fortunately, Buddhism offers a sensible strategy for how to end this hungry ghost cycle. This begins with understanding the concept of *dukkha*—the "pervasive unsatisfactoriness" of all passing things in an imperfect, temporal world. Even those rare experiences that do manage to satisfy us completely will soon enough come to an end, we know, and this knowledge, in the Buddhist view, is exactly what casts the shadow of longing we find ourselves unable to shake. This dissatisfaction with things as they are remains, Buddhists tell us, our main source of suffering. Yet we seem unable to curb our compulsion to make this empty-sense go away.

The drive to fill internal emptiness stems from fundamental doubts about our own existence, the Buddha taught. Looking deep inside our psyche for a "self," humans are forever haunted by the suspicion that there is, in fact, no *there* there. If we continue to peel back the layers of our so-called "selves," Buddhists teach, we will come upon no permanent subject, regardless of how long or hard we try. Because confronting this emptiness feels so scary, we're driven to keep trying to cover it up, to papier-mâché the abyss with stuff.

Yet it is here—at futility's brink—where we can begin to free ourselves. The cycle of craving is interrupted when we learn how to stop. "Sitting with uncomfortable feelings, getting friendly with the hole you really are, you realize that emptiness is not really a problem," says Buddhist teacher David Loy. "It's our ways of trying to escape it that turn it into a problem." When we learn to tolerate this empty feeling within, instead of binge-feeding the hungry ghosts, an important, metanoia-like turnaround occurs (Buddhists call it *paravritti*), when the "festering hole at our core turns into a life-healing flow [springing] up spontaneously from we know not where," in Loy's words. "The empty core becomes a place where there is now awareness of something other than, greater than, my usual sense of self—greater than I understand myself to be."

Nothing can possibly be enough, we now see, because nothing is meant to be enough. We're wise to feel the insufficiency of lives predicated on ephemera (including other people), we are told by the Buddhists. Longing is the point, it seems; *dukkha* is our built-in reminder of what can never be filled (and should not be), *not* so that we cling to our cravings but in order to call the pursuit—and the containers themselves—into question. Fuming over the imperfection of even the most brilliant life is meant to be a goad for discovering what cannot be taken away, for achieving reunion with that sufficient self that lacks nothing, expects nothing, needs nothing in order to feel at home in the world—the self that can stop anytime, anywhere, and know that it belongs. The longing does not disappear, but our story about it does; obscure objects of desire turn into a subject—the true I—whose realization enriches our lives rather than diminishing them.

Destructive as hungry ghosts are personally, their greed writ large now endangers the health of the planet, as ecologists have been warning for decades. Five years ago the writer Bill McKibben found himself standing in Tiananmen Square in Beijing, gazing up toward the sun in the sky—and not being able to find it—when he had a scary revelation about what *enough* really means.

"You could stare straight at the sun if you could even figure out where in the sky it was," McKibben tells me with disbelief. He's on the phone with me at the moment, looking out at pasturelands behind the rural Vermont home he shares with his wife, writer Sue Halpern, and their daughter. "I was in complete shock," Bill admits. Doing the math afterward, he estimated that by the year 2031, barring natural disaster or mass contraception, there will be roughly 1.3 billion Chinese as well off as their American counterparts. "If the Chinese owned cars like we do, they would add one point one billion cars to the eight hundred million already on the road," he says in horror. "If the Chinese ate meat the way we do, they would consume two thirds of the food on the planet. The earth simply cannot support that."

Most of us are already aware of the ways in which greed is depleting the planet. However, we may not have made the connection between this overconsumption and the hungry ghost ethic. Bill McKibben wants to make this clear. "The official idea that more is better, which has been orthodoxy for the past fifty years, no longer matches reality," he explains. "It's as if we've done a controlled experiment to see if materialism [as a path to happiness] works and found it doesn't." With a degree in economics from Harvard, McKibben has made a name for himself doing "coal-mine canary" reporting on issues from overpopulation to global warming. "For all our material progress, all the billions of barrels of oil and millions of acres of trees that it took to create it, we have not moved the satisfaction meter an inch," he says, echoing happiness researcher Dan Gilbert.

The opposite has happened, in fact, with alcoholism, suicide, and depression rates skyrocketing in proportion to the rise in affluence. There even appears to be something afoot that I call "acquired anhedonia syndrome," namely, the inability of people who have too much to enjoy the stuff they already own. This malaise has had a trickle-down effect on our kids. Studies have shown that today's average American child reports suffering higher levels of anxiety than the average child *under psychiatric care* in the 1950s.

Bill found the American dream's shadow side even more troubling when viewed from across the Pacific. In China, he met an eighteen-year-old factory worker named Liu Xian, whom he calls "the most statistically average person on the planet." Bill and Liu Xian struck up a conversation. He told her that he had noticed how many of the girls in the factory dorm had stuffed animals on their beds and asked Liu Xian if she had one. The girl began to cry. "She couldn't afford such an item, she told me," reports Bill. Later, when he brought Liu Xian a stuffed dog, she was as pleased as he had "ever seen a person." The disconnect between her gratitude and his own daughter's disinterest ("she has a room full of Beanie Babies") still affects him. "How could a stuffed animal possibly have the same meaning for her?" he wondered about his daughter. This is why Liu Xian's story continues to haunt him. "In impoverished parts of the world, possessions still deliver," he insists. "Any solution we consider [for redistributing wealth] has to contain some answer to Liu Xian's tears."

Bill decided to try an experiment with his own family. The McKibbens' focus, he determined, would be food. For a solid year, Bill, Sue, and their daughter decided to eat only foods grown locally, to see how it affected their "appetite, budget, community contact, and general sense of fullness." Studies show that the average bite of food an American eats travels some fifteen hundred miles before it reaches our table. It takes a tenth that amount of energy to eat locally, however, and increases our chances of social interaction—the local farmers' market versus Wal-Mart, for example—tenfold as well. Bill hoped that by tipping the balance toward home/local/small, he would dig deeper roots in his beloved Lake Champlain Valley, meet the neighbors, locate his own goods, and even, he hoped, regain a sense of proportion and what it means to have enough.

The experiment wasn't always easy. In the long run, though, it changed Bill's life. While locating and storing his own food proved to be more time consuming than hitting the A&P, Bill and his family actually enjoyed the challenge, cooking at home more, eating higher-quality fare, even making some new local friends (the butcher, the baker, the candlestick maker). Spending a winter without oranges was not nearly as traumatic as he had predicted. This year of eating locally "permanently altered the way I eat in more ways than one," Bill tells me now. "It left a good taste in my mouth. That taste was satisfaction."

It is possible to be satisfied, after all. Enough exists, we come to realize; in fact, we have it with us already. Craving and hunger are not the same thing. Recognizing our hungry ghosts, we learn to discern the important difference between actual hunger and the gap-stuffing reflex that only makes our emptiness worse. Slowly, we begin to recognize the difference between the ghost's voice and true desire, to resist hues and cries against the void, to obey the call of letting things be, and to find satisfaction in doing nothing. Satisfaction is there in the silence, we see, a break from the mind's cacophony. There is always enough, we begin to believe; the emptiness is filling itself. That must be what we can learn from a sabbath. The empty space becomes a spring.

STRESS MATTERS

In a quiet corner of the University of Massachusetts campus, near Worcester, sits a cluster of outbuildings called the Stress Reduction Clinic. Since its opening in 1979, the clinic has helped thousands of individuals suffering from stress sickness to reclaim their peace of mind. In a hyperactive age of time crunching, multitasking, and rampant attention deficit, stress disorders are, indeed, the nemesis of modern life, wreaking epidemic damage on our well-being (some 60 to 90 percent of individuals in hospitals declare stress to be their primary complaint) as well as on our physical health. Luckily, this enemy can be disarmed.

STRESS STOPS HERE, announces a poster on the wall near the clinic's entrance. Indeed, for nearly thirty years the SRC's founders, Jon Kabat-Zinn and Saki Santorelli, have been using a variety of techniques, including biofeedback, meditation, yoga, and cognitive therapy, to help burned-out individuals learn to "unhook" themselves from stressful and painful thoughts. While the human stress response may be autonomic, physiologically beyond our control, its mental triggers can be worked with, which is what I have come to the clinic to investigate.

Saki Santorelli welcomes me with a beaming smile and open arms. A diminutive man with an epic nose and the energy of three people, Saki is a stress guru who's devoted his career to understanding the enemy in our midst in the same way other scientists fight cancer or global warming. "Life is only getting more relentless," he tells me after we've settled in his small office. "People come to us exhausted. Just *frazzled*. They've got ten balls in the air and no sense of how to put them down. They can't give themselves a break, drop off the merry-go-round."

The word *stress* comes from the French for "oppressed," I was not surprised to learn from my own research.

"Stress is oppression," Saki insists.

"So what's the cure for oppression?" I wonder.

"Choice," he tells me. "Plain and simple." Stress, explains Saki, is created from the belief that we are under threat—trapped—and cannot cope. "Shut in," he says.

This reminds me of what a man admitted after surviving a jump off the Golden Gate Bridge: "I instantly realized that everything in my life that I thought was unfixable was totally fixable. Except for having just jumped."

"Realizing that we have a whole repertoire of responses available to us at any moment decreases anxiety right away," Saki tells me. "When people feel that there's no way out of the place they're in, their minds contract. Having choice relieves the stuckness, makes the narrow places wider."

"But how do our lives become so narrow in the first place?" I ask.

"To survive crisis, we narrow our world to a size that feels safe, knowable, familiar, and secure," Saki explains. "But the mind-set that gets us through crisis becomes impoverishing in the long run. We may be *handling* things," he says, "but our lives become small. Patients come here telling us that although they are functioning, they feel stuck in a narrow place they don't like. But if they step outside, they don't know if they'll survive."

In other words, we hide inside safely parametered ruts, then wonder why we feel so stuck. "What gets us through the hardest times does not make us feel content or alive," Saki says. He and the clinic's staff work with patients to help them become more "comfortable with their own discomfort," to "uncouple themselves from anxiety by developing the capacity to feel, see, and actually experience what's going on."

"Instead of what they imagine—and fear—to be going on?" I ask.

"Exactly. People learn to step back and separate their thoughts about what's happening from what is actually happening. This mindfulness creates a bit of space. A toe today, a leg tomorrow. Poco a poco. A bit at a time. Then, when we're not so exhausted from the effort of keeping things at bay, we discover that our lives—that we, ourselves—are much bigger than we think."

Saki discovered his own chill-out mission while still a neurotic undergraduate at university. During a conversation with an esteemed peer, Saki had one of those red-flag, epiphanic moments. "It was thirty-plus years ago," he remembers. "One day, out of the blue, someone I had a great deal of respect for asked me if I was the kind of person who went through the mountain or around the mountain."

"What did you tell him?" I ask.

"I remember pumping up my chest and saying, 'I go through the mountain!'" Saki grins. "That's when this person asked me if I had ever thought of going around the mountain. I have been living inside that question all these years. Wondering what it would mean to go *around* the mountain. When is that the right approach? When does it work better than trying to push through? If we've pushed as hard as we possibly can and the mountain still does not move, can we yield?" Saki asks.

"That's when control issues kick in," I say. "Not wanting to give it up."

"But there are different kinds of control," he insists. Saki tells me about groundbreaking research being done by a team of doctors at Stanford, who have identified two distinct kinds of control. "The first is positive assertive control," he explains. "When we put our noses to the grindstone and see the task through. This is not a stressed-out state. Unless it leads to negative assertive control."

"That sounds bad," I say.

"It is. Negative assertive control means pushing till it hurts." This is the sure path to stress sickness, Saki teaches. "We may have succeeded quantitatively, but qualitatively we're a mess," he explains. "What have we plowed through to maintain control, to achieve our aims? Whom do we grind up in our wake?" In a world piled high with collateral damage, this does seem an important question. But what is the alternative? "There is something known as positive yielding control," Saki makes clear. "This has to do with surrender, acceptance, and choosing your battles. Positive yielding control can have enormously positive effects on people's lives, particularly in situations where survival hangs in the balance."

"Not pushing?"

"Knowing when to stop," he says. "When to go around the mountain. Using the power of choice."

MARK MATOUSEK

In other words, yesterday's steadfastness may be tomorrow's embolism. Undiscriminating effort is a sure path to burnout. Stress relief comes from more choice, less brawn; more patience, less pressure; more stretching, less strife; more stillness, less stipulation. According to Saki, stillness—*far niente*, as the Italians call it—is a largely untapped elixir for counteracting battle fatigue in our frantic lives. "Pascal said that most of our troubles come from the fact that human beings can't be alone with themselves for any extended period of time," he reminds me. "The act of stopping may be uncomfortable at first, but it often becomes revelatory. People begin to have small epiphanies."

All the more reason to observe a sabbath, I note.

"Stillness is what enables us to interrupt the stress cycle," he agrees. "When we unhook from our craving thoughts, we're struck by new possibilities, fresh ideas, more constructive responses." Even small children respond to reconnecting in this way. Saki recalls the story of Maria Montessori, the Italian educator who made important innovations in the field of early learning. Apparently, Montessori, who began her work with poor children in Italy, would give the kids short periods of quiet time throughout the day. "In the beginning the children hated it," he says, "but Montessori had them do it anyway."

He presses his palms together at the side of his face in the international gesture for napping. "When she deliberately took the quiet time away, the children would start yearning for it," Saki says. "They'd ask, 'Could we just put our heads down, please?'"

Then my host gazes out through his office window toward a copse of trees in the distance and takes the words right out of my mouth.

"I know exactly how they feel."

THE WOUNDED HEALER

Medicine is a front seat to mystery, according to one wise physician. While some doctors are emotionally stunted individuals, others surpass our empathic expectations in the course of living through their own hardship. "Only the wounded physician heals," Carl Jung said. Without having been tested themselves, like shamans enduring their rites of passage, it may be fair to ask how much help doctors can really be in helping us survive our own.

Dr. Rachel Remen grew up as the only daughter in a Russian immigrant family of doctors and rabbis when the subway still cost a few cents in New York City. Long before she entered Cornell Medical College, where she trained as a pediatrician, Rachel's personal healing work began following a diagnosis of Crohn's disease at fifteen. An autoimmune disorder attacking the intestine, Crohn's was untreatable and agonizingly painful in those days. Struggling to live a normal life, Rachel braved several major surgeries, as well as the humiliation of wearing an evacuation bag under her sixties peasant blouse.

"I was furious at my disease for a long time," Rachel tells me when we meet. We're seated across from one another at the dining room table of her Olympian home overlooking the bay in Marin County, California. A purring cat curls around my ankle. The house, where Rachel lives alone, is decorated in calming earth tones and filled with Asian sculptures. Beyond the floor-to-ceiling windows, red robins swarm fruit trees across the expanse of manicured lawn. Snowy-haired and owlish in a cream-colored pants ensemble, Rachel is not who I expected her to be. In book jacket photographs, the bestselling author of *Kitchen Table Wisdom* looks like a sweet-natured, *babke*-pushing *bubbe* (a grandma, in other words, offering cake), the kind who kvells and pinches your *tuches*. In person, though, she's more like Bea Arthur, the no-b.s., tough-as-nails sitcom actress best known for playing Maude on TV. Armed with a mystic's awe at the wonder of healing, as well as a scientist's flinty mind, Rachel is quick-witted, formidable, and—though good-hearted—no sufferer of fools.

Her anger at Crohn's brewed a long time before she finally exploded. Offered a prestigious teaching job during her medical residency, the ambitious young woman was forced to turn down the position for lack of sufficient energy. "Here was another dream stolen," she wrote. Severely depressed, the nineteen-year-old escaped to a deserted Long Island beach, where she had her first major healing breakthrough:

> In turmoil, I walked wearily along the water's edge, comparing myself to others my own age, people of seemingly boundless vitality . . . I remember thinking that this disease had robbed me of my youth. I did not yet know what it had given me in exchange . . . A wave of intense rage flooded me, the sort of feeling I had experienced many times before. But for some reason,

this time I did not drown in it. Instead, I noticed it go by and something inside me said, "You have no vitality? Here's your vitality."

Shocked, I recognized the connection between my anger and my will to live. My anger was my will to live turned inside out. My life force was just as intense . . . as my anger, but for the first time I could experience it as different and feel it directly . . . Somehow *this [intense love of life] had grown large in me as a result of the very limitations I had thought were thwarting it* [italics mine]. Like the power of a dammed river . . . I also knew that in its present form, as rage, this power was trapped. My anger had helped me to survive, to resist my disease, even to fight on, but in the form of anger I could not use my strength to build the kind of life I longed to live.

"I was like Zorba the Greek!" Rachel laughs, remembering the angry girl she was and the lust for life trapped inside her. "The shift came when I realized that I could express this power—my power—directly. I didn't need to be angry. But let me tell you something," she says now, fixing me with her fierce dark eyes. "I would never have reached that point if some therapist had worked with me to get rid of my anger."

Rachel sips her tea. "People can get caught in anger, this is true," she goes on. "And that is very limiting as a way of life. But there is a place for anger in the process of becoming a human being." The wonderful Buddhist teacher Rick Fields channeled rage at his own disease into a series of poems—including a doozy called "Fuck You Cancer"—as a means of staying real in the throes of healing. "Without it there's something important that you never get to have."

That thing is authenticity, Rachel believes. Such authenticity signals the deepening of soul that occurs when untrue things are burned from our lives. "What many people don't understand is that it's not enough to survive physically," insists Rachel. "That's too low a goal. The idea is to survive psychologically, as a loving being. To survive as a soul. This is how we begin to awaken."

"To what?" I inquire.

"The beginning of loss is also the beginning of compassion," she tells me. "My experience has enabled me to help a lot of people free themselves where they've gotten trapped. I can be in situations that would terrify most other people."

I do not doubt this for a moment.

Raised in a family where the debate between science and spirituality never stopped raging (until she was twelve she wanted to be a rabbi), Rachel struggled to reconcile these worldviews not only as a physician but also as a patient. Outraged by the arrogance, shortsightedness, and lack of imagination she recognized among medical colleagues, she set out to find a middle path between intellect and intuition. In 1976 she cofounded Commonweal holistic cancer center in Bolinas, California, and has since been a pioneer in the field of mind-body medicine.

Rachel freely admits to having an ax to grind. "I made many of my critical life decisions based on what I was told by doctors," she tells me. "I was told that I'd be dead by forty, so I never got married or had children." That is quite an ax, I think. "Nobody offered the possibility that I might be able to survive," says Rachel, who recently celebrated her sixty-fourth birthday. "It's hard to think outside the box. But that is where life is. Outside the box."

Healing is a mysterious process whose principles often contradict reason. Working with thousands of patients, she has learned how often the body's intelligence defies expectations. "The body is hardwired to persevere," Rachel reminds me. "If I cut you, your body will heal stronger than before. Without this built-in tenacity toward life, even the most sophisticated treatments could not succeed."

The poet Dylan Thomas called this "the force that through the green fuse drives the flower." Rachel vividly recalls the first time she noticed this uncanny power in miniature. "It was one spring day when I was fourteen," she says. "I was walking up Fifth Avenue in New York City and was astonished to notice two tiny blades of grass growing through the sidewalk. Not around, but *through*. They were green and tender, and had somehow broken through the cement. Despite the crowds bumping up against me, I stopped and looked at them in disbelief."

The memory still amazes her. "This image stayed with me for a long time, possibly because it seemed so miraculous. It gave me a very different sense of what power and force look like. There's no violence in real power," she observes, in spite of common, dog-eat-dog wisdom. "There is something much more mysterious at work than our culture would have us believe," she insists. "Confronted by enormous change—losing a breast, a country, a child—we're faced with an important choice. Either we come to surrender, go into the loss, attend to our own responses, and listen to ourselves, or we attempt to put it behind us and get on with the rest of our lives. But does this really work?"

"It hasn't for me."

"Me either," she says. "This is essential to understand. When we try to avoid loss or plow through our pain, our lives are actually diminished. On the other hand, there's an extraordinary wisdom and clarity that emerges in people who genuinely meet their pain, not in theory but in life."

"Why do you think that is?" I ask.

Rachel considers the question a moment. "We realize that there is a larger power operating which can be trusted to sustain us," she says finally. "As any woman who's gone through delivery knows, it's minute by minute when the going gets rough. The forces that are happening are so great that the woman surrenders. She has to. Often it's the moment just before birth." The paradox of this is quite beautiful. "The whole process of awakening, initiation, comes only when things are surrendered. Women talk about this moment and how much they learn from it. Afterward they have a different relationship to life—and to themselves. It is the beginning of trust."

This trust in mystery carries us forward. "An awareness of something larger breaks through," she explains. "There's a core identity shift, not just in ideas about yourself but how you see the entire world." Working with cancer patients all these years, Rachel has witnessed this identity shift quite frequently. "I've often seen that the body can be quite diminished while this other identity has expanded greatly," she tells me. "The *individual* has expanded."

Doubleness, I think to myself.

"The process of wounding actually awakens us to our strength," she says. "It shuffles our values. And the top priority is never what you thought it would be. It's never about perfection or power. It always turns out to be about love."

We decide to take a walk in the garden. Trailing Rachel into the sloping yard, watching her as she pinches seed carefully into a bird feeder, bending ever so carefully to pick up a rag, I'm reminded of how ill my hostess truly is, how meticulously she must measure her energies in order to carry out her many duties. This gives Rachel a sturdy yet frail balance, a poignant and particular strength.

We sit side by side on a bench. The fog is creeping up Mount Tamalpais, blanketing the pine-sided mountain in white. "We forget that there is a flow in things," Rachel reminds me. "That the trick is to get out of the way."

"To get out of our own way, you mean?"

"When you block a river, it finds another way to get where it's going," she says in a soft voice. "When your physical being is changed, you travel in other ways." Rachel scatters a handful of seed for the birds. "Think of trees that go through extreme weather—not only are they strengthened, but their roots grow deeper. They're not straight, but twisted into themselves. Every challenged individual I have ever met comes to this same crossroads, regardless of what's standing in their way. Will they be resigned, or will they surrender?"

"Sometimes these two seem synonymous," I say.

"But that is where our freedom lies," Rachel tells me. "I came to a point where I decided that being ill was not going to stop me from living well. Of course, I'd love to be able to see perfectly!" she admits. Crohn's has robbed her of vision in one eye. "Of course, I'd love to be able to eat whatever I want. I would absolutely love to go mountain climbing. But I can't do those things," she says with a shrug. "What I can do is adapt."

Rachel leans back on the bench. "It's the way in which we move through very difficult circumstances, and not the absence of circumstances, that enables a person at the end of a life to say, 'You know, this has been a great ride,'" she tells me.

Rachel's dark eyes turn silver as she gazes up at the fog. "You see that even though your body has changed, there is a part of you that was never hurt," she explains. "My sense of wholeness has nothing to do with my body." Her confidence does seem to match this claim. "I don't believe that there is something wrong with me," says Rachel, pointing overhead at a golden hawk perched high in an evergreen nearby. The hawk appears to be watching us, too.

"I see the world as a mystery," she says. "Much like a child does."

TRUE CONFESSIONS

For reasons never explained to me, I became our family confessor. From the time I was old enough to listen, my sisters, my mother, their lovelorn girlfriends, the widow Yetta who lived two doors down, with her brick-red hair and bison-sized muumuu, pouring out her big heart over sweet borscht and flanken she cooked for me as a snack on my way to bar mitzvah class—to all of them I was Mr. Lonelyhearts, Mr. Let Your Hair Down, Mr. You Know You Can Trust Me. Sit.

"What d'you know?" Yetta would kvell at me after delivering one of her epic tales of betrayal by her late husband, Mack, stubbing my chin between her fat fingers. It did Yetta's heart good to be heard, she told me. It did me good to listen, I said.

Yetta had a friend named Molly Gross, who needed to talk, the widow told me, like someone begging for oxygen. Molly was a caged bird singing her desperate heart out, married to a miserable surgeon named Sid, who made millions excising brain tumors and did his best, during off hours, to make Molly's life miserable. I first heard about her when I was twelve, but the caged bird and I had never met. Ten years passed. I was in graduate school by then, hardly able to pay my rent. Molly, about to turn eighty-five, was on the hunt for an assistant to help her plow through the avalanche of notebooks she had been keeping for decades, to draw her untold stories from her and then weave this material into a manuscript that would represent her life's work: fifty years of scrawled introspection crammed now, mausoleum style, into a stack of boxes in Sid's closet.

"She's a brilliant woman, misunderstood," Yetta told me over some schmaltzy plate of overcooked food. Molly had been born before her time, the widow believed, and was truly a diamond in the rough, a philosopher, practically, in her own right. Now this unsung old poet lady was afraid of dying without ever having stretched her wings. Someone needed to save her, said Yetta. That was my knee-jerk cue, of course. Needing money—and, even more, to be needed—I made a date to meet with Molly Gross at the penthouse apartment she shared with Sid overlooking Santa Monica Beach.

I shall never forget my first sight of her rushing toward me, wrenlike and breathless, teary-eyed, arms outstretched, a plume of white hair escaping its net as she hurried forward on sticklike legs, bathrobe open, slippers flapping, down the aquamarine-blue hallway carpet, grinning and clutching the Kleenex that never left her hand. I immediately saw that Molly was dying. Her white arms were covered with purple track marks. She squeezed my hands, looked into my eyes, and said, "Oh, honey. He's here at last" to Maxine, the Guatemalan maid.

Molly seduced me for two distinct reasons. The first was that I had never met anyone so ferociously honest—so utterly vulnerable, hurt, and alive, yet giggly over the silliest things—and I am an emotion whore, an addict of intimate connection. Second, this old lady seemed to possess a quality that I'd always yearned for but had yet to encounter: a brazen, unfettered brand of aliveness, a no-holds-barred thrusting into each coming moment-never-to-come-again. Molly and I would gab for hours behind the closed door of Sid's curtained study, seated side by side at a long mahogany table piled with her mass of materials, a hodgepodge of legal pads, paper napkins, dog-eared tomes marked with passages she wanted to quote, other books she all but knew by heart—*The Cloud of Unknowing*, *I Am That*, the *Meditations* of Marcus Aurelius—reams of various sorts of paper etched in her erratic, crooked script. Sometimes Molly would cackle over a delightful memory sparked from this collectanea; other times her eyes grew teary when a painful thought arrowed up from the past, forcing her to look away, to cover her mouth with the crumpled tissue.

During the fifteen months we spent in this passionate mind-meld, Molly continued to unnerve, enthrall, and move me. She spoke with startling conviction about things I knew nothing about, beginning with the spiritual aspects of life. In spite of her frail health, Molly overflowed with spirit—absorbed, reflected, saw and heard more; cared more; suffered more; tasted her existence more deeply than anyone I had ever met. We sifted through her papers, recorded her stories, transcribed the tapes of our interviews. One day Molly might be in cheerful form, peaceful in her circumscribed world; the next day she might be agonized over her quarantined existence. "Honey," she'd tell me with pain in her face, "life is important. People waste it. Please don't waste it."

"I won't," I promised.

Other times Molly would grip my hands, squeeze her eyes shut, and refuse to tell me what was going on. Stymied by one cryptic passage, I asked her *what* was she trying to say?

"You know!" she said, slapping my arm.

"I don't know."

"Oh, you!" She pinched my ribs.

"It's fuzzy," I told her.

"*You're* fuzzy." Molly laughed. She touched me every chance she got, stroking every available surface. One day we came across a particularly koanlike entry. It read, WHAT IS MINE WILL KNOW MY FACE and was written in large capital letters on stationery from the Hotel de la Legion in Paris.

"What does this one mean?" I asked.

Molly tousled my hair. "You know!"

"I honestly don't."

She peered over my shoulder, although no one was standing there. "One day I stopped in the wood and all paths were the same," she whispered, nonsequentially, widening her eyes.

"Stop it!"

"The end of folly is the same as wisdom," she taunted.

"Avoiding the question," I would say. But it was no use trying to stop her. Like a woman drawing a strand of pearls from her bodice, Molly revealed her mystical aperçus one glowing jewel at a time. Mostly, I didn't want to stop her. I'd fallen in love with Molly by then. She believed that my visits were the only thing keeping her alive.

"Somebody sees me!" Molly once said to Maxine, squeezing my hand. My friend had weakened as the year wore on. One day we were eating lunch at her kitchen table, drinking a thimbleful of vodka first, as had become our little custom. Maxine was watching us with a smirk.

"I do see you," I told Molly.

"Eureka!" she squealed, and gripped the table.

"Loud and clear," I assured her.

"Will you publish my book?" she asked.

I promised her that I would try. We had decided to call her five-hundred-page manuscript *Moments of Being*, not knowing that Virginia Woolf had already usurped that title. As I write these words today, Molly's manuscript remains in its same blue binder, tucked away at the top of my living room closet.

"Happy day," Molly said, kissing the tops of both my hands. "Now, you say the prayer, Maxine."

The plump, shy maid closed her eyes. "*O Dios, por favor, Padre Nuestro, denos su mano—*"

"Isn't that just wonderful, honey!" Molly squealed. "Isn't she just beautiful?" Molly laid a kiss on Maxine's cheek. "Look at the three of us here together with all this love like a family, my children. And all the sun and this beautiful food."

Just then, Molly pulled herself to her feet and lifted her knee-length nightgown many inches higher than a woman with varicose veins should have. "I want to dance!" she begged me, holding out her thin arms. "Oh, let's dance and get drunk!" Molly said.

Maxine lowered her eyes and smiled. I watched Molly waltz around the kitchen, embracing an invisible partner, singing a popular song from the 1920s in her trembly voice. "Oh, promise me that someday you and I will take our love together to some sky," she sang. Molly begged me to come and swing her around. "Come to me, my handsome man. This day will never come again."

"*Vaya*," Maxine urged me.

"Hon-eeee!" Molly begged, lifting her nightgown an inch or two higher, prancing around the kitchen. "You will break my heart."

I took her into my arms awkwardly. Molly pushed her slack breasts against me, hooked her hands around my neck, and hung there, smiling up at me. Then she started to sing. "Oh, promise me that someday you and I will take our love together to some sky," she crooned. I heard Maxine humming along and the grandfather clock ticking in the hall, the sounds of traffic below. Molly laid her cheek against my chest.

All sorrows can be borne, Isak Dinesen said, if you put them into a story. Rachel Remen remembers sitting under the kitchen table as a little girl, stroking the purple velvet carpet slippers of her grandfather, an Orthodox rabbi, as he told stories and read kabbalah. Rachel believes that our lost art of telling stories, the pre-e-mail tradition of people sitting around telling stories as a way to pass along wisdom, accounts for a cultural loss of soul and shared insight into how we live. By sharing our stories, she believes, we tap into a largely ignored reservoir of living wisdom.

"When we stop telling each other our stories, we seek out experts to tell us how to live," Rachel has written. "The less time we spend at the kitchen table, the more how-to books appear in the stores. Because we have stopped listening . . . we have stopped learning how to recognize meaning—and to fill ourselves—from the ordinary events in our lives." Storytelling is also a great boon in friendship. I learned of an Israeli woman who'd gone to a therapist because she was having trouble breathing. As they spoke, the shrink noticed the camp numbers tattooed on the patient's forearm. The woman coughed a great deal while telling her story. "When did you start having trouble breathing?" the therapist asked. "When my friend died two years ago," the survivor admitted. "When she was alive," this lady told the doctor, "we could talk about anything. Although she had not been in the camps, she understood. But now there is no one to tell. And the nightmares haunt me. I can't sleep alone in the house. I know that if I want to live, I have to find another friend."

Our stories are meaningful to the degree that they converge, in a meaningful way, with others. One recent afternoon, I found myself with fifteen medical residents, the novelist Michael Ondaatje, and Dr. Rita Charon, who heads the Program in Narrative Medicine at Columbia University's College of Physicians and Surgeons in New York, sitting around a Dorito-strewn conference table, talking about how doctors can learn about patients' inner lives from listening carefully to their stories. Rita Charon has been a pioneer in narrative medicine since its appearance two decades ago. As a young internist, Rita realized that she knew neither how to listen deeply to patients, nor how to interpret the life narratives they were telling her. What better way to learn about stories, she asked herself, than to study great works of fiction? She went back to college for a Ph.D. in comparative literature and emerged with an intriguing theory about how doctors can become better healers by doing what good readers do: ponder character, structure of plot, emotional foreshadowing of the kind that novelists employ and that patients use in bringing personal stories to life in their doctors' offices.

Eric David, a third-year medical student who's fresh today from the OR (where he assisted at a radical prostatectomy), is struggling to make a point. "Doctors dismantle human beings," says Eric, who's shaggy-haired and looks like he's in high school. "It's what separates us from the rest of the world. You have to fight the temptation to turn off. If you remember that everyone has a story, it kind of helps."

Ondaatje, a leonine, big-bellied guy with a white beard and icy green eyes, listens carefully to the young man in green scrubs. The novelist himself got interested in narrative medicine after observing a quadruple bypass, he told me before the class. "I was standing two feet away from the heart," Ondaatje marveled. "Just staring down into the patient's body. What could be more fascinating?"

That heart surgery got him hooked. "I've been fixated on doctors since I was a boy," Ondaatje told me. "I wanted to talk to doctors about books the same way you would x-ray a body, to see how it worked, how it was made."

That seems like such a clinical motive, I said. "No more profound or artistic reason?"

He thought about it a moment. "I suppose it has to do with rescue and healing," Ondaatje offered. "Our lives are all so dangerous, precarious—you could even say abandoned. Rescue and healing are essential things."

Abandoned? I wondered. This seemed like an odd choice of words for describing the human predicament. Abandoned in the world by who—or what? In *The Noonday Demon*, Andrew Solomon describes the outcast state of depression as "the loneliness in us made manifest, a crystallization of the human condition in which each of us is held in the solitude of an autonomous body." If feelings of abandonment do lie at the core of our common longing for connection, it seems even more understandable that religions use confession as a means of healing and that writers such as Michael Ondaatje approach the art of storytelling in almost holy terms.

Back in class, he listens to a female resident who appears to be upset over their reading selection for the day, William Maxwell's novel *So Long, See You Tomorrow*. Wearing a pained expression, the young doctor confesses to having been callous with one of her patients during morning rounds. This man, who was gravely ill, had invited her to sit beside him and listen to one of his stories. The resident made an excuse, she tells us, claiming that she was too busy to stay. Instead, she hurried the lonely man through his tale and then cut him off before the end. She never saw the old man again. "I should have taken the time," she says now.

"Next time," says Rita Charon, the comforting mentor, who's trying to train better doctors, not promote more self-punishment.

When the class is over I walk Ondaatje to the elevator. The novelist appears far away in his thoughts. When the door slides open, it rouses him from his trance and he blinks. "Extraordinary," he mutters aloud, without elaborating on what he's thinking. "I can't forget to write that down." Then the elevator closes behind him.

PROMETHEUS

At a recent Fourth of July barbecue, I find myself seated next to a bouncy brunette who introduces herself to me as Ella. In a movie, she'd be played by Eva Longoria. Ella tells me that she's a nurse as fireworks explode overhead. "I work with miracle kids," she says, dabbing corn-on-the-cob butter from her mouth.

"Miracle?" I ask.

"Heroes," Ella says. "You want to talk about Independence Day? These kids are freedom fighters," she tells me as pyrotechnics kaboom down the beach. Ella is the head nurse of pediatric orthopedics at New York's Beth Israel Hospital. Her boss is a renowned surgeon named David Feldman, who, in addition to a private practice, runs a monthly clinic for severely handicapped public-assistance kids who have nowhere else to turn. "He takes these twisted children and makes them walk," Ella says. "The man is a hero in his own right. A greater heart you have never seen."

The following week, I'm powerwalking behind Dr. Feldman up and down Beth Israel's crowded corridors during rounds, flanked by four residents, a Spanish translator, a rep from a crutch-making company, and Ella. Feldman is a blond-haired, turbocharged Orthodox Jew who dresses slick, barks orders, and walks (when he forgets to hide it) with a limp left over from a childhood illness. Hurrying along the corridors, we're surrounded by crippled kids, lots of them wheelchair bound, others crawling or holding their mothers' hands, feeling their way along the wall. Their eyes light up when they see Feldman. Though gruff, Dr. F. is a natural with these kids, *zetzing* this one in the ribs, tickling another, calling them names, making them laugh.

In the first exam room we find Melanie, a naughty six-year-old with spina bifida, who giggles hysterically when Feldman runs a ruler across the bottom of her clubfoot. Melanie's mother, a squat Latina, crows over her daughter's vast improvement since surgery (Feldman has many more planned to straighten out the little girl's spine). He helps Melanie down from the table and holds the little girl's hands as she slowly, proudly rotates herself across the floor to show him how much better she's walking.

"The boys will be eating out of the palms of your hands," he teases her, carefully measuring the splayed angle of Melanie's ankles, shooting technical info at Ella and the residents.

The girl squeals with delight, leans forward, and falls flat on her face. When Feldman moves to pull her up, Melanie sticks her tongue out at the doctor. "I can do it!" she cries, yanking herself up slowly by the handles affixed to the side of the table. Once standing, Melanie beams at him in triumph. "I told you."

"Yes, you did," says Feldman. Then he adds to the mother, sotto voce, "We'll fix her, Mrs. Padilla. I promise."

In the next room a Hasidic family appears to be in midmeltdown. The high-school-aged patient with bad skin and a faint mustache refuses to stay in his wheelchair.

"He's making me meshuga," cries the mother, a tall, unpleasant-looking person in a bad wig, a baggy dress, and crunching patent leather shoes. "Sit down, Yudi. Sit. Now!"

"You sit!" he shouts back at her, groping his way along the sink toward the window. "I'm tired of sitting."

"He don't listen," mutters the father, an unshaven, hopeless-looking guy wearing side curls and a yarmulke. "Mind your mother," he tells the boy with a shrug.

"I want to walk, Doc!" Yudi tells Feldman.

The mother seems to be davening, clutching at the sides of her face. "You're fine like this," she hisses.

"I want to dance at my prom!" Yudi tells her. He also wants to go skiing, ride motorcycles, and trek in the Himalayas with Sherpas. With each high-risk threat to her dominion, his mother's face goes a shade more livid. "You see what I mean?" she moans to Feldman.

"I think he's ready for surgery, Mrs. H.," says the doctor. "But Yudi, you tell me, where should we start? The ankles? The hip? The back?" Feldman turns the boy back and forth by the shoulders. "I say we go for the back."

The mother looks at the father, who looks at the doctor, who looks at the boy, who appears to be the least scared of all of them. "Tell me the risks first," Yudi says in a calm, grown-up fashion. Feldman lets him know that he could be paralyzed and even less mobile after surgery—although that's unlikely—suffer pneumonia because of his weak lungs, or even die under anesthesia.

"You're fine like this," the mother says softly, reaching out for her son's hand.

"I want to do it, Mama," says Yudi.

Feldman repeats to the parents, "He wants it." The mother

looks positively stricken. The father shakes the doctor's hand and tells him to schedule the surgery. As we leave the room, I look back and see Yudi smiling. He gives me a thumbs-up.

Two hours and thirty children later, David Feldman collapses in his office easy chair, exhausted but visibly happy. "I should have half their chutzpah," he says, waving away a resident. "Half their humor and come-what-may. These kids are my teachers, so help me God. Honestly, I don't know how they do it. They're completely guileless."

"Guileless?" I say. "That's an interesting word."

"They're not hiding anything," Feldman says. "These kids are at the end of the line. They have nowhere else to turn. It teaches you—" The doctor can't find the words. "You just learn what a huge difference little things can make. It takes so little to make them happy."

Afterward, Ella walks me to the elevator. We sit for a few minutes in the lounge. "At first I was miserable working with these children," she admits. "I thought I'd made a big mistake. This work was just too heartbreaking."

"I can understand why."

"But the truth is, I was feeling sorry for myself," Ella admits. She offers me a handful of Skittles. "Then one day," Ella tells me, "a twelve-year-old spastic quadriplegic girl was brought in." I'd just observed Feldman examining a quad with severe spasticity, kicking her feet uncontrollably, arms crunched against her chest as her father cradled the girl in his arms.

"Her name was Lisa," Ella says, remembering this other child. "Her knees had decomposed. She was walking on the sides of her feet, dragging herself along the ground like a crab." Ella pauses to

227

collect herself. "Suddenly she saw me and gave me this beautiful smile. Lisa said, 'Ella, you look so pretty.'"

She blows her nose in a tissue. "My fear started to go after that. Something broke open inside me. I saw the person she was, not the body she was in. It baffles me that these kids aren't angry," says Ella. "It's like they aren't even handicapped. You don't see them making a big deal over their imperfections. They're always asking you how *you* are. They speak to you from their souls. You can see it in their eyes."

"I saw it," I say.

"It all comes down to how they see," Ella tells me. "Lisa's mother saw me watching her that day. There must have been pity in my eyes. The mother looked at me and smiled, probably guessing what I was thinking—the thing I'd never really ask." The memory still amazes Ella. "Then she said it anyway."

"What did she say?"

"'I love her,' Lisa's mother told me. 'She's mine.'"

FOUND ART

Years ago I was waiting on line with a hundred other pilgrims to visit the grave of a long-dead saint in a small town near Poona, in central India. Directly ahead of me was a German mother, her hair covered by a head scarf, helping her crippled Down syndrome child kneel at the side of the marble tomb. The boy, who couldn't have been more than twelve, was having a tough time bending his knees. When he finally managed to lower himself to the ground, the child laid his cheek on the stone for a long time. His mother tried to hurry him along, but the rest of us didn't mind the delay. "Worship is not a ritual, it is an attitude, an experience," this very saint had once suggested. The child's worship seemed to elevate the hearts of the pilgrims standing behind him.

Afterward, in a crowded hall, we listened to the dead saint's closest disciple, an old guy wearing a Rice-A-Roni T-shirt (people bring him mementos from their native towns), as he reminisced about fifty years spent at his master's side. The great man had blessed hundreds and hundreds of thousands of people seeking his *darshan*, or holy touch. "Baba loved everyone," the white-haired secretary explained to us in his pidgin English. "Most of all, though, he liked the scoundrels! The bad ones like me!" The old man's wicked smile made it easy to imagine him as the bad-boy aristocrat he once was, the scion of a wealthy Bengali family, addicted to fast cars, booze, and easy women, till the day his guru spun his head around.

"The naughty ones," the secretary chuckled. "That is who Baba liked the best. Some people would come to him pretending to be holy. They would sit up very straight and tell Baba about how good they were. How pure. How enlightened. Baba would just smile and move them along."

The Down's boy was rolling around on the ground, giggling. His mother gave up on trying to control him.

"God does not need your holiness," the old man said, swatting the H-word from the air and grinning. "God does not need your goodness!"

"What does he need, then?" an Australian woman inquired.

"God wants your humanness, nothing more," replied our host. "Broken furniture, that's what he called them, the people who came without making a pose. Baba loved broken furniture. This is where, he said, Baba could sit the best."

I liked the idea of humanity as a sort of global Salvation Army store filled with derelict furnishings, three-legged chairs and mangy sofas, rickety tables, half-extinguished lamps, neglected armoires empty of drawers, beds too lumpy and slouched to dream in. When Andrea Martin, then Bowlby, was a five-year-old girl in a body cast, bedtime was the most painful part of the day. "I would lie there, crunched up in agony, till morning came," Andrea tells me when I visit her in the rectory of the Episcopal church in Hartford, Connecticut, where she is the junior pastor. A tiny woman with pixie hair and a limp, Andrea is feisty, self-deprecating, extremely smart (she graduated from Yale Divinity School), and honest about the torturous path she followed as a child forced to endure fifteen major surgeries and six months out of every year trapped inside the dreaded cast.

"It's like found art," Andrea says to me now, looking out at the trees in a garden. "You take all the bad things—the pain, the embarrassment, anger, longing—also surprising moments of grace, and form them into something original, unique, which then becomes your life."

Born with a condition known as PPD, Andrea nearly lost her right leg when doctors recommended amputating the drastically shorter limb while she was still a toddler. Luckily, her parents refused. Instead, from age two until twenty-one, Andrea suffered through these leg-lengthening surgeries and the excruciating, racklike procedures that followed.

"It wasn't so much the physical pain as the emotional agony," Andrea says back at her house, fussing over omelets she insists on cooking after christening eight babies ("a train wreck!") at the morning service. "I felt so out of control," she admits, whisking eggs. "I was so much at the mercy of doctors and their decisions. So alienated and ostracized. And so self-conscious!"

Andrea pours the eggs into a pan and offers me coffee. "It was very painful," she remembers. "I was *terrified* of social situations, teased mercilessly by the kids at school." Yet even at that early age, she began to find comfort in her faith. "I was helped by the Christian story of Jesus inviting all the outcast people to be with him," she tells me. "Reaching out to the lepers and the sinners. That had quite an effect on me. Jesus himself was an outsider. That gave me hope."

231

Hopeful, too, was the possibility that Andrea might someday be able to use her personal struggle for a higher good. "Maybe my heart would be different," she says, serving our breakfast. "Maybe God could use my empathy for others in a way I couldn't predict." Adolescence was a nightmare still to be survived, though. "Other girls in school were dating," she tells me. "There was this huge chasm between me and them. I thought, 'Gosh, I've survived all these surgeries, years on crutches, rehabilitation, and now it's become a double whammy, because nobody is going to love me.'" Andrea seems embarrassed by what may sound too much like self-pity. "A man with a limp or scars is somehow attractive to the girls," she explains. "It's a sign of manliness. For a woman, it's total alienation. I thought I'd never get married." (In fact, Andrea's husband of four years, Chris, a Libertarian lobbyist, seems to adore her.)

This confusion in her began to shift during an undergraduate semester in India, where the future priest found her vocation. Andrea had previously planned on being a doctor. "I wanted to minister to sick people the way my doctors did for me," she says. "Treating not just my leg but the whole person." Unfortunately, she did not excel in science. Then one day, in Delhi, Andrea Martin got her calling. "We were visiting Gandhi's birthplace," she tells me over breakfast. "I was on this big, ostentatious tour bus—TVs, velour seats, the whole deal—looking out the window, when these two street urchins came up and looked right at me, reaching out for money or food. The words from the liturgy came back to me: 'Lamb of God who taketh away the sins of the world, have mercy on us.' These two children represented the sins of the world. It was a trace of God calling me," she says. "Reaching out. I finally had permission to follow the path I truly loved."

Her ministry since then has become this unconventional reverend's oeuvre of found art. "My mother used to say, 'Andrea, your struggle right now is very difficult on the outside. But everybody has challenges and hurts and struggles that are not always so visible,'" she tells me. "As a priest, my own struggles are mostly on the inside now. But since I've known what it's like to feel a chasm between me and other people, or me and God—and a longing to close that gap as best as I possibly can—I have increased empathy. I pray every day for the grace to help bring people together. This desire is deepened by the isolation of my own childhood."

Working with her congregation has taught Andrea how pervasive such feelings of alienation, isolation, even abandonment, are among outwardly successful individuals. "There's a huge amount of pressure on people to have it all together, or to look like it at least," she tells me. "Even when they're crumbling inside. My job is to look past the exterior into somebody's heart and soul and know that what's inside can be very different from what they present."

"Appearances are so deceptive sometimes," I say.

"A doctor I know uses discarded junk from the hospital where he works," Andrea tells me, sipping her coffee. "Old x-ray film, IV tubing, gauze, broken casts, to create the most beautiful sculptures." She refills both our cups. "Found art," she says, "from sickness. To me, that is a great metaphor for hope. It's how God acts on our behalf, I believe. When a whirlwind sweeps through our lives, leaving scattered debris and junk, and we're tempted to give up hope, even then God is at work reassembling the junk, the shit of our lives, into something new. When we collaborate with this creative, redemptive spirit, miracles can happen."

Today Andrea can bike, swim, and climb mountains with almost no pain. "God is economical," she says with a smile. "There's no experience that we can endure—short of torture, starvation, or extreme abuse—that God can't use for good. God has a dream for what we might be, and the more we're open to cooperating with that grace, the more we can be sanctified and pulled upward on that spiral to be the person God dreams us to be. Even the most hopeless cases. God takes what's hopeless and turns it into fecundity."

"Broken furniture?" I suggest.

"God may even love the broken ones just a little bit more," Andrea Martin says.

THROUGH WILDERNESS

Visionary power has historically been the shaman's gift, in traditional cultures, only after surviving the wild. Certain individuals are asked to "go walkabout" in extreme terrain; others endure physical torture in order to be "awakened" by pain. Others are called upon to venture into trance states (drug-induced and not), where they undergo terrifying psychological initiations involving "demons" and other dark interior foes. Finally, there are those, like Francis Bok, the escaped Sudanese ex-slave, who, while not indigenous shamans, are thrust as children into trials so extreme that their characters are forged, swordlike, to help them become liberating agents for others braving their way in the dark.

On the list of grueling obstacle courses to wisdom, no path is more savage than incest, or the sexual abuse of children. Molestation by a trusted caretaker tends to split a child's life in two. In fact, according to Ariel Jordan, a pioneer survivor in the field of incest, "Childhood ends the moment that a child is raped," and incest amounts to what he calls "soul murder." In order to heal from such trauma, incest survivors are required to pass through spiritual wildernesses most of us would find hard to imagine, labyrinths whose darkness is matched only by the light that dawns in the night sky of recovered children who've found their way back to the land of the living.

Without documentation, Ariel's story would be hard to believe. A handsome sixty-year-old man with movie-star silver hair, soulful dark eyes, and a bellowslike voice reminiscent of Henry Kissinger's, Ariel was born on a kibbutz in the Upper Galilee, a few years before the state of Israel came into being. His father was an engineer and a pillar of the community. His mother organized the child-care section of the kibbutz. "Throughout my childhood, I was told how very lucky I was to have them as parents," Ariel tells me when we meet in his crowded Chelsea apartment. "I worshipped my parents. Especially my father." He shows me a photograph of himself as a wide-eyed five-year-old being grabbed around the waist by a creepily smiling man.

The boy looks frightened and trapped. I hand the picture back to Ariel. "How explicit do you want me to be?" he asks. Aware that Ariel has testified twice before congressional committees on child abuse, I invite him to be completely candid. His intention is not to shock, he assures me, but simply to shed light on what he calls "society's darkest secret," to draw the murky topic of incest out into the open. There's a cultural block against believing kids, he's learned during twenty years of working in this field. "But children must be heard," he insists.

"Of course," I say. So Ariel leans back in his leather chair and launches into his surreal tale. "My father raped me for the first time when I was four," he tells me without introduction. "He had given me a bath. It felt so good, because my parents rarely touched me," he says. "Israeli boys were supposed to be tough."

My host is speaking matter-of-factly, with no trace of self-dramatization. "My father was drying me off and tickling me," he goes on. "It was wonderful! The two of us alone together, having fun—"

"Where was your mother?" I ask.

"She was there. Somewhere," says Ariel. "But this was time to be with Papa. It was like a game that we were playing. I remember laughing and telling him to stop tickling me. Then my father began to kiss me."

Ariel's face darkens when he says this. "I didn't know what was happening," he admits. "I just knew that my father was no longer playing. He seemed to be in a kind of trance. Then—" He stops to take a breath. "He entered me."

"At four years old?" I ask, unable to mask my own incredulity.

"The physical pain was one thing," says Ariel. "But the body goes into shock. Emotionally, it was much, much worse."

I'm completely speechless.

"It's so terrible that part of you dies. You cease in that moment to be a child. Suddenly you are an orphan," he says. Researching a piece about incest in the weeks after meeting Ariel, I'm shocked to learn that one out of four girls is raped before the age of eighteen, by a family member or another (the number is slightly lower for boys, one out of five). Even Freud had trouble believing the harsh facts and prevalence of incest. The father of psychology was so appalled by patients' memories of sexual abuse that he famously recanted his original theory, fearing the scorn of skeptical colleagues, and blamed abuse memories on "hysteria" and juvenile sexual fantasies. Psychologists since then have used Freud's own reversal as an excuse for discounting incest survivors' stories.

"How long did he do this?" I ask now.

"Until I was fifteen," Ariel says.

"Why didn't you tell someone? Or fight him off?"

"I wanted to make him happy," he tells me, aware of how crazy this sounds. "It is hard to understand, I know. But abused people have strange relationships with their violators. This became our secret. Our secret world. Your survival mechanism tells you not to resist, since they're going to do it anyway. If you collaborate, you'll be like . . . lovers."

Miraculously, Ariel managed to graduate from high school and escape from Israel. Transplanted in London, he earned a degree in cinema and began making documentary films. Far away from home, he was able to nearly submerge his memories of abuse. He was nearly able to convince himself that this dark history was a trick of his imagination. I'm compelled to confess to Ariel that the enigma of recovered memory, common among abuse survivors, is a mystery I've not quite been able to grasp. How can a person who's been through such severe trauma actually function without conscious recall? Sándor Ferenczi, a colleague of Freud's, had a theory about uncontrollable stress of any kind—from wartime combat to serious accidents to sexual abuse—believing it can cause a person to emerge from trauma riddled with mnemonic bullet holes. "Part of our being can 'die,'" wrote Ferenczi. "And while the remaining part of ourselves may survive the trauma, it awakens with a gap in its memory."

Arriving in New York in the early eighties, haunted by his secret past, Ariel was determined to fill in his psychic gaps—to heal himself of the pervasive feelings of shame, impostorhood, and sexual confusion (hyper-promiscuity combined with emotional absence) that were standing in the way of his living a happy life. This was years before incest became a household word—thanks in large part to Oprah Winfrey's publicizing of her own incest story—and Ariel could find no one who would believe him. Finally screwing up his courage to talk to a therapist, Ariel was appalled by the doctor's response. "I poured out my heart for an hour, and you know what this shrink said to me?"

"I'm afraid to ask."

"He put his arm around my shoulder and told me it was all wishful thinking." Ariel chuckles. "I realized in that moment that I would have to do it myself."

Like a shaman in training, Ariel Jordan entered the dark wood of memory armed with nothing but raw nerves and resolve. Determined to confront his demons, he turned to art as a tool for excavating his past and bringing monster feelings to light. He created a roomful of work recalling Francis Bacon's disemboweled-looking paintings, a pictorial season in hell, a place where his subconscious could spew the evidence of what he'd lived through, making the art of that raped child still inside his body, who needed to speak but until then had no voice.

Slowly, Ariel found his way through the forest. He emerged with a technique for incest therapy that has helped hundreds of other survivors through their own mazes, back from soul murder. "Every single survivor I've worked with has at least two personalities," he explains to me. "One is enormously intelligent and functional. The other is a maimed, speechless child who contains, though they can't quite touch these qualities, spontaneity, connectedness, and creative power."

"How can a survivor uncover them?"

"Memory lodges itself in the body," Ariel explains. Though many of his clients have been through decades of talk therapy, recycling known narratives rarely seems to get at the root of the trauma.

"Many therapists prefer rational dialogues," Ariel says. "But the child part of the patient can't even put what happened into words. One must enter the theater of the subconscious like a safecracker and break the child's code that is spoken there. The child mostly needs to scream. In order to survive his trauma, he has learned to function as a fake, an impostor. This disassociation creates enormous existential pain."

Ariel points out that incest survivors, like so many post-catastrophe individuals, often have "an unusual capacity for transcendence." "Survivors are forced to become seekers," he explains. "We learn to take whatever nurturing we can from anything, no matter how small. Like a cactus in the desert."

He remembers doing this himself as a boy when human comfort was nowhere around. "As a child, I would see how nature wakes up after the trauma of winter," Ariel tells me of those early years in the Galilee, "blossoming, blooming, enriched with sweet smells. I remember leaving our house one particular afternoon, after I had left my father. My hair was wet with sweat, and there was a breeze coming through the mountains right into my face. Suddenly, even though nothing had changed, I was happy again."

"How do you explain that?"

"The breeze told me I wasn't alone," Ariel says simply. "It was as if somebody or something was talking to me. Reaching out to touch my forehead."

The room gets quiet for a moment. Ariel seems to be lost in that memory. "A traumatized person becomes the center of his own universe," he goes on to explain. "This is why so many individuals remain stuck and depressed. Connecting to forces beyond yourself helps you realize that your story, painful as it might be, is not finally that significant. When you get that you're part of a larger context, cells in a larger organism, it gives you a huge amount of comfort."

Transcendent connection also allows us to examine our wounds without being consumed by them. "None of us can fulfill our lives without retrieving the truth," Ariel instructs those who come to him. "You cannot heal what you cannot feel. Whatever you are most ashamed of, whatever humiliates you—this is the exact door to your healing."

This does not mean that abusers necessarily need to be confronted, however. Ariel never hashed things out with his father before he died. He has never talked to his elderly mother about what happened. This has not stopped him from finding some forgiveness, though.

"How do you forgive something like that?" I can't help but wonder.

He reminds me that forgiveness is an "inside job," and has nothing to do with our abusers. Forgiveness is an act of self-blessing. This reminds me of Eva Eiger, a German ballerina forced to entertain her Nazi captors in order not to be murdered. In her memoir, Eiger described how it had taken her forty years to begin to forgive her former captors. "You must be strong to forgive," she reminds us. "Forgiveness is not about condoning or excusing. Forgiveness has nothing to do with justice. Forgiving is a selfish act to free yourself from being controlled by your past."

When the interview is over, Ariel Jordan takes me into the adjacent room that stores his latest artwork. The tormented images of yesteryear have been replaced by photographs of shamans and medicine men from around the globe, wild-looking characters in

Ecuador, India, Polynesia, who've passed through hell and emerged as potent healers. These shamans feel like kindred spirits, Ariel tells me. Like him, they have slain their minotaurs, the man-eating monsters who dwelled in the depths of their dark mazes.

"The dark tells you secrets," Ariel tells me. We tend to forget that the beast in Greek mythology is also an angel. In the story about the labyrinth, the minotaur's name is Asterion, "star." Once again, our nemesis is recognized as a beacon after its hidden face is revealed. Working with clients, Ariel witnesses this turnaround often. It's like watching people being reborn, he says; they reclaim some lost part of their innocence. He helps them to use these wounds to deepen. Asterion leads them back into the world. Like the green shoots through that New York sidewalk, trust emerges slowly. Life begins again.

A SPLINTER OF LOVE

Trauma comes from the German for "dream." Like recurring dreams, traumas have an uncanny power to haunt, change form, and remain spectrally part of the present. We actually carry the past inside our bodies, metaphorically as well as literally (biologists now understand that memory imprints itself upon our cells in the form of amino-peptide chains). Each of us is, literally, a container for the sum of our life's experience, even when, as in the case of incest survivors, we lack conscious memory of that experience. The body itself remembers.

That's why *closure* is such a misleading term. What is it that closes exactly? Crisis may end but memory stays open. Even after the worst things pass, a residue of loss remains, a shadow of love over memory. A splinter of love stays caught in the heart. My mother passed away twelve years ago, for example, but my memory of her is as living as ever. The contours of our lives together remain with me as they always have, a few layers down. Scratch most of us in the right place and we're still ten years old, huddled with our parents and siblings. Are those memories that we want to close? we might ask. Would we know ourselves as well without them? Even when those memories include painful details, are they not the shadow that underlies the fullness of who we are and the unique portrait we have painted? Here, in the split between closing and holding, is where the mind and soul diverge. The mind wants neat endings, locked doors, tightened sutures. The mind wants fresh starts without mess left over. But the soul thrives on raggedness, memory, and mess. The soul wants topography, texture, and ruins, like those flour-and-water 3-D maps you made in grammar school, vivid and sloppy and filled with craters. (The mind prefers black-and-white aerial landscapes.) While the reasoning mind wants to cut and run, our souls pursue a different agenda—to remain where love is, even when that love is gone; to ripen open; to be the keeper of sacred memory long after reason has wandered away.

On the morning of October 19, 1973, five soldiers loyal to Chile's new dictator, Augusto Pinochet, landed in the tiny town of Calama, a Wild West–like outpost on the farther reaches of the Atacama Desert. Known as the Caravan of Death, this group of government-sponsored terrorists was already famous across the length and breadth of Chile for its brutality. Now the five men comprising the caravan climbed out of their Puma helicopter and began moving from door to door through Calama, apprehending unsuspecting husbands, fathers, brothers, and sons from their homes and loading them into military vans. As the men were led away in handcuffs, the women of the town watched in horror, and they pounded on the sides of the vans as the vehicles pulled away. This tactic of "disappearing" unsuspecting, frequently innocent, citizens was already a common tactic for the new regime. The women protested to government authorities, who of course ignored them. These twenty-nine Chilean men, ranging from teenagers to seniors, were never seen or heard from again. Their murders were never confirmed nor their remains returned to their families for burial.

Devastated and enraged, the women of Calama took matters into their own hands. Armed with shovels, picks, and kitchen utensils, they organized regular search parties into the Valley of the Moon to look for their loved ones' remains, and continued to do so for decades. Chasing rumors, intuitions, and dreams, disappointed again and again, they returned to the Atacama to dig for bones and teeth, because they could not live without answers.

"No one knew if the men were alive or dead, though the likelihood is that they had been murdered," Paula Allen tells me. We're walking down a beach in Barbados. Paula and I have been buddies since the early nineties. Paula is a documentary photographer who's spent her thirty-year career following what she calls "women's invisible stories" around the globe, spending up to twenty years on a single body of work—from a homeless woman turned streetwalker in Jersey City to gays in Cuba and Irish gypsy lasses living in caravans in Belfast.

On Christmas Day, 1989, sixteen years after the men's disappearance, Paula found herself walking into the Valley of the Moon with the women of Calama at the end of a scorching-hot day, holding a camera and a shovel, scared of what she might actually find. "It was very windy," Paula remembers. "The light was soft and fierce as it is in the desert. Most of the women had on flowered dresses. I remember dresses blowing in the wind and the determination on their faces. I'd never seen determination like this before—how determination turns into action. They could be arrested for what they were doing, but they refused to be silenced. They refused to give up their love."

I had seen the images Paula brought back of weathered-looking women hauling sticks and spades, baskets slung over their shoulders, moving into the chalk-white expanse like explorers on an alien planet, searching for their *desaparecidos*. The plight of Calama's women was heroic yet incomprehensible to me. I could not quite grasp their obsession with touching the remains (that was my mind talking, I now see), their need for physical artifacts if they were to heal.

"When you don't have a body, nothing is certain," said Vicky, one of the widows in the interviews Paula conducted. "It would be easier to stand the pain if we knew the truth." Another reminded Paula that "a mother can never replace her son." "I hear Manuel's voice everywhere. I see him walking on the streets," she said. "There is always the feeling," yet another reported, "that one must search for something." Finally, Señora Leo, the oldest woman among them, summed it up in a chilling phrase: "They buried us alive."

This last phrase seemed to touch the true point. Aside from wanting to honor their disappeared loved ones, and deriving meaning from this pursuit, the women of Calama seemed to be digging for their own lives in the desert, the parts of themselves that had been stolen, the layers of their own severed past, lost somewhere in that vast expanse. Without finding these relics, they could not grieve; without grieving, they could never feel whole. Quixotic as their plight might appear to the eye of reason, it made perfect sense to the soul. Souls seek retrieval and restitution; to the soul's eye, all of our pieces are valuable, especially the broken ones.

When I share these thoughts with Paula, she appears to agree. "They are looking for some kind of wholeness," my friend says. "It's the same thing all of the women I follow are looking for."

"Is that why you call them invisible stories?" I ask. Paula doesn't catch my drift. "Because they're invisible to themselves?"

"They're invisible to the world," she corrects me. "And partly to themselves, too." But the women of Calama have not been engaged in some pop psychology parlor game. Their search is literal, real, and bloody, as hard to them as bones and dust. They have not been digging for metaphors. After nearly two decades of searching, roughly half the men's remains were discovered by a government team in 1990 along the very road the women followed hundreds of times. Paula could not be there for the burials, but the women have since talked to her about the interments, the bittersweet laying of skulls, bone shards, sometimes no more than an article of clothing, finally into the ground. In solidarity, these women continue to help those whose loved ones' remains have yet to be found. Together the women have found new strength and a new sort of family with one another. "We have shared so many intimacies," explains Victoria Saavedra, "the things that fill your life." "The members are my family, united in the same pain," agrees Hilda Muñoz. "We still dream of finding them," says another. "The search has not finished." Near the spot where the mass grave was found, a plaque has been laid in memory of all the disappeared. "Without knowing where they are," it reads in part, "they are with the sun as companion, in the mercy of silence."

In a gorgeous film called *Dance of Hope*, you can see the women of Calama walking together into the desert on the anniversary of the Caravan of Death tragedy, throwing flowers into the air, blanketing the sand with hundreds of red carnations. They have not run away from their memories. Their commitment seems to remind us all that life may be buried under our feet (as memory is buried under the skin), and that soul is revived in uncovering it. The bones—the haunted scary parts; the splinters, failures, disappeared selves; the lovers, secrets, petrified dreams—are important parts of who we are. It may be hard to remember this sometimes but it's always worse to forget. Like trauma, memory haunts only when buried; uncovered it speaks through the heart to the soul, which thrives on cherishing even what's lost: the layers beneath that are no longer seen; history's sediments marbled within us; the full complex beauty of what we have loved.

NAKEDNESS

We must accept heartbreak to be fully human. We cannot love without tasting some blood, nor connect without braving some chink in our armor. Those who are most spiritually naked, most transparent, are also those who see most fully. "Let the scar of the heart be seen," said the prophet Mohammed. "For by their scars are known the men who are in the way of Love." Holy books encourage us to strip ourselves bare—to allow ourselves to be burned all the way through by our passionate quest if we wish to be whole. Avoiding life's shadows makes the heart shallow.

In his play *Orpheus Descending*, Tennessee Williams describes the opposite of such surrender through the invention of a mythic white bird whose entire life is spent in the air—soaring, unsullied, shadowless—touching earth only once, to die. While the desire to avoid pain may be normal, denial as a long-term strategy is a cold, narrow way to live. We may be dodging bullets through extreme self-protection yet find ourselves withering in our distant aeries, too—safe yet only half engaged—armoring our unbroken hearts while remaining secretly loveless, invulnerable, and dry. Such safe-seeming lives may seem charmed from the outside while being still-born inside, closed off from the messes of passion and joy, the pain that always comes with loving. And yet, as lovers and poets both know, the mystery of joy includes its pain. The poet Rainer Maria Rilke, who prided himself on raw, intense living, put it this way:

> It is true that these mysteries are dreadful, and people have always drawn away from them. But where can we find anything sweet and glorious that would never wear *this* mask, the mask of the dreadful? Whoever does not, sometime or other, give his full consent, his full and *joyous* consent to the dreadfulness of life, can never take possession of the unutterable abundance and power of our existence; can only walk on its edge, and one day, when the judgment is given, will have been neither alive nor dead.

While vanity rails against such humiliation and woundsbaring, our hearts thrive on the intimate dropping of masks. Ego may long for admiration, praise, and distance-keeping (as a way to protect its fragile fictions), but soul requires connection and truth. These antithetical human needs help explain the conversion experience, the turnaround in value systems experienced by postcatastrophe people. Unable to hide our humanity, we feel twice born letting down our façades. Hard as we may fight against it, we're grateful in the end for this self-exposure. With less to hide, there's less to defend, freeing our naked selves to love without fear of revealing imperfection.

In the realm of public unmasking and courage, I've never met a braver or more resilient person than my late friend Lucy Grealy, whose memoir of childhood cancer, *Autobiography of a Face*, opened the eyes of thousands of readers to a woman's struggle with facial disfigurement. Diagnosed with a Ewing's sarcoma at nine, Lucy lost half her jaw in an emergency surgery and would spend the next three decades making peace with her own appearance. For years, she spoke publicly about the cost of cancer to her self-esteem and the grueling lessons disease had taught her.

Although Lucy died, famously, of a drug overdose in 2002—a tragedy announced in a *New York* magazine cover story the week after she was buried—her inability to quit a two-year heroin habit in no way diminishes her power to instruct and inspire. Lucy had been told she would be dead by twenty only to survive twice that long, write a classic book, live a colorful (sometimes too colorful) life, teach thousands of writing students, counsel cancer victims, and serve as a great friend to many people, including myself. Her sad end does not subtract from these achievements, any more than Primo Levi's decision to take his own life detracts from his brilliance as a writer on the Holocaust. Lucy descended from a family of Irish alcoholics (she was born in Dublin and came to this country at four), attempted rehab, then tried again. She never stopped attempting to make her life better, and having a tragic flaw did not make Lucy any less of a hero.

She looked like a broken china doll, the scar running down from below her right ear and along her truncated jaw, as if a hunk of porcelain had shattered and then been removed from an otherwise lovely face. Lucy hated her face and believed it was ugly—it *was* disturbing to look at from certain angles. Yet she didn't let this stop her from doing TV talk shows, lecturing in public, or, hardest of all, looking for Mr. Right. Lucy's quest to find a man, like that of many childless women in their late thirties, was primal and relentless.

A few times a month we would sit at our favorite café, commiserating over our twin obsessions, romance and survival. Lucy mostly found the relationship thing hopeless.

"Do you think I'm ugly?" she would ask me constantly, coyly turning her face to its better side, smiling, winking. She would be wearing her oversized arctic wool turtleneck sweater, skintight jeans, and knee-high, leather sex-getting boots (she could be a serious minx).

"You're not ugly," I would say. "But you are unbelievably vain."

This remark would cause her to slap me and order a drink. Lucy knew that she had certain attributes—beautiful Irish blue eyes, blond hair, a peachy complexion, hot legs, a lithe gamine's body—but such information would not stick. She'd grown up being called Dog Girl in school, and was taunted mercilessly from the age of nine, when—after being hit in the face with a ball—she was rushed to the doctor's office and was discovered to have a virulent stage-four tumor in her mandible. In the operating room, Lucy's jaw was sliced in half; then, when she returned to the fifth grade, her education in affliction began in earnest. Physical suffering aside, how could the normal people around her not realize how lucky they were? Lucy would ask herself. In her book *As Seen on TV*, she described her first post-cancer Halloween.

> I breathed in the condensing, plastic-tainted air behind the mask and thought that I was breathing in normalcy, that this joy and weightlessness were what the world was composed of, and that it was only my face that kept me from it, my face that was my own mask that kept me from knowing the joy I felt sure everyone but me lived with intimately. How could the others not know it? Not know that to be free of the fear of taunts and the burden of

knowing no one would ever love you was all that a person could ever ask for?

Self-pity was never an option. Lucy's mother begged her not to cry. While this may sound cruel—and it was—Lucy believed that her mother's sternness had also helped her. Childhood trauma often produces high-functioning, extremely rational people with a disproportionately acute sense of responsibility toward others but a void where their own self-feeling should be. This disproportion, though ultimately problematic, can work to a survivor's benefit during times when we're barely making it through. "I was blessed from the beginning that I never felt bitter about what happened to me," Lucy told me, without sounding self-righteous. "I never asked, why me? From the beginning, it was always, why *not* me?" She said this in a tone like *duh.* "It takes emotional intelligence to realize that feeling bad about yourself is just another form of narcissism," Lucy said. "It's really easy to see your own suffering as another excuse to build up your ego. Poor me!"

This refusal of self-pity in a woman who had trouble eating and drinking in public (for fear of dribbling) was extremely humbling. "That's where the philosophical part comes in," Lucy said. "In the hierarchy of suffering out there, there's a lot worse. People think how strong—how *big*—you must be to get through something. But it takes a lot of courage to admit how small you are. And that your problems don't really amount to very much." This echoed the words of Ariel Jordan, the incest survivor. "Not to turn that into a punishing, depressive act, but as a bridge to compassion," Lucy said. "I know what it's like to suffer."

She described what having cancer was like in 1970, when chemotherapy was even cruder than it is today, the goal being to "poison patients to the brink of their own death." Lucy, the good Catholic girl, at first tried to "sacramentalize" her pain, to render her own suffering holy. The ten-year-old would pray for saintly purification after these horrendous treatments. "I'd sit on the toilet in the hospital bathroom reading two pieces of graffiti over and over," Lucy told me once. "One said GOD IS NEAR. The other said BE HERE NOW. It set up an inquiry in me, and the search for meaning gives you strength."

Lucy became an expert in suffering, eventually, a black belt in the martial art of cancer. She learned that pain, too, has a hidden face. "You begin to see other possibilities in the midst of your hardship," she explained to me. We were driving to Connecticut after Lucy's final pre-op hospital stay before her big surgery. She had been promised that this time her doctors would get her jaw right, make the fix she'd been waiting for, to give her face symmetry. Lucy couldn't wait for the operation but needed to recover in the country first. The pastures of Cos Cob were flying by as she talked about what she had learned. "I experimented with different ways of thinking and feeling about things," she said of those first years after surgery. "Beginning with joy. People think of joy as something rare, something to be acquired." She lit a cigarette. "What I've learned is that joy is simply the absence of suffering— sometimes on a physical level, sometimes the stopping of mental punishment."

"Isn't that an amazing thing?"

"You have to suffer very often for a long time in order to have these experiences," she insisted. "I learned that when pain subsided just a little, I'd have these moments of intense euphoria. I didn't know it was unusual to have moments of deep joy on a regular basis, because suffering always *does* subside for moments," Lucy said. "That's why torture is so effective. Torturers don't give prisoners a moment to have an epiphany about it."

Lucy looked at me. "I've had these moments of intense euphoria throughout my life, but it was the joy that came about simply because I felt a little bit better," she said. "Not through the acquisition of anything outside of me. *The joy was already there.* I just needed the pain to let up a little, and there it was. It's a really profound, miraculous thing."

Lucy's visible defect used to draw people toward her, especially those who knew her story. They adored her by the auditoriumful, magnetized by her naked scar. The thing that she wanted to change was the very wound others found most inspiring, the vulnerability that drew them out and taught them to be more fearless about their own shortcomings.

"Openness, honesty, vulnerability, nakedness are the key to everything," Lucy once said to me. "You've got to be honest with yourself, to face the depth of your own distress. Otherwise it turns to depression," which Lucy described as "avoidance of larger pain."

"Neurosis is always a substitute for legitimate suffering," Jung once said. Lucy could not have agreed more. "People avoid being burned through by things," she insisted. "Instead, they create these holding cells for their feelings. To keep volatile, extreme feelings at bay. That's how depression makes you helpless. It shuts you down. But when people actually let themselves feel these things, the emotions burn hotter and pass more quickly."

"Would that it were so easy," I said.

"Easy?" Lucy asked. "I'm talking about real life."

"Oh, that."

"You saw it after nine-eleven. People immediately wanted to alleviate suffering by creating suffering for somebody else," Lucy told me. "Nobody knew how to feel ambivalence about *not* knowing what to do. Retaliation, acting out, was more comfortable than being in anguish."

Indeed, Lucy's own ability to bear anguish—and emerge bright-eyed—was preternatural to behold. She could land on her feet with the ease of a cat hurled from a top-floor window. Even when things went extra-badly, she comported herself with stoic grace. When the long-promised surgery failed to improve Lucy's face (her jaw had been over-irradiated), she rallied with gusto even then. Her face swollen beyond recognition, a pneumatic tube of transplanted flesh hanging around her neck like a tire, Lucy was bedridden and in extreme pain, yet still managed to retain her unsinkable black humor. I climbed into the bed next to her and she held my hand, with her friend Ann Patchett watching us from a chair. Lucy tried to turn her awful appearance into a joke.

"Helium by Maybelline," she gurgled, turning her bubble face back and forth. She let us know how extremely fortunate she truly was to have such loyal friends, since now she would be alone forever for sure.

"Am I not a lucky girl?" Lucy blubbered, fingering her alien neck, unable to blink her black-and-blue slit eyes.

Ann gave me a pained look.

"I mean it," she said. "I love you guys."

"Oh, shut up," said Ann, who knew her humor.

"Bitch," said Lucy.

"Slut," said Ann. Then both of them dissolved into giggles.

Three months later, on the night that she died, Lucy left a message on my answering machine, to thank me for being such a good friend and tell me how much she loved me. I didn't know that it was the last time I would hear her voice. She had recovered from the surgery, gone back to dating, persevered on her long-awaited novel—even considered going to medical school. Only days before that good-bye message, we'd been laughing over coffee at our favorite café. Lucy was reminding me again about how crazy romance can be, how obsessive insecure men are when it comes to strong women, and why, next to dental work, dating is the cruelest and most horrible thing civilized people actually pay for. Lucy seemed okay to me that afternoon, better than she'd been in a while. Her eyes were especially clear and blue. Did she know what was coming? I ask myself now. Or was her death an accident? I will never know the answer, of course; nor will I ever stop thinking about it. This splinter of love will not go away. As I pass the table where we used to sit, there are ghosts in the corner of my eye. I can almost see Lucy sitting there still, asking me if I believe that she will ever find a man. I'm telling her again that yes, she will, if she finally stops settling for Peter Pans. I'd be watching her face as she laughed and moaned, then ordered herself another drink. Lucy would be leaning forward and purring, getting ready—as always—to talk about love. Her determination—again—would amaze me.

KILLING PETER PAN

Philosophers from Plato to Kierkegaard to Gurdjieff have taught that the path of the soul involves a progressive series of disillusionments. The mirror must crack if we want to evolve. The earthbound lessons of aging, disenchantment, and passing beauty must crack the mask for the soul to breathe. Lucy had learned this lesson in spite of herself, although she still wanted a prettier face. Still, vanity resists the path that leads to this more enduring beauty. No one wants to be discarded by an appearance-crazed, youth-obsessed world.

In a culture that celebrates narcissism, the soul can become a fugitive. "The great malady of the 20th century, implicated in all our troubles and affecting us individually and socially, is 'loss of soul,'" religious writer Thomas Moore wrote. Like water invisible to fish, narcissism is so ubiquitous that we hardly see we're swimming in it. We're inducted into this illusory self-understanding before we are even aware of it. Once, a scholar explained to me that narcissism is born the first time a child looks into a mirror and realizes that this "thing" is what others take to be itself. This knowledge exiles us from the garden; holistic innocence comes to an end. We see ourselves as "things" in a world of other "things," rather than souls looking through these masks. This trance of mistaken identity causes us enormous trouble, psychologists tell us, beginning with alienation from others and excessive attachment to this "reflection." As we age, this obsession only gets worse, our fears of physical loss and change of appearance masking—à la Peter Pan—a self-destructive denial of death.

At eighty-four, Jungian pioneer James Hillman has spent decades singing the praises of soul and warning against excessive narcissism. "Remember what Anna Magnani said when they tried to make her look younger in *The Rose Tattoo?*" Hillman asks me over coffee in a Tribeca diner, referring to the earthy Italian film star. "'Don't take out a single line. I paid for every single one!'" The godfather of archetypal psychology in this country, Hillman has argued in dozens of books, including *The Soul's Code*, that narcissistic culture has it all wrong, exhorting the self-improvement-obsessed to appreciate their so-called weaknesses, embrace their chronic weirdnesses, rough spots, absences of virtue, physical peculiarities—the places where they fall short and never measure up—as integral to their multiplex beings and the texture that gives them character.

Hillman looks much younger than he is, in fact, tanned as toast and surprisingly buff, wearing Levi's and aviator glasses. "When we see an old wall, an old teacup, an old tree, we appreciate these things precisely for their oldness," he tells me, "the increased beauty of their years and the memories they contain. Objects seem to gain in value as they age, but we deny this same respect to people."

He's right. "Yet the oddities and flaws that make you different only increase with time and become the most interesting part of who you are," Hillman insists. "These changes form our character"—a word derived from the Greek for "etched, cut, or engraved," he reminds me.

"Who wants to be engraved?" I ask, half-seriously. "We want to cheat time and look ageless."

"But there is a great deal of human life that cannot be measured by time," Hillman says. "The deepening and refining of personal vision, how we appreciate the world, our increased sense of beauty." Longevity for its own sake doesn't interest him much; it's what we do with our years that determines their worth. "Longevity for its own sake is rarely concerned with what came before you or what will come after," Hillman says.

"Old people can be quite selfish," I agree.

"Obsession with staying alive can lead to a kind of geriatric heroism," he says, referring to our fixation on what's in the mirror. "Beating the odds, lowering our cholesterol levels, outliving statistical tables. But life moves in *three* directions."

"Three?" I ask.

"Backward, forward, and outward," Hillman says.

"Sorry, but I don't follow."

"There is the longevity of extending life backward through memory," he explains, reminding me of the women of Calama "extending" life by digging for their loved ones in the desert. "There is the longevity of concerning yourself with the coming generations," Hillman goes on. "Not only your grandchildren and great-grandchildren, but down to the seventh generation, as the Bible says. This extends your life into the future as you reach forward. Finally, there is the longevity that comes from extending your life *outward* by becoming responsible to the place where you live and the society around you."

Our lives, in other words, are never merely personal affairs, despite what the mirror may tell us. Our culture's tendency toward planned obsolescence—cultivating the myth of perpetual youth—distorts the wisdom we might glean from soul. "Each stage of life has its own meaning," he explains. "What's unique about surviving into old age has nothing to do with being young. In Rome a man put on the *toga senilis*, or 'toga of old age,' at age sixty. But our culture is so concerned with quickness and speed, people don't have the patience for slowness."

"We equate slowness with being washed up," I remind him.

"But slowness is another kind of adventure," he insists. "When you're old, you don't even know if you're going to get out of the bathtub! But there is an adventure in that. If you think about it, there's the same challenge and achievement as climbing mountains. You hold on to something, you watch your foot as it moves, the whole adventure is right there in miniature. This is the adventure of slowness."

It is also, Hillman has learned, the adventure of love. As character deepens, so does an eros more nourishing and durable than lust, he believes. Embers are better for cooking than flame, as the saying goes. "A certain love for the world deepens the recognition of its beauty," he says. "It's amazing how some people who had miserable lives are grateful in old age just to have been here, to have gone through it all." I've often noticed this myself, I tell him. "Relationships can become richer, provided people aren't trying to recapture the experiences of their youth," he continues. "There's more acceptance in love between old people, more respect for the other person and their foibles."

"The mirror is no longer the last word?"

"We learn to appreciate our partner's oddities," Hillman

stresses, "and to realize what a miracle it is that we're here, still together." He looks out the window at traffic on Hudson Street. "We take more interest in one another. Not what medications we're taking, or what our pulse rates might be, but what we're reading and dreaming about, what memories are returning to us, what peculiar reflection just turned in our minds, something we haven't thought of for years. We become more interested in each other's souls. That is the truly interesting part."

"I thought only superficial people don't believe in appearances," I kid him, citing a joke from Oscar Wilde.

"'In the final analysis, we count for something only because of the essential we embody,'" James Hillman replies, throwing a line from Jung back at me. "'If we do not embody that, life is wasted.'" He chuckles and sits back in his chair. "Try wiggling out of that one."

THE WATER OR THE WAVE?

Time is a cruel bitch goddess. We measure our lives in coffee spoons and wonder why we feel so crushed by the ticktock of minutes piling down on us through the burying years. We chop existence into nanoseconds and struggle to fill up every one, fearful of wasting a moment to leisure, hoarding time as if it really were money. Rushing through the measured world, we forget that ours is the first civilization in history to be so obsessed and bedeviled by time. The unhelpful image of God as a celestial clock keeper, stopwatching our every move from above, has shown (in our attention-deficient times) no sign whatsoever of blinking.

Yet philosophers have insisted for centuries that there are in fact two kinds of time operating in the world—man-made time and soul time—and that it is vitally important that we remember both if we wish to remain sane. *Nunc fluens* is their name for hourglass time, the relentless metronome that frays your nerves, grays your hair, forms rings inside the trunk of a tree. *Nunc stans*, on the other hand, denotes time as seen through eternal eyes, the timeless sense we may feel in nature, while reading a great book, creating artwork, having sex, or praying—peak-and-valley moments—when *nunc fluens* seems to stop, dropping us through the mental scrim that separates our everyday minds from great silence. Spaced-out as this sounds to the stressed-out psyche, we're actually more awake than usual during *nunc stans* moments, able to see more clearly, to operate more effectively, than we can while hugging a clock. Contrary to the puritan belief that time-gripping keeps us on the ball (and keeps our great assembly line ticking along), the opposite appears to be true. *Nunc fluens* without *nunc stans* behind it creates an assembly line to madness.

A mountain climber who'd been part of the first team to scale Mount Everest described how the discovery of soul time changed his life. Returning from the peak, the hiker paused on a high pass to admire the stupendous view. As he turned around, he saw a small blue flower in the snow. "I don't know how to describe what happened," he reported later. "Everything opened up and flowed together and made some strange kind of sense, and I was at complete peace. I have no idea how long I stood there. It could have been minutes or hours. Time melted. But when I came down, my life was different."

These blue flower moments are happening all the time, but few of us pause to pay attention. The workaday mind needs a slap—or a climax—to stop it in its habitual tracks. When this happens, we may find ourselves dropped into this timeless dimension. Problems suddenly seem to shrink down to size when seen against this spacious backdrop. Artists, seekers, lovers, adventurers, people like R.D. who like to trip, all recognize the freedom of such moments when the mind quiets down and affords us a taste of that gorgeous expanse.

Still, we tend to fear *nunc stans* and its freedoms. We cling to our wristwatches for dear life. Until we're torn somehow from our habitual grid, we may even doubt that eternal time exists. After we glimpse it, though, we begin to see our lives differently—to perceive the world stereoscopically, like the double-faced Roman god Janus on the threshold between two realms, facing both directions at once, the physical and the invisible worlds. Reality seems to turn almost translucent sometimes, as if eternity itself were peeking through this time-stopped thinning of veils.

In the Andaman Sea of Indonesia, there lives a group of nomadic tribesmen whose lives are virtually untouched by time as we know it. Spending up to eight months out of every year traveling from island to island, living on their primitive boats, the Moken are among the peoples of the world least touched by modern civilization. They are born on the sea, live on the sea, and die on the sea. They understand the moods of the ocean better than any marine biologist. Constantly moving from island to island, they learn to swim before they're walking and are more or less amphibious. The Moken can see twice as clearly as the rest of us and are able to lower their heart rates automatically to stay underwater twice as long. They catch sea cucumbers and eels at low tide, dive for shellfish when the water is high, and enjoy as close to an Edenic existence as seems possible in this time-obsessed world.

Nunc fluens does not exist for them. If you ask a Moken how old he is, he may have trouble telling you. Conspicuously absent from their language are terms for "when," "want," and "worry." If you show up at a Moken village after a twenty-year absence, locals will greet you as if it were yesterday. They have no words for "hello" or "good-bye." *Nunc stans* is their everyday state. This allows them to exist in a unity with their environment that most of us would find hard to imagine. No reaching backward or forward in time—no longing, projecting, hurrying, or reminiscing—upsets their daily round.

It is not surprising to learn, for this reason, that the Moken were the only Indonesian group to suffer not a single casualty in the 2003 tsunami that claimed three hundred thousand lives. This was thanks to a sixty-seven-year-old fisherman named Satha Kathaleway, who was mending his nets on the beach when the first signs of trouble appeared. The cicadas, whose loin-rubbing causes a ruckus here nine months a year, suddenly fell silent. In all of his years, Kathaleway, who's gray-haired and nimble, had never heard anything like it before. The dolphins made for deeper water as the tide receded abnormally far. Livestock stampeded for higher ground. Kathaleway warned his fellow Moken that the *lumbi*, the great man-eating wave described in a popular myth, was about to descend on them. His fellow tribesmen followed the old man up the mountain, and their lives were spared, all because this "primitive" fisherman was watching the world instead of a clock.

One crisp fall afternoon, I make my way to Rhinebeck, New York, to have a conversation with Eckhart Tolle, the German spiritual teacher whose book *The Power of Now* introduced the concept of *nunc stans* to millions of readers trapped in their time-obsessed heads. According to Tolle,

> the mind, to ensure that it remains in control, seeks continuously to cover up the present moment with past and future . . . as the

vitality and infinite creative potential of Being, which is insepa-
rable from the Now, becomes covered up by time, your true nature becomes obscured by the mind.

I loved that. "The accumulation of time in the collective and individual human mind," he concluded, "also holds a vast amount of
residual pain from the past."

I find Eckhart waiting for me on his bungalow porch, an elfin
man with a gnomelike beard reminiscent of a character out of *The
Hobbit*. He's wearing an Alpine-style vest and a Nehru shirt, his
voice a sort of amused hush. When Eckhart offers me his hand,
it's as light as a feather. He pours us tea and we take our seats in
the dimly lit cabin he's calling home during the weeklong silent
retreat that he's leading.

"Human history has largely been a history of insanity," Eckhart
begins cheerfully. "The manifestation of a sort of collective mental illness." His steady gaze makes me realize how frazzled I'm
feeling after my two-hour drive north. Why is this? I wonder.
"Everyone has the roots of this illness to a greater or lesser degree," Eckhart assures me. "But in order to understand this, we
need to look for a moment at how the human mind works."

He sips his tea and begins to explain. "The mind finds labels
and concepts to describe and interpret things and people," Eckhart tells me. "Clouded by labels and concepts, the mind becomes
unconscious. Jesus's last words are borne out in the truest sense—
'they know not what they do.'"

"Okay," I say. But what does this have to do with time?

"The mind is essentially a survival machine," he goes on,
approaching my question from another direction. "In the most

primitive sense." "Fighting, defending, storing information, analyzing—this is what the conventional mind is good at," Eckhart has written, "but it is not at all creative. All true artists create from a place of no-mind, from inner stillness, whether or not they're aware of it."

Blue flower moments, I think. "Even the greatest scientists admit that their creative breakthroughs come at times of mental quietude," Eckhart says. "When we quiet the mind, we can be present. Right now. In this very moment." He gazes out the window at a squirrel nibbling leaves on the lawn. "When we can yield, accept, be open to our lives, a new dimension of consciousness opens up," Eckhart says. "If action is possible or necessary, your action will be in alignment with the whole and supported by creative intelligence. Circumstances and people then become helpful, cooperative. Coincidences happen. If no action is possible, you rest in the peace and inner stillness that come with surrender. You rest in God."

"Otherwise?" I ask.

"You get resistance, an inner contraction, a hardening of the shell," he tells me. "You close yourself off from reality, and whatever action you take will only cause more resistance." I've noticed this often in my own life. "If the shutters are closed, the sunlight cannot come in. The universe will not be on your side; life will not be helpful," says Eckhart.

While *nunc fluens* is necessary for organizing our daily lives— your wristwatch gets you to the dentist's office on time—life is more than a dentist's appointment. Without tapping into *nunc stans*, Eckhart teaches, we divorce ourselves from the big picture. "It wasn't through the mind, through thinking, that the miracle that is life on earth or your body were created and are being sustained," he has written.

> There is clearly an intelligence at work [inside us] that is far greater than the mind. How can a single human cell measuring 1/1,000 of an inch in diameter contain instructions within its DNA that would fill 1,000 books of 600 pages each? . . . When the mind reconnects with that, it becomes a most wonderful tool. It then serves something greater than itself.

"Yes, we need the mind to function," he says. "But there comes a point where it takes over our lives, and this is where dysfunction, pain, and sorrow set in." When we balance the tyranny of *nunc fluens* with the spaciousness of soul time, we free ourselves from past and future and realize how much unhappiness we create with our constant mental time-jumps backward and forward, often missing what's in front of our eyes. This habit is comparable to driving a car while staring into the rearview mirror (and reading traffic signs *way* up the road at the same time). What we get are accidents and the smell of burning rubber, not realizing that the emergency brake is still on. Such time distortion is even more hazardous during times of crisis, Eckhart tells me. "Whenever loss occurs, you either resist or yield," he says. "Some people become bitter or deeply resentful. Others become compassionate, wise, and loving. The intensity of the pain depends on the degree of resistance to the present moment," he explains. "What could be more futile, more insane, than to fight something that already is? It means you're opposing life itself, which is now and always now. Say yes to life, and see how things start working for you rather than against you."

When the bell rings to call retreatants into the meditation hall, I realize that I haven't looked at my wristwatch for over half an hour.

"When we are caught in the timekeeping mind," Eckhart says, "we think our lives rather than living them. We have relationships with our ideas of people rather than with the people themselves."

Is he saying that our approach to time affects how we think about other people?

"Of course. The moment you put a mental label on another human being, you can no longer truly relate to that person."

"I understand that—"

"The more mental labels you have for other people, or groups of people different from the group you identify with, the more you deaden yourself to the aliveness and the reality of those people," he tells me. "It then becomes possible to perpetrate any act of violence."

In other words, the mind's blinding concepts—aimed at time, other people, or ourselves—prevent us from seeing clearly. I am writing these words on August 15, 2007, but what does this numerical series have to do with the humid New York afternoon, the actual sunlight warming my window, the rain clearing out of the late summer sky? Is it August in the eye of the soul? we might ask. Or is it just today?

Eckhart excuses himself to rest before his evening's talk. Driving home, I listen to one of his hypnotic tapes as I navigate my way down Route 9. Near Poughkeepsie, I'm startled by a car's horn blaring directly behind me. I've been moseying along at thirty miles an hour in a fifty-five-mile-per-hour zone, I realize. Perhaps this is a sign of progress? Eckhart's soft voice on the tape continues.

> Imagine the earth devoid of human life, inhabited only by plants and animals. Would it still have a past and a future? Could we still speak of time in any meaningful way? What time is it? The oak tree or the eagle would be bemused by such a question. "What time?" they would ask. "Well, of course it's now. The time is now. What else is there?"

WHAT TIME IS GOOD FOR

While our obsession with *nunc fluens* can become a straitjacket, history (time's overcoat) can be useful for cinching in our woes and warming the soul in harsh weather. The knowledge that others have lived through worse troubles than ours can provide comfort and courage in times of duress. "I cried because I had no shoes till I saw the boy who had no feet," my own mother used to say when we whined about our welfare-grade life. Though I'd never actually met a footless person, the suggestion helped me anyway. Stop complaining, my mother would tell us, you've lived through nothing, we've got a free country, your grandma stuffed kishke to get out of Poland.

After 9/11, Americans were invited to use history in a similar way: to feel less sorry for ourselves. One risked sounding hardhearted at first, reminding fellow citizens that genocide did not actually begin on that September morning. Still, it is helpful to remember that tragic events carry their own centripetal force, sucking attention toward themselves and away from other suffering beings. Self-privileging is a terrible trap, especially when we're trying to heal. As incest survivor Ariel Jordan put it, remaining the center of our own cruel universe is a sure way of remaining stuck. Connection of any kind will free us. In times of historic-scale tragedy, only history is forceful enough to pry the victim mentality loose and release the pretense of specialness.

"History is the great leveler," says historian Doris Kearns Goodwin in the aftermath of the 9/11 attacks. "History helps us to survive," she tells me. "If *they* did it, we say, we can, too."

"We forget that worse things have happened—"

"Listen," Doris interrupts me. "We tend to think of past wars from the victory backward," she says. "World War Two came out well, but in the beginning there was an enormous amount of uncertainty about whether or not we could match Germany's weaponry. In 1940 Germany had the most powerful army ever amassed on the face of the earth, and our armed forces were rated eighteenth in the world. By the time Pearl Harbor came, we were much better prepared, but there were many months of losses before that situation began to turn around."

"Necessity forced invention," I say.

"As it always does. Americans are still reeling after nine-eleven," Doris says. "But it might help if we remembered the London Blitz. There were fifty-seven nights of continuous bombing. Londoners had to live through massive uncertainty. Twenty-three thousand people were killed. But just as Hitler failed to break the will of the British people, citizens in this country have proved that their will has not been broken either."

"On the contrary," I say.

"Indeed. Churchill insisted that theaters in the West End remain open, remember?" Doris reminds me. "When there were air raid sirens, people put on gas masks and sang songs until the 'all clear' was sounded. Tube stations were turned into underground shelters with libraries. Stores opened with signs on their shattered windows that read, MORE OPEN THAN USUAL. Life went on!" she insists. "This is when Churchill said, 'If the British Empire and its Commonwealth last for a thousand years, men will still say this was their finest hour.' Knowing that people had the ability to sustain themselves through this barrage, and somehow endured it, should give us hope that we can do it as well."

"We had our illusion of safety destroyed."

"That's true. But you see how we've risen to the occasion?" Doris asks. "When people band together to defy the enemy, what you see is that fighting spirit. Not allowing the terrorists to win by breaking us. It's not that fear is taken away, but this passion not to be broken becomes greater than fear. Being part of a group gives you courage that you might not have individually. That's why the massive show of flags and feeling of being a nation have been so important during this time."

I admit that the flag-waving scares me a little.

"Most of the time, nation is an abstraction," she explains. "But when a crisis happens, you remember in your heart what it means to be someone living in this country. Being part of something larger than yourself gives you an extra sense of strength. During World War Two almost everyone was involved in doing something to help: planting victory gardens, sending in their dogs' rubber toys, collecting aluminum. That's why people remember the war with such a positive feeling. Surviving nine-eleven has been a major shift for Americans," she acknowledges. "And not at all part of the ethos of recent years. In the decades since the war in Vietnam, we've been more private and individual-oriented. This disaster is awakening that other side of people, infusing the leaders of the future with a deeper public consciousness."

"I hope you're right," I say.

"One feels enlarged during times such as these," Doris tells me.

From the patio of her home in Marin County, Chilean novelist Isabel Allende agrees that history is the best antidote to both victimhood and hubris.

"We have been privileged in this country to believe that life is secure, that our rights—including the search for happiness—are sacred," Isabel tells me over the phone. "But most of the world has lived with uncertainty for millennia. I lived in Chile, a country that had one of the oldest democracies in Latin America," she says. "We never thought that anything like a military coup could happen to us. Those only happened in banana republics! Until one day it did happen, and the brutality lasted for seventeen years."

Pinochet's coup had taken place on September 11, 1973, coincidentally. "This was a military coup orchestrated by the CIA," Isabel says, sounding angry. "It was a terrorist attack against a democracy!" I'm reminded of the Caravan of Death arriving in their Puma helicopter. "The extraordinary thing is that in twenty-four hours you learn to adapt."

"How?" I ask.

"You go on with your life, because life goes on," says Isabel. "You see this in anyone who has survived a traumatic situation. My own daughter died, for example." Her only daughter, Paula Frias, died of porphyria in 1992 at the age of twenty-seven. "At first you think you can't live with this," says the author, who just turned sixty-five. "It's just too much. Then life begins to take over. One morning you wake up and you want to eat chocolate. Or walk in the woods. Or open a bottle of wine. You get back up on your feet."

"When you can, right?"

"You have no choice!" Isabel insists. "You cannot let the bullies keep you on the floor! I have been on my knees a thousand times, and I always get up. This is the message we must give to our children. You must get up off the floor! Sooner or later everybody suffers. Grief and darkness are a part of life."

"That's what nine-eleven has taught us."

"Americans," she says, chuckling. "When I moved to this country twenty years ago, I fell in love with a lawyer, the kind who sues the city when you fall on a banana peel. I couldn't believe it! Accidents are accidents. If you slip and fall, it's your own fault."

"Tell that to people who are suing McDonald's for making them fat."

"There is no insurance for happiness or safety! That's impossible," Isabel exclaims. "Life is difficult, painful, and wonderful. But we are a society that expects to be happy and entertained all the time, a spoiled society that hasn't had war in its territory in more than a century, though we contribute to war in other countries all the time. We support many of the worst dictatorships in the world. It is we who helped create the Taliban."

"That may be true. But how can we live differently now?" I ask.

"By becoming citizens of the world. Americans cannot have a gated-community mentality anymore, or believe that we can keep ourselves safe while there's so much inequality and poverty in the world. More than eight hundred million people on this planet are hungry. The distribution of wealth is completely unfair. This creates conditions for hatred and violence. How can this continue forever without paying the consequences?"

Isabel steps off her soapbox and gets to the point. "I learned something in Chile at its time of terror. We tend to focus on the negative because that's what makes the news. But for every terrorist and torturer, every person who commits a crime, there are a thousand people who are willing to risk their lives to help and do good," she says. "We forget this. But if it weren't true, we would still be in the Stone Age. Why has humanity evolved? Because there are more good guys than bad guys, even though the bad guys make more noise."

That is why post-catastrophic times like these are rich in potential for metanoia. "We can come together," Isabel agrees. "Make changes. Begin to reflect. We now have a chance to grow up. Make peace. Become aware. Renew our spirits."

"Otherwise we're on the floor?"

"That's right," answers Isabel Allende. "And life on the floor is terrible."

For the past fifty years, Holocaust survivor Elie Wiesel has been exhorting us to remember the past in order not to repeat it. The Nobel Peace Prize winner warns that forgetfulness is our greatest public danger, since tyrants prey on ignorance. While memory is sometimes a heavy burden, it is the price we pay for wisdom.

"This is the choice we must make as humans," Wiesel tells me from his office at Boston University. "The quest for knowledge is what makes humans survive, even if it hurts." I have trouble imagining that this éminence grise was once a sixteen-year-old Hungarian boy in a death camp. "There's a troublesome verse from Ecclesiastes about this," he tells me. "It says that the more we know, the more pain we have. But because we are human beings, this must be. Otherwise we become objects rather than subjects."

He pauses for a moment to let this sink in. "Of course, it hurts when we see pictures of people throwing themselves out of windows, children who are orphaned, the widows," Wiesel says. "But there is no way out of what we've seen."

"And how do we live with what we know?" I ask

"How can we live with *not* knowing?" He says this as if it's the only true question. "We have more responsibility now."

"More fear, too," I say.

"But fear is a natural ingredient in life. If a child is afraid of fire, that's good. Fear is only unhealthy when it becomes excessive. Courage has an important role to play in how we cope with what we know. Courage," Wiesel maintains, "means doing the impossible within the possible."

At first, I have trouble unscrambling this. "We have learned so much from nine-eleven about what makes human beings noble," he says. "When people are in need, you must be present. When people suffer, you must let them know you're suffering with them."

"The good side of bad acts?" I say.

"I would not say that from horror comes goodness. That would be giving horror too much credit. But goodness prevails in spite of horror."

"That's amazing in itself," I say.

"And finally we must have hope," he tells me.

"Did you have hope when you were in Auschwitz?" I ask.

"Even when there is no hope, as Albert Camus said, we must invent it."

AT SEA

In the period between January 1994 and April 1996, I experienced depression for the first time. Though I was outwardly healthy, my T cells were gone, I was running on empty, treatments were barely on the horizon, and one day, during a monthly checkup, I was told by my then-physician to begin prophylactic treatment at once or invite an opportunistic infection. I knew what such infections looked like; I'd nursed my share of dying friends. So I agreed with the doctor's futile, expensive recommendations, none of which had been proved to work, and changed overnight from a person who resisted swallowing aspirin to taking fifteen toxic pills a day and hanging out twice a week in this doctor's death salon with vitamin C dripping into my arm through an IV, surrounded by dying people wrapped in blankets. The time I spent in that ghostly place is the nadir of my life to date.

Every day became an ordeal. Minor efforts required Herculean strength; a ring of sullen hopelessness seemed to orbit every moment, mocking every prospect for improvement with a devil's sneer. Finally, I felt paralyzed and had trouble even leaving my tiny apartment. This reminded me of how a plane crash survivor described the last moments before impact. When the plane first began to malfunction, passengers were hysterical, sobbing, uncontrollable. Then they began to quiet down, prayed, clasped hands with strangers, and wept as the aircraft spiraled toward the ground. Finally, the survivor reported, even these movements stopped— passengers sat glued to their seats, too frozen and numb to even cry out. This is exactly how I was feeling, as if strapped inside a hurtling vehicle, frozen, asphyxiated, and plunging.

For the first time in my whole life, I was unable to function. I sought the help of a psychiatrist, who prescribed a drug called Paxil, whose only visible effect was to make it impossible for me to cry. I tossed the stuff in the trash. While I was at it, I fired Dr. G. and ditched those purgatorial treatments. Somehow, refusing to be deadened by narcotics (and my physician's hopelessness) lifted my spirits a tiny bit. Shafts of hope, fragile but real, began to dispel the depressive cloud. This clearing left me motivated enough to seek out the advice of a new physician and create a semblance of normal life until better treatments did arrive.

Once you've traveled this road, though, you never forget it. Never again is depression just a word to you. It's a visceral absence, a soul's negation. As author Andrew Solomon put it in his atlas of depression, *The Noonday Demon*, it is "the flaw in love."

Andrew's own descent into purgatory began insidiously and with no tangible cause. The scion of a pharmaceutical fortune (his father got rich from manufacturing the antidepressant drug Celexa, coincidentally), Andrew was a beloved child of privilege, educated at Yale and Cambridge, embarking on what promised to be a formidable career as a writer, surrounded by friends, in peak physical shape—circumstances, he assures me when we meet, that "in no way entitled me to misery." A deceptively cheerful, sweet-natured guy in an oxford shirt and herringbone blazer, Andrew is almost anachronistically cordial, the sort of "swell" guy you'd expect to meet at a garden party written by Edith Wharton, with a rising hairline and blue eyes that do appear, as one reporter described them, to be gazing perpetually out to sea.

"It began quite slowly," Andrew tells me at a café in our mutual neighborhood. "It was around the time that my mother died." A few weeks after her sixty-fourth birthday, Carolyn Solomon, who was losing her battle with uterine cancer, warmed herself some tea and muffins, called her prewarned husband and two sons to her bedside, swallowed forty Seconol capsules, and died before their eyes. His mother's last words to her younger son were "Enjoy what you have"—advice that became Andrew's recrimination after his depression took hold. Having published his first novel, an intensely emotional story about a mother and son ominously titled *Stone Boat*, the first-time author was about to set out on a reading tour when his melancholy turned clinical.

"For someone who hasn't been through this, it's almost impossible to imagine," he tells me. "I was excruciatingly afraid all the time. Tied up in knots, just petrified. As if I were about to explode."

"What were you afraid of?" I ask.

"You know the moment before your hands shoot out to break a fall if you trip or something?" says Andrew. "When you feel the ground rushing up at you but you can't stop yourself? That passing fraction-of-a-second terror?"

I know this feeling well, I say.

"I felt that hour after hour after hour," he tells me. "Just being awake—being alive—was acutely painful. I had no idea how to deal with it. People would say, 'Oh, it's just a phase. You'll get through.' I would think, No, I can't get through another fifteen minutes of this, much less another day."

His therapist was no help at all. "I was in analysis with an incompetent who failed to recognize what was happening," he says. The memory still makes him angry. "He said it was very brave and heroic of me not to take drugs. The truth is that if I had gone on medication six months earlier, I would never have gotten to the point I did."

Andrew reached his low point during the summer of 1994, when he was no longer able to leave his bedroom. "One day I couldn't get up," he tells me. "I was actually too frightened to get out of bed. I lay there for hours and hours after I woke up, wondering how I could put on a pair of socks. I stared at the phone for seven hours till finally it rang. I said to the person who called, 'I'm really in a bad way. I have to get some kind of help.'"

He compares this smothering darkness to a vine choking a tree, a crushing, parasitic force that will not stop till its host is dead. "Compacted and fetal," as he writes in *The Noonday Demon*, he found himself "depleted by this thing that was crushing me without holding me. Its tendrils threatened to pulverize my mind and my courage and my stomach, and crack my bones and desiccate my body. It went on glutting itself on me when there seemed nothing left to feed it."

Fortunately, there were loved ones around to help him fight off this killer. Nurturing friends circled around him; his mogul father, not one for touchy-feely affection, insisted on cutting his grown son's food. Slowly, Andrew began to improve. He dumped his useless analyst and found his way to a psychopharmacologist who was finally able to stabilize his moods with a cocktail of medications. He vividly recalls the moment in 2001 when his life force revived for a moment. "I was with my father, looking out of a window," he says with a smile. "Suddenly I saw a patch of gray sky pull apart, and the sun came blazing through before the clouds came together again. I know it's the most cliché image, but it was incredibly apt for me at the time. I felt okay again for maybe five minutes, which gave me the exultant sense that I might actually feel that way again."

An agnostic, nonpracticing Jew, Andrew is careful not to gloss his recovery in supernatural terms, but does admit to a certain spiritual boon to the terror he lived through. "It's the thing with feathers at the bottom of my box of miseries," he says, borrowing a phrase from Emily Dickinson.

"Major depression is a birth and a death," he says. "Before this happened, I had this idea of myself as a very strong person. In a concentration camp, I always figured I'd be one of those prisoners who managed to sing while they worked." This heroic self-image now makes Andrew snicker. "The idea that I might actually be one of those who fell to pieces, faded and died very quickly, involved a complete readjustment of who I thought I was. The idea of being captain of my own ship, the grand master of my own life, has completely gone out the window. I'm more tolerant now and far less judgmental. There is a fluidness, a fragility I did not previously have. I thought I was a rock." He laughs. "It turns out that I'm a river—or something idiotic like that."

Indeed, this witty man's own definition of courage—what it means to be a courageous person—has done a complete about-face.

"There are two ideas of bravery I like to play with," he now says. "Is the brave person the one who rushes in and goes to the front line because he doesn't feel fear? Or is the brave person the one who is completely petrified but does *something* . . . not as much as the first person, perhaps, but done against the weight of their own fear?"

"The first one might just be impetuous," I say.

"I am more fearful than I used to be. But I am also more rigorous about pushing myself past that fear. It's made me aware of how much I depend on other people. But," he makes clear, "I'm also much more careful about which people I do depend on, because I recognize my vulnerability—the profound fragility we all share." Andrew weighs his words with care, wary of sounding too maudlin or glib. "I have found that there is a kind of bliss that only comes to those who've known deep suffering," he tells me, echoing Lucy Grealy.

"What do you mean?"

"There is a kind of ecstatic delight when things are going well, a kind of joy I could never have known about if I had not been so depressed." Andrew even alludes to the discovery in himself of something akin to soul. "A part of myself I could never have imagined until one day, seven years ago, when hell came to pay me a surprise visit," as he wrote in his book. "It is a precious discovery."

As Julia Kristeva, the Bulgarian psychoanalyst, wrote in her own memoir about coming through darkness, "I owe a supreme, metaphysical lucidity to my depression. Refinement in sorrow or mourning are the imprint of a humankind that is surely not triumphant but subtle, ready to fight, and creative."

I walk Andrew home after our interview. Near his landmark brownstone is the building where the poet Emma Lazarus lived, whose most famous poem ("Give me your poor, your huddled masses . . .") is inscribed on the Statue of Liberty. The irony of this message almost next door is hardly lost on this clever man, with its themes of exile, resurrection, sail-setting for a country whose standard is freedom. "So lies the world before us," as Andrew described it in his wise book,

and with just such steps we tread a solitary way, survivors as we must be of an impoverishing, invaluable knowledge. We go forward with courage and with too much wisdom but determined to find what is beautiful. It is Dostoyevsky who said, "Beauty, though, will save the world." That moment of return from the realm of sad belief is always miraculous and can be stupefyingly beautiful. It is nearly worth the voyage out into despair.

THE MOTHER (OR ALOHA OY)

A Jewish intellectual had gone to Hawaii to live with a local family. After several months, the head of the family informed their visitor that the clan was ready to introduce him to the family whale. There was a whale that the family revered, he told the Jew. The animal responded to their calls and played with the family at a secret place on the island. They called this whale the Mother.

I can just imagine the Jew's reaction. Aloha oy! Thanks, but no thanks. My people do not hunt or take risks in goyish locations involving harpoons. The Jew must have thought that his host was bonkers, but since these kind people were putting him up, he pretended to consider it. The Jew was also curious. A whale that came on command? he thought. Nothing in this neurotic man's life came on command.

"I'm not a swimmer," he told the elderly Hawaiian, hoping that would end it.

Not to worry, his host assured him. "Just cling to a rock. The Mother will do the rest."

The Jew felt himself starting to tremble. He had spent his life being afraid of everything, most of all death. He'd tied a tourniquet around his passions. That is why he had come to Hawaii: to wake himself up, to set himself free. The Jew decided to meet the whale.

On the given day, the family traveled together to a secluded cove surrounded by black volcanic rock. The Hawaiians watched their visitor strip down to his bathing suit, and laughed at his petrified expression as he lowered himself down into the water, clutching the rocks like a monkey. Slowly and in unison, the family began to chant (think of Enya in a hula skirt), their voices carrying over the water as the Jew shivered, awaiting his fate.

Then the most astonishing thing happened. About five hundred yards away, the biggest black whale he'd ever seen surfaced calmly in the water. He was terrified and nearly jumped out of the sea. In spite of his rational mind's protests, however, the Jew stayed where he was. What he felt in his heart seemed to contradict everything he had believed possible until that moment. The Jew sensed that the whale was aware of his terror and was sending him great, warm, enveloping waves of something he could only call love—a strong, immense, impersonal warmth that actually began to calm him down. He was certain that the whale not only could feel his fear, impossible though it seemed, but also knew that he couldn't swim. His only task, the Mother appeared to be telling him, was to stay in the water and feel that great warmth, to trust its heat and go on trusting.

Slowly, the whale began to float toward him, sending miniature geysers from her blowhole as if to introduce herself. The Jew was overwhelmed and stayed perfectly still as the great beast moved in his direction. Then the elder Hawaiian said, "Touch the Mother."

With shaking hands, the visitor reached out and touched the

whale's slick, ebony skin. The moment he made contact, the Mother tilted her body so that he could run his hand along her side. Miraculously, the Jew wasn't frightened. Wonder burned his fear away. He stayed like that for several minutes, with his local friends crooning in the background. Finally the whale slipped away. At that moment, he stopped clutching the rocks and waded into the water, marveling at his own buoyancy.

Why had he ever doubted this, the Jew asked himself, feeling water as if for the first time—his body as if for the first time, too. Afterward, the world seemed changed; there was awe in him where there had been terror; a confident yes where there had been maybe; courage where caution and doubt had lived; trust in his formerly cynical heart, the desire to swim replacing the notion that letting go, he would sink like a stone.

He never saw the Mother again. But the world was lightened in the Jew's eyes. He had stepped through the back door of his own mind. He no longer knew what was possible. Nothing in the world seemed beyond his touch.

ROPE BURN

The day before my mother died, we were in her bedroom passing the time, with Mom's head on my lap and a wall clock ticking, when suddenly she opened her eyes and blinked at me through the morphine haze.

"What is it?" I asked. She blinked again, then whispered the first words she'd uttered for days, in a dreamy growling voice. "Easier," my mother was saying. "It's easier when you let go."

This startled me, coming from her of all people, a stubborn, cantankerous, fighting broad who didn't enjoy introspection. Still, I had noticed a subtle change in her, beyond what was happening to her body, without quite being able to name it. My mother seemed to be suffering less, to be more peaceful. There was something making way in her, helping her to loosen her grip. I resolved then to remember this when my own time came.

Saint Augustine said that we can only know what we love. And to know something is to know it's not yours. We're guests in this hotel, after all; even the ashtrays will have to stay. Still, attachment

289

is bound to happen. We imagine our lives to be an accretion, an increase of layers solidifying the identity that holds us down to the ground. But what if the opposite's even more true, that we're winnowed away, worn down by time, pushed into transparency? What if we're humbled, without being severed, in order that we may move through the world with less friction, less regret but more desire, less protection but more love?

Babies only learn this with time. At first they must cling if they hope to survive. Deprived of touch, infants will rock and rock themselves to sleep, as a volunteer at a foundling hospital told me. "They would sit there with their arms wrapped around themselves on their beds, just rocking and rocking," she said. There are orphans, both actual and self-imagined, who crave being held this way their whole lives, trapped in the psychic bodies of infants. How many times have you heard someone say that if so-and-so doesn't love them, they will just die? It's sad but also clearly a throwback to what they longed for as unmothered children.

One snowy day in the Berkshire Mountains, Buddhist teacher Joseph Goldstein is talking to me about love and strangling. We're in his house adjacent to the Insight Meditation Society, which Joseph cofounded thirty years ago with fellow Americans Jack Kornfield and Sharon Salzburg. "We assume that clutching and caring go hand in hand," Joseph tells me, crossing his size-14 feet on the table between us. A towering man of sixty, Joseph, though single, is no monkish stranger to human tangling. As he talks about pain and clinging and emotional vampirism, he could be any person who's been wounded in love. "We assume that attachment equates with love," says Joseph. "But just look at these forces closely and you realize how different they actually are. When we feel most loving, we feel most *open*hearted. Attachment isn't a giving energy. When we're attached, it's a subtle contraction, the heart holding on, saying, 'Please don't leave me.'" He compares the pain of this to rope burn.

"But we're human," I say. "We get attached."

This teacher reminds me that the alternative to rope burn is not some chilly pseudo-detachment, apathy masked as enlightenment. It's *commitment*. "Attachment wants things to stay the same, especially in relation to us," he says. "Since everyone and everything is always changing, this is obviously doomed. Commitment, on the other hand, does not say things must stay the same for us to be happy, but that we will abide with ourselves affectionately throughout these changes."

Abide? I ask.

"Otherwise we only create more suffering. Attachment and commitment are different," Joseph says.

Then he stops talking. The room grows quiet. It must be weird to live like a monk, I think, cutting ties instead of tightening them, relinquishing rather than gathering up. Once upon a time, Joseph was a Jewish intellectual himself, seeking far and wide for inspiration, for something to awe him out of himself. He let go of the rocks when the dharma rose enormous-bellied on the horizon. He touched the Buddha's slippery back. The Four Noble Truths became his lovers. Solitude has left him young.

"Imperfect life," I say stupidly, backing off from the silence Joseph loves.

He smiles again, seeing my *spilkes*. "'Love your crooked neighbor with your crooked heart,'" Joseph says, pretending to instruct me with W. H. Auden's words.

"You do the best you can," I say.

My mother loved us at the end. Ida's lobster shell fell off. She allowed us to touch her in a way she'd never been comfortable with before, as Samuel's Israeli baker father had blessed his own son in the end. I laid my mother's head in my lap, a tiny skull with gray flattened wisps, and stroked the skin without hurting her. This woman whose attention I'd craved my whole life was now humbled enough to finally surrender. No sign of rope burn anywhere.

"Am I dying?" Mom asked the day before she did. She was leaning against the bathtub on her knees, smoking her last cigarette, flicking the ashes down the drain.

"It doesn't look good," said my sister Belle.

My mother looked more puzzled than scared. Then she said, "It's not that bad."

WHAT MAKES THE
ENGINE GO?

When I first meet him, a few years before his death at the age of one hundred, poet Stanley Kunitz is a living example of how *viriditas* works, a photosynthetic phenomenon whose lust for life and singular spirit overflow with ever-greater intensity with each coming year. "I don't wake up as a nonagenarian," Stanley will tell me when we meet. "I wake up as a poet! It is only the body that wears out. The imagination remains as intense and glowing as ever."

Stanley answers the door of his New York apartment, bright eyes popping, waving his hands, dressed in funny blue tennis shoes and a shabby tweed jacket. "Welcome, welcome, welcome!" he sings, hunched at a sixty-degree angle, leading me at a healthy clip down a long hallway lined with canvases by Stanley's famous friends Franz Kline and Robert Motherwell (as well as abstracts by his wife, painter Elise Asher), piles of books, and a bronze bust of Stanley worthy of a past poet laureate. We settle in opposite high-backed chairs in the large, sunny sitting room. Elise and an assistant field a constant stream of phone calls from a nearby office.

"There are penalties one pays for a long existence, but I am happy to pay them!" Stanley smiles and sighs. He looks dwarfed in his large chair, fingertips pressed together under the chin of his ancient, spritely Semitic face. Despite his working-class Jewish background, Stanley speaks in lofty Bostonian Brahmin tones, unfurling one carefully manicured phrase at a time.

"Reinvention is my philosophy, if you want to call it that," he says, looking out the window. "Imagination is the key to creating a life that is ever new." Stanley turns his eyes to me. "We are each of us a changeling person," he says. "We are not going to be the same decade after decade. Wisdom results from confronting not only one's desires and capacities but also one's limitations."

"The Layers," one of Stanley's best-loved poems, is his crystallization of this wisdom.

I have walked through many lives,
some of them my own,
and I am not who I was,
though some principle of being abides
from which I struggle
not to stray.
When I look behind,
as I am compelled to look
before I can gather strength
to proceed on my journey,
I see the milestones dwindling
toward the horizon
and the slow fires trailing
from the abandoned camp-sites,
over which scavenger angels
wheel on heavy wings.

Oh, I have made myself a tribe
out of my true affections,
and my tribe is scattered!
How shall the heart be reconciled
to its feast of losses?
In a rising wind
the manic dust of my friends,
those who fell along the way,
bitterly stings my face.
Yet I turn, I turn,
exulting somewhat,
with my will intact to go
wherever I need to go,
and every stone on the road is precious to me.
In my darkest night,
when the moon was covered
and I roamed through wreckage,
a nimbus-clouded voice
directed me:
"Live in the layers,
not on the litter."
Though I lack the art
to decipher it,
no doubt the next chapter
in my book of transformations
is already written.
I am not done with my changes.

Dynamism in the midst of our "feast of losses," metamorphosis
among the ruins, self-creation inside our own changing story,

reconciliation to the dangerous knowledge that while we may no longer be who we were, "some principle of being abides"—the authentic, immutable inner voice from which, like the poet, we struggle not to stray. With such directions Stanley has mapped a strategy for weathering time, change, and sorrow without losing our élan vital. Curiosity goads this appetite. Whether fortune is smiling, or not, our lives shaped as we'd like them to be, or not, the future seemingly navigable, or not, we remain intensely curious about our own unpredictable changes, all that has yet to be revealed. Curiosity is the link to this green source; so is the courage to remain creative and not cede rule to our screeching demons. The choice of renewal over resignation—truthfulness over the status quo—transforms day-to-day life into evolution.

We long to puncture the heart of things, to touch the pulsating rawness of being, especially in difficult times. It's no accident that after 9/11, poetry became a national obsession—Auden's "September 1, 1939," for example. Poetry is the language of survival linking us to the green source, bridging divides of culture and time. During crisis we long for simple things, since only the simplest, truest things are broad enough to carry us across.

"What makes the engine go?" Stanley wrote on his eightieth birthday in a poem to his wife. "Desire, desire, desire."

The road to where Stanley is sitting today has been marked by catastrophic detours. Before he was born, his father had poisoned himself in the main square of their town, Worcester, Massachusetts, leaving the sickly boy and his mother to find their own way in the world. Though he excelled enough in his studies to be hired by Harvard (Stanley graduated in 1924), the university suddenly reneged on its own employment offer for fear that "Anglo-Saxon students might resent being taught by a Jew." Soon afterward he fell in love with a poet named Helen Pearce while both were fellows at Yaddo, the artist colony in Saratoga Springs, New York, married her, and moved with his new bride to a hundred-acre farm in Connecticut. One April day, with no warning, Helen Pearce disappeared from the farm without a trace. To this day, Stanley doesn't know what happened.

"The heart breaks and breaks and lives by breaking," Stanley wrote in "The Testing Tree." His willingness to be broken, then remade, his commitment to the belief that such destruction is natural and fruitful, has led to a life of constant self-reinvention. "Whatever we create is made of the materials of life," explained Stanley during a period of tremendous grief. "We should never think of the life—our life—as being the enemy of whatever we aspire to create."

A protégée of Stanley's, the gifted poet Marie Howe, received a dose of her mentor's wisdom during a period of great loss. "I came to Stanley when my brother was dying," Marie tells me. "I told him that it felt as if something had me in its mouth and was chewing me up. Stanley said, 'It is, and you must wait to see who you are when this thing is done with you.'"

With his first wife gone and his wunderkind career stalled, Stanley was thrust into the darkest period of his life, a phase that lasted for nearly a decade. Then one day in 1936 he opened the door and found the well-known poet Theodore Roethke standing on his porch with a copy of Stanley's latest commercial failure in his hands—and the offer of a teaching position at his college. "How he found me I shall never know," Stanley says now, "but that moment will remain with me always. Roethke made it possible for me to live."

"In a dark time, the eye begins to see," Roethke himself had written. Since that time, in addition to being poet laureate, Stanley has published dozens of volumes and received nearly every major literary honor available in this country. Even during the hardest of times his inspiration has rarely flagged. "Poetry is like breathing," he likes to say, likening each encounter with a poem to meeting a new bride. "One never retires from art, any more than one retires from breathing. I say in one of my poems, 'Maybe it is time for me to practice growing old.' I meant it as a joke."

Stanley turns a hooded eye to one of his wife's bold canvases on the wall behind me, his stubbled chin resting on his chest like a bird's. For a moment, I'm not sure where he is—then the old man swoops back. "Keats has a great phrase in one of his letters, describing what he values most. He refers to 'the holiness of the heart's affections,'" he says. "I remember when I first read those words, recognizing that this holiness would be something that would be forever meaningful to me, a foundation stone of my life. And it has been."

In his stress on reinvention, Stanley shifts emphasis from the endurance of loss to becoming more essentially oneself. "Every artist I've known has been distinguished, almost from birth, by knowledge of the need to become a self, not just a living body," he tells me.

"Isn't that true of everyone?"

"Yes." Stanley smiles. "I suppose that it is."

"How does it feel to be almost a hundred years old?"

He looks positively jubilant at the question. "I feel I have found myself," he tells me. In another interview, he elaborated on this point. "I feel in possession of my destiny, That I am not a victim of it." "Look at this beautiful day, for example," he tells me now, smiling at a sunlit tree. "I've been through so much these last few years, but I don't feel I'm powerless at all. There is a sense of another level, a state of being, that is both yours and not yours."

"Has the world become a more dangerous place?" I ask.

"Sometimes one does fear for the future," says Stanley. "One fears the loss of the search for the sacred, for the beautiful, for the true. One fears that the dynamics of modern society point toward the practical rather than the spiritual. But I think there will always be individuals who will carry on the great tradition of the prophets and poets. I have such a fierce conviction about the value of existence, the importance of life, that I know that there must be many, many others who feel the same way, and will always be here on earth. That gives me hope."

The last time I see Stanley, two years after our first interview, he's reclining in a hospital bed in the same living room where we first spoke, drifting in and out of consciousness, looking more bemused than uncomfortable. Conversation is no longer easy for him. Stanley listens to me, smiles, shrugs his shoulders, his delight in being here at all still palpable. When I stand up to leave, he squeezes my hand for a long time. Crossing the green parquet floor, I catch sight of a first edition of Stanley's collected poems lying on a table. The final lines of "The Round" have remained with me since I first read them.

I can scarcely wait till tomorrow,
when a new life begins for me,
as it does each day,
as it does each day.

NOTES AND SOURCES

Magical Thinking: See Joan Didion's *The Year of Magical Thinking* (New York: Alfred A. Knopf, 2005) for more on "the American way of grief." John Leonard's introduction to Didion's collected nonfiction works, *We Tell Ourselves Stories in Order to Live* (New York: Alfred A. Knopf, 2006), is also an excellent introduction to Didion's cultural profile ("a poster girl for anomie").

The Roar of Freedom: For more on "The Roar of Freedom," see *Dialogues with a Modern Mystic*, by Andrew Harvey and Mark Matousek (Chicago: Quest Books, 1994).

The Day of Laughter: Stephen Batchelor's *Buddhism Without Beliefs* (New York: Riverhead Books, 1997) is an excellent, lingo-free introduction to the Buddhist way of life.

Om Mani Padme Hum: *The Tibetan Book of Living and Dying*, by Sogyal Rinpoche (San Francisco: HarperSanFrancisco, 1992), provides a strong framework for understanding impermanence as an element of spiritual practice, as well as the path of the bodhisattva.

Dragons at the Gate: See the Willises' memoir, *But There Are Always Miracles* (New York: Viking, 1974), for more on their story. Mary Willis's autobiographical novel, *Papa's Cord* (New York: Alfred A. Knopf, 1999), provides background to her journey with Jack.

Superman's Ghost: For more on Jim MacLaren, see http://JimMacLaren.com. Deep thanks to Elizabeth Gilbert for turning me on to Jim with her article "Lucky Jim" (*GQ*, May 2002) and asking him the two questions that interested me (about metaphysical pain) before I could get there.

Home in the World: My article "The Crucible of Homelessness" (*Common Boundary*, Spring 1992) rounds out this discussion of homelessness as metaphor. Jonathan Kozol's book *Rachel and Her Children:*

Homeless Families in America (New York: Fawcett Books, 1988) and Eve Ensler's play *Ladies* (New York: Central Park Locations, 1989) provide illuminating case studies of homeless individuals.

The Art of Losing: Viktor Frankl's *Man's Search for Meaning* (New York: Pocket Books, 1984) is required reading for anyone wishing to understand survival, dignity, and how meaning is culled from life in extremis. Francis Bok's *Escape from Slavery* (New York: St. Martin's, 2003) gives the full story of Francis's life before and after he came to the United States.

A Quarter Inch from Heaven: Shunryu Suzuki Roshi's *Zen Mind, Beginner's Mind* (Boston: Shambhala, 2006) remains the best introduction to Zen practice that I know of.

Going to Tahiti (or Raising Heaven): For more on Ram Dass's thoughts about conscious aging, see his *Still Here: Embracing Aging, Changing, and Dying* (New York: Riverhead, 2000) and Mickey Lemle's documentary *Fierce Grace* (Zeitgeist Films Ltd., 2002).

The Net of Indra: Daniel Goleman's *Social Intelligence: The New Science of Human Relationships* (New York: Bantam Books, 2006) is an eye-opener regarding neuroplasticity and the science of relationships. Ken Wilber's *No Boundary* (Boston: Shambhala, 2001) provides a philosophical basis for understanding interdependence (the Net of Indra) in daily life.

Reinventing Your Wife: For more on Henry Grayson's theories, see his *The New Physics of Love* (New York: Gotham Books, 2004).

Praying: Three excellent sources on prayer are *Story of a Soul: The Autobiography of St. Thérèse of Lisieux* (New York: Tan, 1997), Kathleen Norris's *The Cloister Walk* (New York: Riverhead, 1996), and Sharon Salzberg's *Faith* (New York: Riverhead, 2002).

Demon Lovers: For more on Michael Klein's life, see his *Track Conditions* (New York: Persea, 1997) and *The End of Being Known* (Madison: University of Wisconsin Press, 2003). Identifying details have been changed in Kathleen's story to protect her anonymity.

Questioning (or The Sphinx): Byron Katie's book *Loving What Is* (New York: Three Rivers Press, 2002) is a thorough introduction to The Work.

The Terrorists Within: For more on metanoia, see *The Passionate Life*, by Sam Keen (San Francisco: HarperSanFrancisco, 1984). C. H. Waddington's *The Ethical Animal* (London: Allen & Unwin, 1960) provides a hard-science background to terror as an evolutionary element in history.

Earth Angel: See *The Protean Self: Human Resiliency in the Age of Fragmentation*, by Robert Jay Lifton (Chicago: University of Chicago Press, 1993), for more on shape-shifting and the trickster archetype in human adaptation.

Something Else Is Also True: Maria Housden's memoirs, *Hannah's Gift: Lessons from a Life Fully Lived* (New York: Bantam, 2002) and *Unraveled* (New York: Harmony, 2004), offer poignant and inspiring insights into "child wisdom" and grief as a prelude to self-discovery.

Pain Passes, but the Beauty Remains: This story is adapted from Bo Lozoff's short story "The Saddest Buddha," with great thanks to the author.

Hedonics: For more on the science of happiness, see *Stumbling on Happiness*, by Daniel Gilbert (New York: Alfred A. Knopf, 2006), and *Full Catastrophe Living*, by Jon Kabat-Zinn (New York: Dell, 1990). For more on Colette, take a vacation with Judith Thurman's *Secrets of the Flesh* (New York: Alfred A. Knopf, 1999).

Original Blessing: To more deeply understand the importance of blessing, see *Original Blessing*, by Matthew Fox (Santa Fe, NM: Bear and Co., 1983), and *Dialogues with a Modern Mystic*, by Andrew Harvey and Mark Matousek (Chicago: Quest, 1994).

Enough: Rabbi Rami Shapiro's discussion of the sabbath in *Minyan: Ten Principles for a Life Worth Living* (New York: Bell Tower, 1997) is worth reading. David Loy's *The Great Awakening: A Buddhist Social Theory* (Boston: Wisdom, 2003) is useful in understanding the hungry ghost dilemma. Bill McKibben's *Deep Economy* (New York: Henry Holt and Co., 2007) elucidates the East-West consumer crisis and the virtues of local consumption.

Stress Matters: Saki Santorelli's *Heal Thy Self* (New York: Bell Tower, 1999) is a great overview of stress, its discontents, and treatment.

The Wounded Healer: For more on Rachel Remen, see her *Kitchen Table Wisdom* (New York: Riverhead, 1996) and *My Grandfather's Blessings* (New York: Riverhead, 2000). Also see www.commonweal.org.

True Confessions: For more about narrative medicine, see Dr. Rita Charon, *Narrative Medicine: Honoring the Stories of Illness* (New York: Oxford University Press, 2006).

A Splinter of Love: See Paula Allen's *Flowers in the Desert* (Santiago: Cuarta Propio, 1999) for photographs and more stories about the women of Calama. Also see Deborah Shaffer's wonderful documentary film *Dance of Hope*.

Nakedness: Lucy Grealy's *Autobiography of a Face* (Boston: Houghton Mifflin, 1994) gives a deeper look into Lucy's story. Also see Ann Patchett's *Truth and Beauty* (New York: HarperCollins, 2004).

Killing Peter Pan: For more about the loss of soul in modern life, see *Care of the Soul,* by Thomas Moore (New York: HarperCollins, 1992), and *The Soul's Code,* by James Hillman (New York: Random House, 1996).

The Water or the Wave?: Eckhart Tolle's *The Power of Now* (Novato, CA: New World Library, 1999) is indispensable to a deeper understanding of *nunc stans* and the relationship between conflict and mental labeling.

At Sea: For more about Andrew Solomon, see his *The Noonday Demon: An Atlas of Depression* (New York: Scribner, 2001). Also see Julia Kristeva's memoir, *Black Sun* (New York: Columbia University Press, 1992).

Rope Burn: Joseph Goldstein's books, including *One Dharma* (San Francisco: HarperSanFrancisco, 2002) and *Seeking the Heart of Wisdom* (with Jack Kornfield; Boston: Shambhala, 1987), are treasures for understanding Buddhist wisdom.

What Makes the Engine Go?: For more on Stanley Kunitz's life and work, see *The Collected Poems* (New York: Norton, 2000). Also, special thanks to Genine Lentine for *The Wild Braid* (New York: Norton, 2005) and for arranging my last visit with Stanley.

ACKNOWLEDGMENTS

Every book has a back story—some more epic than others. Five years, three publishers, four editors, two coasts, a season in hell, two funerals, one wedding, and multiple drafts later, I am indebted to many souls.

My agent, Joy Harris, is a writer's dream; Barbara Graham is a sister in all things; Eve Ensler, my greatest inspiration and heart; Robert Levithan, best friend and brother; Florence Falk, my beautiful *bechert*; Maria Housden for unfailing courage; Marcia Lippman for joie de vivre; Catherine Ingram for wisdom in exile; my sister, Belle Heil, for constant kindness; Dr. Paul Curtis Bellman, for faith and nerve; and Amy Gross, dear friend, for suggesting that I write about this in the first place.

Deep thanks to Karen Rinaldi (the first person in publishing to recommend never to rush a book, coincidentally, years before she was my publisher); to Terra Chalberg for comfort in limbo; to Amanda Katz for leading me to my wonderful editor Kathy Belden, whose taste, humor, and indomitable patience showed me what I'd been waiting for all these years. The team at Bloomsbury—especially Sabrina Farber, Annik LaFarge, Maya Baran, and Sara Mercurio—have been wonderful. Special thanks to Jill Hughes and Greg Villepique for their exacting eye on detail.

Profound gratitude to my close friends Michael Klein, Hugh Delehanty, Martha Cooley, Sharon Salzberg, Samuel Kirschner, Paula Allen, Joe Dolce, Andrew Hood, Katharina Tapp, Susan

Dalsimer, Gwenyth Jackaway, Karen Fuchs, Ed and Deb Shapiro, Dr. Sue Grand, Sally Fisher, Billy Blechen, Rabia Halim, and Gary Lennon for love and conversation; to Cynthia O'Neal, Robbie Stein, Marie Howe, Elizabeth England, Ram Dass, Lisa Cornelio, and Roger Housden for writerly strength; and to the many people, including Betsy Carter, Deborah Copaken Kogan, Tyrone Thompson, Ella Pasqueriello, and Dr. David Feldman, who were generous enough to tell me their stories. Deep thanks to Louis Morhaim, my greatest teacher. R.I.P.

And to Marco Naguib, most of all. "Set me like a seal upon thy heart, love is as strong as death." *Semper fi.*

ABOUT THE AUTHOR

Mark Matousek is the author of two memoirs, *The Boy He Left Behind* and *Sex Death Enlightenment*. He is a contributing editor for *O* and *Tricycle* and has served as senior editor of *Interview*. He has written for the *New Yorker*, the *New York Times* magazine, *Vogue*, *Yoga Journal*, and others. His most recent book, also published by Hay House, is *Ethical Wisdom: What Makes Us Good*. He lives in New York City.

www.markmatousek.com

Hay House Titles of Related Interest

BROKEN: A LOVE STORY: A Woman's Journey Toward Redemption on the Wind River Indian Reservation, by Lisa Jones

EVERYTHING I'VE EVER DONE THAT WORKED, by Lesley Garner

FEEDING YOUR DEMONS: Ancient Wisdom for Resolving Inner Conflict, by Tsultrim Allione

THE MINDFUL MANIFESTO: How Doing Less and Noticing More Can Help Us Thrive in a Stressed-out World, by Dr Jonty Heaversedge and Ed Halliwell

OUT OF THE DARKNESS: From Turmoil to Transformation, by Steve Taylor

All the above are available at your local bookshop, or may be ordered by contacting Hay House (see opposite page).

We hope you enjoyed this Hay House book.
If you would like to receive a free catalogue featuring additional
Hay House books and products, or if you would like information
about the Hay Foundation, please contact:

Hay House UK Ltd
292B Kensal Rd • London W10 5BE
Tel: (44) 20 8962 1230; Fax: (44) 20 8962 1239
www.hayhouse.co.uk

✳✳✳

Published and distributed in the United States of America by:
Hay House, Inc. • PO Box 5100 • Carlsbad, CA 92018-5100
Tel.: (1) 760 431 7695 or (1) 800 654 5126;
Fax: (1) 760 431 6948 or (1) 800 650 5115
www.hayhouse.com

Published and distributed in Australia by:
Hay House Australia Ltd • 18/36 Ralph St • Alexandria NSW 2015
Tel.: (61) 2 9669 4299; Fax: (61) 2 9669 4144
www.hayhouse.com.au

Published and distributed in the Republic of South Africa by:
Hay House SA (Pty) Ltd • PO Box 990 • Witkoppen 2068
Tel./Fax: (27) 11 467 8904 • www.hayhouse.co.za

Published and distributed in India by:
Hay House Publishers India • Muskaan Complex • Plot No.3
B-2 • Vasant Kunj • New Delhi – 110 070.
Tel.: (91) 11 41761620; Fax: (91) 11 41761630.
www.hayhouse.co.in

Distributed in Canada by:
Raincoast • 9050 Shaughnessy St • Vancouver, BC V6P 6E5
Tel.: (1) 604 323 7100; Fax: (1) 604 323 2600

✳✳✳

Sign up via the Hay House UK website to receive the Hay House
online newsletter and stay informed about what's going on with
your favourite authors. You'll receive bimonthly announcements
about discounts and offers, special events, product highlights,
free excerpts, giveaways, and more!
www.hayhouse.co.uk

JOIN THE HAY HOUSE FAMILY

As the leading self-help, mind, body and spirit publisher in the UK, we'd like to welcome you to our family so that you can enjoy all the benefits our website has to offer.

 EXTRACTS from a selection of your favourite author titles

 COMPETITIONS, PRIZES & SPECIAL OFFERS Win extracts, money off, downloads and so much more

 LISTEN to a range of radio interviews and our latest audio publications

 CELEBRATE YOUR BIRTHDAY An inspiring gift will be sent your way

 LATEST NEWS Keep up with the latest news from and about our authors

 ATTEND OUR AUTHOR EVENTS Be the first to hear about our author events

 iPHONE APPS Download your favourite app for your iPhone

 HAY HOUSE INFORMATION Ask us anything, all enquiries answered

join us online at **www.hayhouse.co.uk**

 292B Kensal Road, London W10 5BE
T: 020 8962 1230 E: info@hayhouse.co.uk